Promoting Gender Equality at Work

Promoting Gender Equality at Work
Turning vision into reality for the twenty-first century

EDITED BY
EUGENIA DATE-BAH

A study prepared for the International Labour Office
within the framework of the Interdepartmental Project
on Equality for Women in Employment

Zed Books Ltd
LONDON AND NEW YORK

Promoting Gender Equality at Work was first published by
Zed Books Ltd, 7 Cynthia Street, London N1 9JF, UK
and Room 400, 175 Fifth Avenue, New York, NY 10010,
USA, in association with the International Labour Office,
4 route des Morillons, CH–1211 Geneva 22, Switzerland.

Cover designed by Andrew Corbett.
Printed and bound in the United Kingdom
by Biddles Ltd, Guildford and King's Lynn.

A catalogue record for this book is
available from the British Library

US CIP data is available from the Library of Congress

ISBN 1 85649 453 5 Cased
ISBN 1 85649 454 3 Limp

Distributed exclusively in the USA by St Martin's Press,
Inc., 175 Fifth Avenue, New York, NY 10010, USA.

Contents

Preface

For the past two decades, increasing attention has been given to the situation of women within the context of the world of work in the light of the many changes that have taken place in the world economy. Indeed the Fourth World Conference on Women, held in Beijing in 1995, identified this issue as a critical area of concern if the condition of women is to be improved. Statistics indicate that there has been some progress, especially in terms of the increase in the female labour-force participation rate over the past 10 years. This has not, however, been matched by gender equality in opportunity and treatment in the workplace.

Women have borne the brunt of the social costs of the changes in the world economy such as globalization and increased international competition, structural adjustment, the transition to a market economy and other economic reforms, and technological changes and their impact on the organization of work. Women have tended to be negatively affected by the precariousness of employment, deterioration of the quality and conditions of work, and reduction of resources for social protection in many parts of the world in the wake of these changes. Women continue to labour under stereotypes in the workplace, and find themselves as a result clustered on the lower rungs of the career ladder and in sectors outside the purview of existing labour legislation. Few countries have explicit policies to provide adequate social support for workers with family responsibilities. There has been a tendency also for women's work to be undervalued, with statistics failing entirely to reflect the amount of work women perform for no wages at all.

This volume, which presents contributions from 12 experienced gender specialists, examines the various developments and elements that impact on the participation of women as equal players in the workplace, and conveys a number of messages to guide policy and action. It draws attention to the unambiguous need to formulate more viable and effective policies and strategies that take due account of the diverse economic, legal and social factors crucial for the improvement of women workers' situation. It encourages the promotion of training to enhance women's occupational and employment opportunities. It draws attention to the need to make evident the economic contribution of women by removing the methodological and conceptual problems that perpetuate the dearth of reliable empirical data on women workers. It underlines the importance of the legislative environment that would guarantee quality working conditions for women, gender-sensitive labour-market policies, appropriate social protection, and adequate arrangements for workers with family responsibilities.

The volume demonstrates the relevance of international instruments, including international labour standards, in ameliorating the plight of women workers. It enumerates as worthy of special attention a number of International Labour Conventions and the United Nations Convention on the Elimination of All Forms of Discrimination against Women. It draws attention to other laws of importance, such as those on land ownership, property rights, family and marriage, inheritance, contracts and banking, which could constrain or facilitate women's capacity to embark on economic and other activities, and to be treated equally in the workplace.

Other messages relate to the positive impact that would be achieved if women were mobilized to articulate their concerns themselves and if the representation or participation of women at decision-making levels of work groupings is improved. It further stresses the need to marshal the involvement of all relevant actors in the world of work, such as governments, employers' and workers' organizations, grass-roots associations and other non-governmental organizations (NGOs), in order to improve the situation of women. The most important message, however, is the resounding call for the adoption of an integrated, comprehensive strategy for tackling the issues which influence the condition of the woman in the workplace, in recognition of the interlinked and multifaceted nature of the problem.

The Fourth World Conference on Women placed great emphasis on the effective follow-up of the Conference conclusions. This book's publication so soon after the Conference, and its coverage of different countries, both developed and developing, is opportune, as a major input into the design of policies and strategies, in moving the recommendations contained in the Platform of Action from mere words on paper to realization, and in advancing the debate on policy and action concerning women and gender equality in the world of work. It should be an invaluable reference, therefore, for policy-makers, as well as for the international community, researchers and lobbyists, and scholars interested in gender issues. It should also supplement existing publications and other documents in this field for the burgeoning women's and gender studies programmes at universities and other institutions of higher learning.

Mary Chinery-Hesse,
Deputy Director-General,
International Labour Organization (ILO),
Geneva, Switzerland.

Acknowledgements

The contributions assembled in this volume constitute part of the output generated by the Interdepartmental Project on Equality for Women in Employment, implemented from January 1992 to February 1994 in the ILO (see the annex for a full list). Attempts have been made to incorporate into the contributions new developments since the project's completion.

The editor of the volume would like to thank in particular: Jack Martin, her Director during that period, for his inspiration and guidance in the immense challenge of managing this complex multi-disciplinary project; professional colleagues on the project for their team spirit, which greatly facilitated the task; various local consultants and others who made valuable inputs; and Marie-Madeleine Boiron, the secretary at that time, for her considerable dedication and loyalty.

With specific reference to this volume, its preparation was facilitated by the co-operation she received from not only the multi-disciplinary contributors from different parts of the world but also the Office of the ILO Special Adviser on Women Workers' Questions. Several colleagues including Richard Anker, Andrew Dale, Naziha Gaham-Boumechal, Christine Elstob, Elizabeth Goodson, Margaret Martens, Liba Paukert, Jean Perret, and Carmen Solorio acted as 'sounding boards' for ideas, both technical and editorial. The editor also greatly appreciated the assistance of Kathi Hill, Valeria Morra, Susan Peters and the ILO Publications Bureau, and the encouragement of other colleagues, family and friends to persist with the volume's completion. The typing of the manuscript was undertaken principally by Sarah Horekens and Catherine Taylor, to whom the editor is grateful.

The editor, as manager of the Interdepartmental Project, hopes that this volume will contribute to the debate on the multifaceted nature of women's concerns in work, and to the continuing struggle against gender inequality.

April 1996

Contributors

Sally Baden is a British economist. She is currently manager of the programme 'Briefing in Development and Gender' at the Institute of Development Studies, Brighton, England.

Anne-Marie Brocas is a French specialist in social security who has served as a consultant to the ILO. She works at the Ministry of Finance, Bureau of Social Transfers in France.

Eugenia Date-Bah is a Ghanaian sociologist, formerly senior lecturer at the University of Ghana, manager of the ILO Interdepartmental Project on Equality for Women in Employment and senior technical specialist on women workers' and gender questions. She is now co-ordinator of an action programme on post-conflict countries, ILO, Geneva, Switzerland.

Barbara Einhorn is an economist from New Zealand who has published a considerable amount of research on Eastern and Central Europe. She is a research fellow at the Research Centre for Women's Studies at the University of Sussex, Brighton, England.

Evance Kalula is a Zambian labour lawyer and a university senior lecturer. He is currently the co-ordinator of the Southern African Labour Project, Labour Law Unit, University of Cape Town, South Africa.

Yoke Wan Lee is a Malaysian who studied law and economics and is currently research and information manager of the Malaysian Employers' Federation (MEF), Kuala Lumpur, Malaysia. Her responsibilities include conducting surveys on salary and fringe benefits, publishing the Federation's monthly newsletter and annual reports and organizing conferences.

Guy Mhone is a Malawian economist who was formerly a university professor in the United States, head of the economic division of SAPES Trust in Harare, Zimbabwe, and ILO official in Lusaka. He has also worked as chief technical adviser of a manpower project in Lesotho.

Swasti Mitter was born in Calcutta, West Bengal. She is the deputy director and a professorial fellow of the United Nations University Institute for New Technology, Maastricht, the Netherlands. She has written extensively on the impact of technological changes and emergent management practices on women's work.

David Tajgman, from the United States, is a senior specialist in international labour standards in the ILO multidisciplinary team, based in Harare, Zimbabwe. He was formerly with the Application of International Labour Standards Branch of the ILO in Geneva and also practised labour law in Los Angeles, California.

Rachael Taylor is a law graduate from New Zealand. She has worked on various occasions as an intern with the ILO. She is currently examining the social and legal aspects of occupational health and safety.

Constance Thomas is a labour lawyer from the United States, formerly with the Equality of Rights Branch at the ILO. She is now a senior technical specialist on international labour standards and women workers' questions in the ILO multidisciplinary team for the Caribbean, based in Port-of-Spain, Trinidad.

Linda Wirth is an Australian specialist on gender and working conditions. She works with the ILO's Conditions of Work Branch, Geneva, Switzerland.

1
Introduction

EUGENIA DATE-BAH

Background

Women's work is of such critical importance for their social, economic and political empowerment, for family livelihoods, economic efficiency and the sustainable development of society that it must be given emphasis in any serious development agenda. The Fourth World Conference on Women (September 1995) and its preparatory process at national, regional and international levels provided an opportunity to assess progress in this and other areas during the previous decade. While there has been significant progress, the pace has been slow and considerable problems remain. New risks and opportunities have also emerged with the globalization of the economy, and with changes in technology and the labour market, all of which have had different repercussions for female and male workers. This portrait at the close of the twentieth century poses an enormous challenge for promoting the advancement of women workers and gender equality in the twenty-first century. A bold and innovative strategy is required.

This volume focuses on such a strategy above all, and in doing this attempts to convey a number of messages. One is that the situation of women workers and gender equality in the world of work is a complex, multifaceted and cross-cutting issue, which requires a comprehensive integrated strategy – economic, legal, social and political – for effective action. It is through such a broad-based attack that sustainable positive change can occur for women at work. The volume attempts, therefore, to examine several different critical elements of the comprehensive approach. Space constraint prevents full treatment of all the elements.

A second message is that the present rapidly changing socio-economic climate cannot altogether be termed an enabling environment for the promotion of the quantity and quality of women's employment, and also for gender equality, unless conscious and deliberate strategies and interventions are implemented. The world today is characterized by major changes in the economic, social and political spheres. Apart from rapid expansion in the globalization of production, trade and markets and the emergence of regional economic and other blocs, others include recession, the transition to market economies in Central and Eastern Europe, structural adjustment and other economic reforms in other parts of the world. Moreover, there are ongoing transformations in technology and work organization. New skill needs have emerged in the labour market. Furthermore, rapid urbanization is being experienced in some regions, and there are also demographic changes, such as the upward trend in both internal and international migration in some regions, in population ageing, and in the numbers of female heads of households. These changes continue to have far-reaching direct and indirect impact on the world of work with both positive and negative consequences on its participants, which are not gender neutral. This therefore constitutes an area for urgent action in the follow-up to the Fourth World Conference on Women. Indeed, this issue is reflected to some extent in the Platform for Action, adopted by this Conference, as well as in the regional platforms and plans of action adopted by the preparatory conferences in different parts of the world in 1994.

A third message is the relevance of international labour and other instruments, especially those on equality, for providing the appropriate parameters for the required comprehensive strategy. These include International Labour Conventions Nos 100 on Equal Remuneration, 1951; 103 on Maternity Protection (revised), 1952; 111 on Discrimination (Employment and Occupation), 1958; 156 on Workers with Family Responsibilities, 1981; 175 on Part-time Work, 1994; and 177 on Home Work, 1996; as well as the United Nations Convention on the Elimination of All Forms of Discrimination against Women (1979).

This introductory chapter provides an overview of the current situation of women workers and gender equality. It introduces the comprehensive integrated approach needed for urgent action and, in this context, the key issues covered in the ensuing chapters. Getting to grips with these critical issues is an essential part of the armoury required to combat effectively women's predicament and gender inequality in the world of work.

Women workers and gender equality at the close of the twentieth century: a brief overview

It should be pointed out at the outset that limitations persist in data collection, which continue to undercount women's economic activities and to under-assess their economic contribution, especially their non-market and informal work (Anker, 1994; Goldschmidt-Clermont, 1994). The available data indicate that women's economic activity rates and share of the labour force have been increasing in most regions of the world in recent decades, unlike men's, which have been stagnating,[1] a trend referred to in some of the literature (ILO, 1994a; Date-Bah, 1995a) as the 'feminization' of the labour force. Globally, the ratio of women to men in the economically active population has risen from 37:100 in 1970 to 62:100 in 1990 (UN, 1995a). Forty-four per cent of women aged 15 years and above are currently reported to be economically active (ILO, 1995c). In absolute numbers they constitute about 854 million women (UN, 1995a). There are, however, variations between regions, and a situation of near parity even exists in a few areas, such as the Nordic countries. In 1990, female economic activity rates were 58 per cent for Central Asia and Eastern Europe; 56 per cent for East Asia; 50–54 per cent for South-East Asia, sub-Saharan Africa, Western Europe and other developed regions; 44–49 per cent for the Caribbean, Oceania and South Asia; 30–34 per cent for Western Asia and Latin America; and 21 per cent for North Africa (UN, 1995c).

In almost all regions, with the exception of sub-Saharan Africa and East Asia, these percentages are higher than those in 1970. For example, they were 55 and 56 per cent for Central Asia and Eastern Europe; 37 and 40 per cent for Western Europe and the other developed countries; 38 and 22 per cent for the Caribbean and Latin America; and 8 per cent for North Africa (UN, 1995c). In OECD countries, women's economic participation rate is growing at the rate of 2.1 per cent per annum, which is more than double that of men – 0.8 per cent (ILO, 1995c). In 1992, 169.4 million women were in the labour force in this group of countries, representing an increase of 33 million since 1980 (ILO, 1994c). In Central and Eastern European countries, female participation has remained high despite the loss of some state-funded infrastructural social facilities, women's inability fully to tap and exploit the emerging entrepreneurial opportunities arising from the liberalization of the economy, and the re-emergence of traditional prejudices against women. This demonstrates women's 'strong labour force attachment' (Paukert, 1994). For example, in the Czech Republic and Slovakia, the crude female participation rates were 50 and 46 per cent respectively in 1989, compared to 54.9 and 51.1 per cent for men, and 44.8 and 45.3 per cent in 1992, compared to 52.4 and 49.2 per cent for men. In Poland, the figures were 57 per cent in 1988 and 54.2 per cent in 1992 for women, and 74.3 and 70 per cent for men (Paukert, 1994; ILO, 1992a).

The upward trend in some parts of Asia can be illustrated by the cases of China and Sri Lanka. Female economic activity rates for China and Sri Lanka rose from 44.25 and 18.05 per cent respectively in 1970 to 53.9 per cent in 1990 for China and 26.6 per cent in 1992 for Sri Lanka.

In South-East Asia, women form 80 per cent of the labour force in the export processing zones (ILO, 1995c). In Africa, the slight decline in female economic activity rates in official statistics[2] can be illustrated by the cases of Kenya, Nigeria and the United Republic of Tanzania. In Kenya, for example, the decline was from 35.15 per cent in 1980 to 31.3 per cent in 1990. In Nigeria, it was from 28.9 to 25.45 per cent. In the United Republic of Tanzania, the activity rate declined from 49.45 to 44.2 per cent during the 10-year period.

Regional differences also exist in the proportions of women in the different economic sectors. In the developed world, Latin America and the Caribbean for example, economically active women are more likely to be in waged employment, while those in Africa and Asia tend to be found more in rural agriculture and the urban informal sector.

Substantial progress has also been achieved in the adoption of equality instruments, such as pay equity schemes, affirmative action, and other measures by governments, some employers and trade unions. Furthermore, with the expansion in women's education,[3] training and skill diversification, there has been a gradual shattering of the 'glass ceiling' (the invisible barrier preventing women from reaching top positions) with the slow but steady entry of women into managerial and decision-making positions, and into non-traditional careers and so-called 'male' occupations and jobs. The glass ceiling, however, remains unshattered. In the United Kingdom, for example, women formed only 11 per cent of managers and 3 per cent of directors at the end of 1995 (*Financial Times*, 11 December 1995). Globally, women's participation in trade unions has also been rising, but is still unequal to that of men in most countries and regions, especially in leadership positions (Date-Bah, 1995b).

Despite these positive trends, there have been growing numbers of women among the unemployed, underemployed and workers in precarious employment. Even the increase that occurred in women's labour force participation was only 3 per cent during the 20-year period from 1970 to 1990 (UNDP, 1995). There is still a substantial gap between men and women in their economic activity rates. Women continue to shoulder the bulk of unpaid work, performing more than 70 per cent of it (INSTRAW, 1995). Economic restructuring programmes, by reducing employment opportunities in the public sector, have forced many women in sub-Saharan Africa into overcrowded informal sector work such as petty trading and home-based production. At the same time, the reduction in state financing of social services has increased women's unpaid work (ILO, 1994c, 1995c). Women's economic position and their social burden have, therefore, worsened under economic adjustment. In Europe, a number of the emerging employment opportunities for women have been in small-scale enterprises, in part-time, casual, temporary and other atypical forms of work (Meulders, 1994; Bettio, Rubery and Smith, 1996). Many women still face insurmountable inequalities in their preparation for entry into the labour market in terms of type and level of education and vocational training, skill diversification and flexibility and access to productive resources. In many developing and developed countries, for instance, women remain grossly under-represented in scientific, technical and vocational education and also have limited access to credit,[4] land, appropriate technology, agricultural extension services and other essential productive resources. Difficulties persist in women's reconciling of productive and reproductive functions, owing to men's inadequate sharing of family responsibilities and the limited availability of child-care facilities, parental and paternal leave and other relevant social support measures, not only for the care of the young but also for the aged. Furthermore, the ageing population trend has compounded women's caring responsibilities towards the elderly. Few countries have concrete and effective public policies to provide adequate programmes to support workers with family responsibilities. Furthermore, few enterprises provide family-friendly workplaces. There is also only limited enforcement of equality provisions resulting in discrepancy between *de jure* and de facto equality.

Horizontal and vertical job segregation and gender wage differentials remain universal features of the labour market, even though slight reductions have been reported in some countries in recent years. Women currently earn an average of between 50 and 96 per cent of men's pay, but there are significant variations between countries and regions (ILO, 1995c). For example, women's earnings as a percentage of men's earnings in non-agricultural employment stand at between 90 and 96 per cent in Australia and Turkey, but between 57 and 60 per cent in Cyprus and Korea (ILO, 1995c). Recent data (for example, ILO, 1993a; Gunderson, 1994) show that even if productivity-related factors are taken into account, a major male-female wage gap still remains, indicating the persistence of discrimination against women workers. Women continue to be concentrated in a narrow range of jobs, often at lower levels, and to be poorly represented in management and decision-making positions. *Women in a changing global economy* (UN, 1995a) reports that the ratio of women to men in decision-making positions is only 34 per cent, and that there had been no significant increase in many regions during the previous decade. It has been estimated (Ducci, 1993; ILO, 1995c) that it would take 475 years for gender parity to be reached in this sphere at the present rate of progress. Even when women have been able to overcome the barriers to entry into managerial positions, they face the inhospitable 'male environment' of the corporate structure and other barriers which rarely enable them to reach the top. Thus, with few exceptions, they often end up in low-power and low-status managerial positions.

The positive development in women's quantity of work has, therefore, not been matched by any similar trend in quality. Furthermore, working and living conditions of vulnerable groups of women workers, such as informal and rural-sector workers in the developing world, the disabled, migrants and female heads of households remain grave. Also alarming is women's growing and unfair share of poverty, the trend towards the 'feminization of poverty' (Buvinic, 1995; ILO, 1995c, 1995d; UN, 1995a, 1995b; Mhone, 1995), and the horrendous impact on women of the expanding incidence of civil strife and other wars around the world (Date-Bah, 1996). The recent Declaration of the World Summit for Social Development acknowledges this problem when it states that 'More women than men live in absolute poverty, and the imbalance continues to grow, with serious consequences for women and their children' (UN, 1995b). Women constitute 70 per cent of the 1.3 billion poor people in the world (ILO, 1995c).

Equality of opportunity and treatment between men and women in the world of work thus remains an intractable problem as the twenty-first century dawns, in spite of the progress achieved since the United Nations Declaration of International Women's Year over 20 years ago. The current trend is the net effect of a number of factors which affect men and women differently. It is thus essential for each of these factors to be taken into account in a holistic framework in any serious effort to promote the situation of women and gender equality at work.

The need for urgent action and an effective comprehensive approach

The current world attention being given to democracy, human rights and the achievement of sustainable development should, in addition to events such as world conferences on women, also imply more serious commitment to improving women's situation and visibility and gender equality in the world of work, and to creating an enabling environment for such an improvement to occur and for it to be sustained. The urgent need for such action is portrayed in the conclusions of a number of meetings organized recently (ILO, 1995a), the Declaration and Platform for Action of the Fourth World Conference on Women (1995), the various regional platforms and plans of action (1994), and the

Declaration and the Programme of Action of the World Summit for Social Development (1995). For example, among the 12 critical areas of concern identified by the Platform of the Fourth World Conference on Women are the persistent and increasing burden on women of poverty; inequality in economic structures and policies in all forms of productive activities and in access to resources; and lack of respect for and inadequate promotion and protection of the human rights of women (which also include women workers' rights). In relation to poverty, for example, governments are called upon to generate economic policies with a positive impact on women workers' employment and income in the informal and formal sectors and adopt specific measures to tackle women's unemployment.

The regional platforms of action adopted by the preparatory conferences for the Fourth World Conference also pinpoint a number of critical labour-related issues in relation to women and gender equality where action is urgently required. For instance, the regional platform for action for Europe specifies 'insufficient de facto gender equality in employment and economic opportunity and insufficient policies and measures to reconcile employment and family responsibilities'. The Arab plan of action mentions 'strengthening the capabilities of Arab women to enter the labour market and to achieve self-reliance'. The Jakarta declaration for Asia and the Pacific talks about 'inequality in women's access to and participation in economic activities', while the African platform covers, *inter alia*, 'women's lack of economic empowerment'. In addition, all the various regional platforms draw attention to women's increasing poverty. Focusing on women and gender equality questions in the world of work with a view to enhancing the pace of progress in this area could thus be perceived as one of the essential follow-ups to the Fourth World Conference on Women. The Summit's Declaration, for example, apart from emphasizing the 'goal of full employment as a basic priority' also stressed that particular attention should be paid to 'women's access to employment, the protection of their position in the labour market and the promotion of equal treatment of women and men, with respect to pay'.

The insights gathered in recent years (see for example ILO, 1995a, 1995b; Date-Bah, 1995a) throw light on the diverse variables and the interrelationships between them which should constitute the integrated strategy for sustainable change. The strategy should not separate women and gender equality issues at work from the formulation and implementation of macro- and microeconomic policies relating to growth and development.[5] A supportive legislative framework and its adequate enforcement is necessary. It is also essential to tackle the obstacles that women encounter in the labour market in terms of preparation (education and training, skill diversification and flexibility); quality of work and working conditions (pay, occupational health and safety, job and social security and sexual harassment); access to productive resources and to a wide range of employment opportunities; and various forms of discrimination. Furthermore, action to create more employment avenues is also required, such as through entrepreneurship promotion. There is a need to emphasize reconciliation of productive and reproductive roles. Affirmative action and other measures continue to be necessary in the short term to increase women's representation in decision-making and management. Furthermore, apart from governmental action, measures by the trade unions, employers' organizations, grass-roots and other organizations of civil society, including the mobilization of women, dialogue and collaborative action, are vital for women's empowerment.

Availability of relevant data is indispensable both for detailed elaboration and effective monitoring of the strategy's implementation. The development of appropriate concepts and measurement instruments and the generation of up-to-date, gender-disaggregated and reliable data therefore require emphasis in the comprehensive approach. As indicated in *The world's women 1990* (UN, 1991), 'Words advocating the interests of women, however plausible and persuasive they may be, need numbers to influence policy – and to change the world'. Furthermore, *The world's women 1995* (UN, 1995c) points out that improved statistics can 'inform and focus the debate' on women and gender issues and also contribute to a 'better understanding of women's and men's contributions to society (which) is essential to speed the shift from agenda to policy, to practice'. The design of appropriate statistical instruments, such as for measuring job segregation and wage differentials between men and women, is of particular importance for generating valid data required, for instance to determine the extent of gender inequality, to monitor trends and to underpin appropriate interventions such as labour-market policies. Current work (ILO, 1993a) on statistical measurement of gender wage differentials indicates, for example, that different methodologies exist that do not all measure the same thing and therefore hinder comparisons of gender wage differentials between countries. There is a need for appropriate methodology or methodologies that can disentangle the variety of factors contributing to women's wage disadvantage, including lower educational attainment and other human capital traits, seniority, productivity, employment pattern, non-pecuniary benefits and discrimination in the labour market.

It is only through such an all-inclusive attack that both the practical and strategic needs of women can be addressed to bring about effective change for women and gender equality in the world of work. The need for such a comprehensive approach can also be gleaned from some current resolutions (ILO, 1991, 1995b, 1995c). For example, the Resolution concerning ILO action for women workers, adopted by the International Labour Conference in 1991, urged governments, workers and employers' organizations 'to adopt comprehensive strategies to eliminate continuing barriers to equal participation of women in employment' (ILO, 1991).

Lessons gathered by some recent studies can serve as a useful basis for elaborating the required comprehensive and integrated agenda for future action. Among such studies is a multidisciplinary research initiative of the International Labour Organization – called the Interdepartmental Project on Equality for Women in Employment[6] – implemented from 1992 to early 1994 as part of the preparations for the Fourth World Conference on Women. The data generated by the project, some of which are assembled in this volume and others already disseminated through various publications and seminars, are of relevance in this respect as they portray the different facets of the required broad-based approach. The ILO's launching of this project reflects the fact that the promotion of equal opportunity and treatment in the world of work has always been one of the Organization's guiding principles since its inception in 1919. The ILO, one of the specialized agencies of the United Nations, has pursued this goal as a matter of social justice, human rights, equity and economic efficiency.

Elements of the comprehensive approach reflected in the current volume

The contributions in this volume touch on a number of critical issues in relation to women's work and gender equality within the changing global environment. Such issues include the macro- and microeconomic environment, notably the impact on women of recession and structural adjustment, the transition from planned to market economies, globalization and changes in work organization and technology to show the extent to which these changes have created an enabling as well as a disabling environment for the quantity and quality of women's work. Other issues considered include social security, sexual harassment, a supportive legal framework, and enforcement of equality provisions. The last two chapters deal with the role of the trade unions and employers' organizations. In almost all cases, the chapters examine policy implications geared to ensuring that women and gender equality questions in the changing world of work receive greater attention in the future. Among the challenges is how to accelerate the process of gendering the world of work and to improve upon women's situation, especially that of the more disadvantaged, in it. The analyses in the various parts of the volume provide a compelling case for adopting a comprehensive integrated strategy.

There are variations between the chapters in approach and method-ology. While most treat the issues by providing worldwide overviews, regional comparisons and cross-national data and examples, two (Chapters 8 and 11) employ the case-study approach, focusing on a specific country. In addition, some of the chapters are analytical and others descriptive. Furthermore, the chapters inevitably reflect the dis-ciplines of their authors, who include economists, sociologists, other social scientists and lawyers. Furthermore, the geographical coverage of the volume is wide and includes both the developing and developed worlds.

Apart from the introductory and concluding chapters, the volume is divided into four parts. Part I focuses on the macroeconomic context; Part II on working conditions and social security; Part III on enhancing the enforcement of equality legislation; and Part IV on the role of some relevant institutions in promoting women workers' concerns and gender equality in the world of work.

The macroeconomic context

Part I of the volume augments the data available (such as ILO, 1994a; Palmer, 1991; Commonwealth Secretariat, 1989) on the impact of macroeconomic changes on the labour market generally, and with particular reference to their differential impact on women and men. Changes in the global environment have contributed to increasing in-terdependence and internationalization of labour markets, and sectoral shifts such as growth in the service sector, which have created consid-erable employment opportunities for women. These have, however, tended to be flexible and precarious forms of work, such as part-time, temporary, home-based and casual. They provide poor working condi-tions, inadequate social protection and low quality of work. With the economic reforms, there have been cutbacks in public spending and retrenchment and privatization of parts of the public sector with an adverse impact on employment opportunities, especially for women, since the public sector has tended to be, in many countries, a significant employer of women. Other changes in the formal sector include the growth of the lean organization and subcontracting, stagnation and even loss of formal sector jobs in response to the exigencies of recession and increasing economic competition. There is a growing trend towards overcrowding in the informal sector in many developing countries, and 'informalization' of employment patterns in the developed countries. Indeed, there is a tendency towards the blurring of the formal and informal sectors (ILO, 1994a). The expanding labour supply, with about 43 million jobseekers annually entering the labour market in recent years, has compounded the high levels of unemployment and underemployment. These changes have affected both women and men, but differently, as demonstrated by some of the chapters in this volume.

With respect to recession, structural adjustment and women, Chapter 2 by Sally Baden brings out, *inter alia*, the methodological and data limitations. This chapter points out the regional similarities (in relation to declines in formal sector employment and expansion of the informal sector) in addition to the regional differences (such as between sub-Saharan Africa and Latin America and the Caribbean) in terms of the extent of wage declines. She examines a number of hypotheses including the 'added worker' effect, whereby women enter the labour force in increasing numbers and often at low wages to compensate for falling real household incomes; and the 'discouraged worker' effect, by which some women withdraw from the labour force as labour market conditions worsen. Women continue to have an unfair share of unemployment and underemployment. She observes that the compensatory programmes initiated to mitigate the adverse impact of structural adjustment, especially on the poor, have been ineffective in sustained employment creation and also have failed to address the specific problems of unemployed women.

The process of transition from centrally planned to market economies, which began in 1989 in Central and Eastern Europe, has been associated with declines in real incomes and standards of living and, therefore, an increase in poverty up to 1992–94[7] (Paukert, 1995). The transition has also had an impact on women's labour force participation. Paukert observes that women's labour force participation continues to be high in Central and Eastern Europe compared to the average for European women as a whole. Especially among the active age group, women still have a strong labour force attachment, perhaps linked to the great need for a double income by most households. Another significant observation relates to women's slower entry, compared to men, into entrepreneurial activities and private sector employment. While a number of factors are identified to explain this trend, family responsibility, in the wake of the reduction in state-funded social support in this area, is perceived to be the key factor. One major consequence, in the long term, of women's limited participation in entrepreneurship and the privatization process is perceived to be an 'exclusion of women from the business community with far-reaching consequences for the status of women in the years to come' (Paukert, 1995). In Chapter 3, Barbara Einhorn provides a further analysis of the effect on women of the current transition from centrally planned to market economies. She points out that despite the fact that under the centrally planned economy women were almost half of the labour force and had comprehensive child-care and other social support facilities, the labour market remained 'gender segregated', with women workers predominantly found in 'light industries ... retail and service sectors'. They were also inadequately represented in the top echelons of the occupational and managerial hierarchy. Furthermore, there was a gender differential in pay. In the transition, women appear to have been more adversely affected than men and currently outnumber men among the unemployed.[8] They have also lost many state-funded and other social supports.[9] The old prejudices against women have resurfaced and, therefore, women face discrimination and other difficulties in seeking re-employment and opportunities for retraining. Although an increasing number are entering into entrepreneurial activities, women remain a minority in this sphere. In the above situation, the chapter concludes that state intervention in the form of anti-discrimination legislation is necessary to guarantee that women do not lose out in the transition to a market economy. It should also be pointed out that there is a need to enforce the already existing anti-discrimination legislation, and to encourage and assist women to become entrepreneurs, such as through giving them better access to credit.

Globalization is one of the principal features of the current world. The recent successful conclusion of the Final Act of the Uruguay Round of multilateral trade negotiations has added a further dimension to this development. Unfortunately, little attention has been given to the differential impact – actual and potential – on women and men of this trend. Regions differ in terms of their degree of incorporation into international trade, the overall globalization process and the world economy. Few attempts have so far been made to analyse the globalization trend in Africa. While the trend in Africa can be described as less pronounced than in the other regions, Guy Mhone, in Chapter 4, is able to show that since the 1980s the process has gradually been growing, with a number of countries in the region putting in place various measures to attract foreign investors, in addition to embarking on economic reforms and market liberalization. While foreign investment confidence in the region remains low, an increasing number of African countries now have export processing zones. However, not much effort has been made by governments to protect the working conditions, occupational safety and health, freedom of association and other rights of the workers, mainly women, who work in them. In some countries, the existing labour relations and factory inspection systems are not made applicable to the EPZs. This predisposes the workers to exploitation. One of the observations made by the chapter is that, while the EPZs may be contributing to meeting the practical needs of women, especially young migrant women from rural areas, in terms of income, they do 'little to enhance their strategic interests'. Furthermore, the skills imparted by the EPZs to their employees tend to be quite limited because of the relatively low level of education of these workers. On the whole, foreign companies appear to find it cost-effective to relocate to Africa enterprises that mainly utilize workers with little education. With respect to rural and informal sector women workers, Mhone points out that one of the impacts of globalization has been to undermine the products of their activities, especially those that can be produced in bulk and cheaply by the EPZs.

Chapter 4 also examines other relevant concerns in Africa today, namely the impact of AIDS, drought and civil conflict and the fact that these problems have worsened the situation of women by making their multiple work burden more onerous. It also analyses the increasing feminization of poverty in the region, emanating, *inter alia*, from women's over-concentration in poor rural areas and also in low-income activities in urban areas, as well as their higher levels of unemployment, the short-term impact of structural adjustment policies, the inadequacy of social safety nets and other services provided by the state, gender biases and the large numbers of female heads of households.

The impact of current changes in work organization and technology on women's employment has not yet received much focus in research. Chapter 5, by Swasti Mitter, is one of the few efforts undertaken in this area. The chapter focuses first on the just-in-time (JIT) model which stresses quality, lean management, flexibility and 'quick response'. In terms of JIT, costs are reduced by working with a network of subcontractors, mainly small-scale units in which women tend to be engaged. This trend is occurring not only in the manufacturing sector but also in services within the context of new information technology and telecommunications. Such subcontracting or 'production decentralization' to small business units has generally provided employment opportunities for women. However, some conditions of work such as pay, occupational health and safety and social protection tend to be unfavourable. One of the features of the external side (subcontracting) of just-in-time is off-shore decentralized work, especially of information-intensive jobs, such as off-shore data-processing, currently found in several relatively poor countries. Mitter points to differences between the working conditions of off-shore and on-shore data processing workers in terms of status and occupational health and safety. JIT is also associated with changes internal to the organization, such as 'streamlining of work'. It stresses total quality control and, therefore, a team approach to work and multiskilling. The impact of internal JIT on women has not yet been widely examined. Mitter therefore points to this as a possible area for future work.

The second half of Chapter 5 examines the issue of new technologies, mainly biotechnology and computer technology, and their implications for women's employment. Women's employment prospects with biotechnology are observed to depend on the extent to which they are able to acquire the new technical skills required. With computer technologies, the impact has been 'complex'. In some areas, it has reduced women's work opportunities, especially for those with few skills. On the basis of data assembled in the chapter, a case can be made that concern for gender equality in employment should also involve assessment of the gender differential impact of changing work organization and the introduction of new technologies.

Working conditions and social security

Examples of inequalities in working conditions and social protection are pay, sexual harassment, job security, promotion prospects, occupational health and safety, measures to reconcile work and family responsibilities, and social security coverage. Improving these conditions and, therefore, the quality of women's work is essential for economic efficiency, owing to the beneficial impact of improved working conditions on productivity and the morale of workers.

Sexual harassment has been identified in a number of recent studies (for example Rubenstein, 1988, 1992; ILO, 1992c) as a major problem at the workplace with an adverse impact on workers' morale, health and performance as well as on employers' costs in terms of lost production and legal expenses. Although both women and men are subjected to sexual harassment, the available data (Rubenstein, 1988) confirm that more women encounter this problem than men. Chapter 6, by Linda Wirth, investigates the nature and extent of sexual harassment at work in developed and developing countries, as well as the means adopted by governments, employers, trade unions and non-governmental organizations to combat the problem. The chapter refers to surveys conducted in a number of countries, which indicate that sexual harassment does affect a significant number of employees. Recognizing that sexual harassment is indeed a serious problem is the first step to be taken in tackling it. The chapter points to growing awareness that sexual harassment is not just a private matter and that employers are increasingly concerned by its potentially negative effects on employees' relations, workplace effectiveness and company image. It also illustrates the range of definitions developed and used in the different countries and how they can vary according to cultural and social norms.

Combating sexual harassment involves both preventive and remedial measures. A description is, therefore, given of the different legal approaches adopted by some developed and developing countries, policies and procedures formulated by enterprises, and actions undertaken by governmental and non-governmental organizations and trade unions to raise awareness and to provide training and advisory services. Action undertaken at the international level is also covered.

The current shift in emphasis from protection of women workers to promotion of equality of opportunity and treatment between men and women in employment can be observed in international labour standards, national legislation and in calls for equality between men and women in social security benefits and in family responsibilities. The heavy burden borne by women in the care of children and the elderly continues to hinder their enjoyment of equal opportunity and treatment at work and their equal treatment generally in the labour market. The Preamble of the UN Convention on the Elimination of All Forms of Discrimination against Women, which was adopted by the United Nations General Assembly in 1979 and came into force in 1981, points out that the 'upbringing of children requires a sharing of responsibility between men and women and society as a whole' and that a change in the traditional role of men as well as the role of women is needed to achieve full equality between men and women. The ILO Workers with Family Responsibilities Convention (No. 156) and Recommendation (No. 165), adopted in 1981,[10] call on states to make it an aim of national policy to enable workers with family responsibilities to engage in employment without being subject to discrimination and, as far as possible, without conflict between their employment and family responsibilities. Measures compatible with national conditions and possibilities should be taken to permit workers with family responsibilities to exercise their right to free choice of employment, and to take account of their needs in terms and conditions of employment and in social security.

Some current trends in arrangements developed in several parts of the world to reconcile work and family responsibilities are analysed in Chapter 7 by Anne-Marie Brocas. The chapter also reviews present trends in social security coverage of women in relation to changes that have occurred in the economy (such as the growing number of women in paid employment) and also in family structure (such as the increase in the numbers of female heads of families). While significant progress has occurred in social security coverage of women as a result of the increasing participation of women in the labour market, full equality does not currently exist in this sphere. Existing provisions in many instances still reflect traditional male-as-breadwinner family models and other assumptions, and do not adequately take into account the specific features and situations of women and men, such as differences in conditions of employment, life expectancy, family status, family responsibilities and the changes in family structure. Furthermore, those provisions that are employment-related tend to manifest the prevailing labour market inequalities. In addition, precarious forms of employment in the developed world and the rural and urban informal sector in the developing world, in which a growing number of women engage, are often outside the purview of existing schemes. The extension of social security schemes to cover these categories of workers should, thus, constitute an integral element in the promotion of gender equality in this sphere. In the analysis, the ongoing debate in relation to derived versus individual rights is examined, but a clear-cut solution is not altogether offered owing to the complexity of the issue.

Enhancing effectiveness of legal enforcement

While the importance of a supportive legal framework in the promotion of equality of opportunity between men and women workers is acknowledged, the discussion of it tends to be confined to labour law. Women's situation in the world of work and the gender inequalities and discrimination faced by women are sometimes linked also to women's treatment under laws other than labour, such as the rights and restrictions contained in laws on the family, inheritance, land, property ownership and contract. Thus, to promote equality, it is necessary to examine these other laws, in addition to labour law, to identify the contradictions that could hinder equality of opportunity and treatment in employment. This is particularly so in developing countries where the majority of women workers operate outside the formal sector and tend to be outside the purview of existing labour law. Thus, to promote a legislative framework for equality, it is also necessary to examine not only labour law but also the other laws – modern and customary – and indeed the country's whole legal system to identify any inconsistencies which could hinder equality of opportunity and treatment at work. Some of the recent investigations of this issue (ILO, 1993b, 1994b) indicate that reform of a broad range of laws is crucial for the elimination of the legal impediments to equality posed by some provisions outside labour law.

Chapter 8, by David Tajgman and Evance Kalula, reviews a national legal system and identifies the legal impediments for the promotion of gender equality at work. This case-study illustrates the required broad legal framework beyond the arena of labour and employment laws. This is one of the complex set of factors that explains why Basotho women, despite their uniqueness in significantly outnumbering men in numbers and in education, even at higher levels, are under-represented in decision-making (ILO, 1994b).

While most countries now have some form of equality legislation at national level, and many have ratified the relevant international conventions on equality,[11] recent reports (ILO 1994a, 1994b, 1995a) demonstrate limited legal literacy and enforcement of equality provisions and, therefore, inadequate observance of women workers' rights. This hinders women's achievement of de facto equality with men. Chapter 9, by Constance Thomas and Rachael Taylor, examines the issue of enforcement and reviews the different mechanisms for enforcing equality provisions. Such mechanisms include: administrative bodies (such as labour inspection and other specialized enforcement bodies, the office of the Ombudsman) and legal aid to supervise and to enforce compliance with the legislation; and judicial action, such as cases brought, initiation of complaints by individuals, representation and group action, remedies and sanctions as well as the enforcement of judgements. The effectiveness of these mechanisms is assessed in two main ways: the intended beneficiaries' capacity to invoke the mechanisms in a judicial process, and the mechanisms' abilities to produce their intended results. The chapter also considers constraints faced in the enforcement of equal pay provisions. Furthermore, relevant information from international labour standards is provided on enforcement.

The role of the relevant institutions

The strong commitments and the individual and collaborative roles of governments, employers' and workers' organizations to addressing women's strategic and practical needs and to promoting gender equality at work often depend on the degree of these bodies' gender sensitivity and on the extent to which women are represented in their structures and leadership positions. Unfortunately, women's representation among employers' and workers' organizations, as well as in government, continues to lag behind that of men despite considerable positive developments. Furthermore, even though there is growing gender-awareness among these bodies, as demonstrated by the policies and other measures adopted by them, this remains inadequate, and intensification of action to enhance women's participation and mobilization within their structures and to promote adequate reflection of women and gender equality concerns in collective bargaining requires emphasis.

Chapter 10, by Eugenia Date-Bah, provides a worldwide overview of current trends in women's situation in the trade unions. The chapter shows that in all five regions of the world women's representation in unions has been increasing, although there are differences in terms of the extent of this increase. It is observed that with current changes in the labour market, the trade unions have other reasons, apart from equity and democracy, for making an effort to increase female representation and participation in their activities. An increasing number of women have also realized the need to mobilize for their empowerment and advancement. The chapter reviews some of the strategies adopted by unions in this regard, pointing out that, despite these efforts, women's representation in many unions remains unequal to that of men, and women are very under-represented in union leadership positions, except at the local level. A number of proposals are made for further action, not only by the unions but also by governments and employers in terms of creating an enabling environment, and by women themselves. In addition, the chapter stresses the need for unions to compile sex-disaggregated statistics to permit monitoring of trends in women's unionization and to serve as a basis for policy formulation.

In some regions, especially in the developing countries, the bulk of women workers is in the informal and rural sectors, which are often outside the purview of union activities. Enhancing women's participation in the unions and the relevance of the unions for all workers, especially the more vulnerable groups, should imply that unions also try to involve and assist these workers. The chapter ends with a review of the few efforts undertaken so far by unions in Africa in this area and looks at the outcome in terms of gains for women and unions. It analyses some of the strategies adopted, which have to be different from the traditional ones often employed by trade unions, because of the different characteristics of informal and rural sector workers. It emphasizes the need for more union action in this field.

Chapter 11, on employers' organizations and other bodies in the promotion of gender equality in employment, by Yoke Wan Lee,[12] provides a brief description of the roles of government and non-governmental organizations in addition to giving practical guidance on the roles employers can play to promote gender equality. The latter includes the elaboration of an equal opportunities' policy in companies, development of training programmes for management development and entrepreneurship promotion, research and other relevant functions.

Promoting improvements in women workers' situation is not only required for efficiency but is an integral part of the social responsibility
of business. The chapter concludes by stressing the importance of
monitoring the implementation of these programmes.

National women's machinery and other important bodies at the
national level, whose roles regarding women's work should be examined
in such a volume, are only covered in passing, owing to space restrictions. In the outputs of the four world conferences on women (1975,
1980, 1985 and 1995), governments have been urged to set up and
strengthen such machineries to provide relevant advice and to monitor
effectively the implementation of policies regarding women's advancement in society. Recent reviews (such as UN, 1995a) indicate that while
most countries have established various forms of women's machinery,
their effectiveness is greatly constrained by inadequate financial and
human resources, as well as by limited authority and linkages with other
relevant bodies in civil society, such as workers and employers' organizations, non-governmental and grass-roots women's organizations and
other structures and departments within government. The strengthening
of national women's machineries can enhance their role in the promotion of women workers' rights and the general improvement of
women's situation in society. Brief references to this issue are provided
in Chapters 4 and 11.

Apart from the relevant bodies at the national level, essential roles
can also be played by regional and international organizations. The
European Commission has, for example, adopted a number of recommendations and decisions covering equal pay, sexual harassment and
other concerns of women workers. Examples of the United Nations'
roles in recent years include adoption of the Convention on the Elimination of Discrimination against Women, convening four world conferences on women, which have served, *inter alia*, to draw attention to the
plight of women in different areas of societal life and to identify concrete strategies for action (Steady and Touré, 1995), and other activities
of specialized and other agencies within the United Nations system. In
this regard, attention needs to be drawn to ILO's special role, since
within the system the ILO has the mandate relating to employment.
This, for example, includes setting standards[13] (such as on some of the
key gender equality concerns – equal remuneration, maternity protection, sharing of family responsibilities and part-time work); provision of
technical co-operation assistance and advisory services to governments,
employers' and workers' organizations, to empower disadvantaged
groups of women workers; publications and information dissemination.

A number of concluding observations are provided in Chapter 12 by Eugenia Date-Bah. She underscores the need for considering all the diverse critical areas within a comprehensive integrated framework for effective policy-making and action. A summary is provided of the gaps identified in data collection, conceptual and analytical work on working women and gender equality. Focusing on their remedy and the collection of up-to-date gender disaggregated statistics to enhance women's visibility is emphasized as an integral part of the comprehensive approach.

Promoting gender equality and the advancement of women in the current rapidly changing world of work is an extensive process. The different chapters draw attention to the varied measures necessary for effective action within an integrated framework. The insights provided are geared to invigorating policy formulation, practical action, raising awareness, advocacy and further research. By pointing to the range of critical issues for effective change, the volume can be perceived as a contribution, in the realm of employment, to the Fourth World Conference on Women's follow-up. Focusing on the broad-based approach should feature in serious commitment to accelerating the process of positive change for women workers and for the attainment of genuine gender equality in the twenty-first century.

Notes

1. The activity rates of men aged 15 years and above were 76–90 per cent in 1970, but 72–83 per cent in 1990. Those of women, 8-57 per cent in 1970, were 21–58 per cent in 1990 (UN, 1995c).

2. The persisting problem of under-reporting of women's work should, however, be borne in mind.

3. The UNDP *Human Development Report 1995*, for example, points out that, in the developing world, between 1970 and 1990, female adult literacy and school enrolment rates increased twice as fast as those of males. With respect to educational enrolment at the tertiary level, the female proportion increased from less than one-half to more than 70 per cent of the figure for males during the same period. Globally, there was 'a two-thirds increase in female adult literacy and school enrolment' from 1970 to 1990 (UNDP, 1995, p. 4).

4. The UNDP *Human Development Report 1995* (p. 4) states, for example, that women represent as little as 7 and 11 per cent of the beneficiaries of credit programmes in Latin America and the Caribbean, respectively. INSTRAW (1995) reports that globally women obtain less than 5 per cent of the credit issued by lending institutions.

5. Mention has also been made of the need to engender the development paradigm, for instance by widening the choices of people, particularly women, to gain greater access to economic and political opportunities (UNDP, 1995).

6. This research project covered, *inter alia*, the development of appropriate statistical methodologies (such as for measuring gender wage differentials and job segregation); enhancement of the effectiveness of (and dissemination of information

about) equality in legislation; promotion of gender equality in social security; tackling women's obstacles in the labour market (such as sexual harassment and limited skill diversification); strengthening the roles of the relevant bodies in the world of work – governments, employers' and workers' organizations; and elaboration of policies and action to promote gender equality in the world of work.

7. The extent of the decline has begun to improve in a few of the Central European countries. For example in Poland, the GDP started to grow again in 1992. There has been a similar positive trend in the Czech Republic and Slovakia since 1994.

8. Hungary and Slovenia are, however, exceptions in this respect.

9. At the same time, there has been a growth in the privately run fee-paying child-care facilities.

10. These standards provided a broader coverage, in terms of being applicable to both men and women, than the earlier Employment (Women with Family Responsibilities) Recommendation, 1965, (No. 123) which, as the ILO's first attempt to guide policy regarding the reconciliation of work and family responsibilities, focused only on women. From a realization that the latter emphasis could reinforce the traditional image of women, a change in the traditional role of men was also perceived to be necessary. Therefore, facilities and measures established to assist workers to reconcile their work and family responsibilities should be equally available to men and women.

11. For example, by August 1995, 139 states had ratified the United Nations Convention on the Elimination of All Forms of Discrimination against Women (1979); and 123 countries had ratified International Labour Convention No. 100 on Equal Remuneration (1951).

12. The original draft of this chapter was commissioned by the ILO's Bureau of Employers' Activities to supplement the work undertaken by the Interdepartmental Project on Equality for Women in Employment.

13. By June 1996, 180 Conventions and 187 Recommendations had been adopted, which are of relevance to both men and women workers. A few among them are of particular interest to women and can constitute an essential framework for national equality legislation and the elaboration of the required integrated comprehensive strategy.

References

Anker, R. (1994) 'Measuring women's participation in the African labour force', in A. Adepoju and C. Oppong (eds), *Gender, work and population in sub-Saharan Africa*, London, James Currey and ILO.

Bettio, F., J. Rubery and M. Smith (1996) 'Gender, flexibility and employment relations', European Seminar on Women and Work in Europe, Turin.

Buvinic, M. (1995) 'The feminization of poverty?: Research and policy needs', in J. Figueiredo and Z. Shaheed, *Reducing poverty through labour market policies*, Geneva, International Institute for Labour Studies.

Commonwealth Secretariat (1989) *Engendering adjustment for the 1990s*, London.

Date-Bah, E. (1995a) 'Women in the global labour market: Empowerment and enabling environment for progress', in F.C. Steady and R. Touré, 1995.

— (1995b) 'Towards gender equality in the unions: A worldwide overview', draft manuscript, ILO.

— (1996) 'Post-war efforts for sustainable peace after war: Arguing the need for gender perspectives and a special focus on women in employment', Geneva, ILO.

Ducci, M.A. (1993) 'Women in authority: The ideal and the reality', in *World of Work*, No. 2, Geneva, ILO.

Goldschmidt-Clermont, L. (1994) 'Assessing women's economic contributions in domestic and related activities', in A. Adepoju and C. Oppong (eds), *Gender, work and population in sub-Saharan Africa*, London, James Currey and ILO.

Gunderson, M. (1994) *Comparable worth and gender discrimination: An international perspective*, Geneva.

ILO (1991) *Resolutions adopted by the International Labour Conference at its 78th Session*, Geneva.

— (1992a) *Yearbook of labour statistics*, Geneva.

— (1992b) *World labour report 1992*, Geneva.

— (1992c) *Conditions of work digest: Combating sexual harassment at work*, Geneva.

— (1993a) *Statistical measurement of gender wage differentials: A practical handbook*, Geneva.

— (1993b) *A comprehensive women's employment strategy for Indonesia*, Bangkok.

— (1994a) *World labour report 1994*, Geneva.

— (1994b) *Promoting gender equality in employment in Lesotho: An agenda for action*, Turin.

— (1994c) *The changing role of women in the economy*, Document GB261/SP/2/2, Geneva.

— (1995a) *Women workers: An annotated bibliography, 1993–94*, Geneva.

— (1995b) *Gender equality at work, strategies towards the twenty-first century: Results of ILO preparatory meetings for the Fourth World Conference on Women*, Geneva.

— (1995c) *Press kit on women workers*, Geneva.

— (1995d) *Gender, poverty and employment: turning capabilities into entitlements*, Geneva.

— and International Institute for Labour Studies (IILS) (1994) 'Framework paper on women workers in a changing global environment', paper prepared for the International Forum on Equality for Women in the World of Work, Geneva, June.

INSTRAW (United Nations International Research and Training Institute for the Advancement of Women) (1995) *Beijing and beyond*, Santo Domingo.

Mhone, G. (1995) 'African women workers, economic reform, globalization, AIDS and civil strife', Document IDP Women/WP-23, Geneva, ILO.

Meulders, D. (1994) 'Employment, unemployment and new forms of labour', paper presented at European Seminar on Women and Work, Turin, ILO.

Palmer, I. (1991) *Gender and population in the adjustment of African economies: Planning for change*, Women, Work and Development Series, No. 19, Geneva, ILO.

Paukert, L. (1994) 'Gender and change in Central and Eastern Europe', paper presented at the International Forum on Equality for Women in the World of Work, Geneva, ILO.

— (1995) 'Economic transition and women's employment in four Central European countries 1989–1994', paper presented at the Technical Meeting on Enterprise Restructuring and Labour Markets, Turin, ILO, 31 May–2 June.

Rubenstein, M. (1988) *The dignity of women at work: A report on the problem of sexual harassment in the member states of the European Community*, Luxembourg.

— (1992) 'Dealing with sexual harassment at work: The experience of industrialized countries', in ILO, 1992c.

Siltanen, J. *et al.* (1995) *Gender inequality in the labour market: Occupational concentration and segregation, A manual on methodology*, Geneva, ILO.

Steady, F.C. and R. Touré (1995) *Women and the United Nations, reflections and new horizons*, Rochester, Schenkman Books.

UN (1991) *The world's women 1990, trends and statistics*, New York.

— (1994) 'Women in extreme poverty', Women 2000 1994, No. 1, New York, Division for the Advancement of Women.

— (1995a) *Women in a changing global economy, 1994 world survey on the role of women in development*, New York.

— (1995b) *Declaration and programme of action of the world summit for social development*, Copenhagen, Doc A/CONF.166/L.3/Add.1, New York.

— (1995c) *The world's women 1995, trends and statistics*, New York.

— (1995d) *Report of the Fourth World Conference on Women*, Beijing, China, 4–15 September, Doc.A/CONF 177/20.

UNDP (1995) *Human development report 1995*, New York, Oxford University Press.

UNECLAC (1994) *Women and urban employment in Latin America: The significance of changes in the 1990s*, Document DDR/3, Integration of women into the economic and social development of Latin America and the Caribbean, Argentina.

PART I
The macroeconomic context

2
Recession and structural adjustment's impact on women's work in selected developing regions[1]

SALLY BADEN

Existing literature, conceptual and methodological problems

This review focuses on trends in women's employment in two developing regions most severely affected by recession – Latin America and sub-Saharan Africa – in the 1980s. In relation to sub-Saharan Africa, adjustment policies form the framework for much of the existing analysis. The material on Latin America and the Caribbean, however, is set mainly within the framework of examining the effects of recession on women's work, with stabilization and adjustment seen in this context.

Most major studies on the effect of adjustment programmes have been primarily concerned with macroeconomic performance and, more recently, with the economic and political sustainability of adjustment programmes (e.g. Mosley *et al.*, 1991; Corbo *et al.* (eds), 1992). There is also a small but significant body of literature addressing the poverty and distributional consequences of adjustment but with little specific focus on gender equality (Bourguignon and Morrisson, 1992; UNICEF, 1987). Similarly, the mainstream work on adjustment and labour markets does not comprehensively address the effects of changes on women's work (e.g. Fallon and Riveros, 1989; Colclough, 1991; Horton *et al.*, 1991). Few sources have attempted systematically to analyse the gender-differential effects of labour-market changes under adjustment, or to develop a framework for doing so (Gindling, 1993 on Costa Rica; Appleton *et al.*, 1990 on Côte d'Ivoire).

Most literature on women and adjustment originates in the 'women in development' and feminist traditions. Few studies have attempted to develop a framework for analysing the gendered consequences of adjustment policies (UNICEF, 1989; Commonwealth Secretariat, 1989; Palmer, 1991). There is also some rather patchy case-study material with a gender perspective on adjustment, but few such studies attempt to isolate the effects of adjustment from other factors, and most do not include the data necessary to make rigorous empirical assessments (e.g. UNICEF, 1989; Deere *et al.*, 1991; Commonwealth Secretariat, 1991; Benería and Feldman (eds), 1992). Much of the gender-related literature on adjustment focuses on agriculture in sub-Saharan Africa and the urban (particularly informal) sector in Latin America, perhaps reflecting the more long-standing concerns of scholars of women and development. More empirical study is needed of the impact of adjustment on women in formal sector employment where problems of gathering data on women's work might be presumed to be less than for rural or urban informal settings.[2]

There are inherent conceptual and methodological problems in trying to separate the effects of adjustment from those of recession and also from longer-term trends. The secular rise in female labour force participation in most countries over recent decades and the longer-term shifting patterns of sectoral representation of women workers need to be separated from the impact of recession and adjustment.

Any attempt to examine empirically the impact of recession or adjustment on women's work is further complicated by the lack of unbroken time series of sex-disaggregated employment data (i.e. yearly or monthly sex-disaggregated data, with no missing figures, which are generated using the same methodology and are therefore comparable) for many countries (especially in sub-Saharan Africa), which might reveal trends. Inasmuch as such data do exist, their accuracy and comparability is constrained by both conceptual and collection problems (Benería, 1992). Moreover, in the context of developing economies undergoing recession and adjustment, the significance of standard unemployment and labour force participation data itself becomes increasingly limited, as processes of casualization of employment and movement into the informal sector are intensified.

Disentangling the effects of adjustment from those of recession is not self-evident, particularly given very variable regional and country experiences. The length and nature of the pre-adjustment economic crisis (if any), the timing and phasing of the introduction of adjustment programmes,[3] the mix of adjustment policies[4] – particularly the degree of demand reduction induced, the level of external financing, and the degree of implementation of adjustment programmes – are interlinked factors that render systematic comparison difficult.[5]

Approaches which have been used to evaluate the impact of adjustment programmes include matching pairs of adjusting and non-adjusting countries (Mosley *et al.*, 1991) or control groups, an approach generally favoured in World Bank studies. Variously, these attempt to control for different degrees of implementation and levels of finance, or for the intensity, timing or perceived success of adjustment. However, there is inevitably a strong element of subjective judgement. There is not enough detailed evidence here to relate systematically the 'success' or otherwise of adjustment programmes to their outcomes for women's work, although inferences will be drawn where possible.

Examining the impact of recession and/or adjustment in developing countries is further complicated by regional and between-country variations in the depth and timing of cyclical movements, as well as in the timing and consistency of implementation of adjustment policies. In sub-Saharan Africa particularly, and also in many parts of Latin America, lengthy periods of stagnation or recession dating back to the mid and late 1970s have preceded adjustment, and many would argue that excessively deflationary adjustment policies have themselves led to more protracted recession (UNICEF, 1989; ECLAC, 1992). On the other hand, adjustment programmes in Asia have generally been implemented in a context of relatively sustained growth, except for brief periods of recession (such as 1984-85 in Malaysia). Some countries in Latin America initiated their own adjustment programmes prior to the onset of recession in the region in the early 1980s and many introduced 'heterodox' adjustment packages in the mid-1980s (UNICEF, 1989). In addition, there have often been reversals of adjustment policy, or else programmes have been interrupted by periods of recession and austerity (Horton *et al.*, 1991).

Given these methodological and empirical problems, a rigorous analysis that separates the effects of recession and adjustment on women's work is not yet possible. Nevertheless, the effects of recession on employment generally and women's work particularly can be viewed in terms of the impact on labour force participation rates, on under- and unemployment and on real wage levels; and those of adjustment primarily in terms of sectoral shifts in employment patterns and in wage differentials between sectors.[6] Some of the limited literature on the impact of recession on women's employment in developing economies has highlighted the 'added worker' effect, whereby women enter the labour force in increasing numbers and often at low wages to compensate for falling real household incomes. Others note the withdrawal of some groups of women from the labour force (the 'discouraged worker' effect) as labour market conditions worsen. Sectoral shifts in labour demand and changing working conditions under recession are also highlighted, particularly in women's participation in informal sector activity or casual forms of labour.

With all the complex forces at work, it is not surprising that no general conclusions have been drawn about the employment effects of recession and adjustment. Nevertheless, one or two overall summary assessments have been made which illustrate different viewpoints. One account of the effects of the crisis in Latin America and the Caribbean concludes that:

> The effects of the crisis on the labour market in Latin America and the Caribbean included a slump in the rate of job creation, changes in the type of employment created and a drop in wages. Between 1980 and 1985 ... the number of unemployed rose at a cumulative annual rate of 8 per cent per annum ... the changes in the structure of employment ... reflect an increase in the proportion of jobs characterized by the greatest degree of underutilization of labour, as manifested in informalization, tertiarization and an increase in employment in the public sector ... the rapid expansion of the urban informal sector ... is indicative of a worsening of the employment situation mainly affecting the lowest income sectors of the population[7] ... the share of agricultural population has once again started to grow, as a result of the slump in employment in the cities. (ECLAC, 1992, pp. 25–26)

Another overview of the effects of adjustment on labour markets in both Latin America and Africa finds that:

> In Latin America and Africa ... there has been some of the desired shift into tradables, but largely due to the shift back into agriculture and out of government employment. Manufacturing sector employment frequently seems to have suffered during years of crisis and not to have recovered during adjustment. This is perhaps a not surprising result of policy changes which depreciate the exchange rate but at the same time reduce tariffs. Although the former benefits agricultural exports, the possible benefits to manufactures are offset by decreased protection. (Horton *et al.*, 1991, p. 30)

Recession, adjustment and labour

Decomposing the relationship between recession, adjustment and labour

Conventional adjustment programmes affect employment and working conditions through a variety of direct and indirect mechanisms. Crudely, policies of demand restraint (through reductions in government/overall borrowing) lead to downward pressure on output prices, cutbacks in production and hence in the demand for labour, particularly in the formal sector. In standard theory, the effect on employment levels depends on the flexibility of wages: where wages are not flexible downwards, net losses in employment are liable to be greater. This is often the rationale for removing minimum wage legislation, or for the de-indexation of wages[8] under adjustment. However, there is evidence that wages have proved remarkably flexible downwardly in most adjusting countries, even in formal sector labour markets, yet unemployment levels have persisted or risen at the same time. It is possible that the demand effect of the fall in wages/employment may lead to persistent unemployment, even where wages have fallen, due to the lower propensity to consume on the part of profit-earners compared with wage-earners. Persistent unemployment could also be the result of imperfections or rigidities in markets other than that of labour (Horton et al., 1991).

Policies of cuts in public expenditure, privatization and public sector enterprise reform lead to public sector recruitment freezes or retrenchments. Wage freezes, the removal of minimum wage legislation and the effects of general inflation (which some would argue are exacerbated under adjustment through devaluation) lead to reductions in real wages.

The shifts in the incentive structure brought about by changing relative prices (particularly through devaluation) under adjustment potentially lead to shifts in employment patterns, with new jobs being created in some sectors as jobs are lost in others. In theory, the temporary wage differentials created under adjustment act as the mechanism for the reallocation of labour between sectors. However, the existence of wage differentials themselves does not indicate that labour reallocation is occurring – it is important to look at actual employment shifts. It is also possible that in sectors of shrinking labour demand, wages may rise if lower-paid labour is shed first. In practice there may be institutional and other barriers, including gender-related constraints (see below) to the reallocation of labour under adjustment. The lack of functioning of other markets, such as credit markets, may also act as a constraint to labour reallocation.

In theory, adjustment brings about increased incentives to the production of tradables (exports and import substitutes) relative to non-tradables (goods which are only consumed domestically, particularly many kinds of services). However, tradability is a slippery concept related to transportation costs and protection policies. Thus, the same goods/economic activities may be tradable in one context but not in another, and their tradability may change over time. This makes it very difficult to predict the employment effects of adjustment according to this schema.

The effects of adjustment on relative wages depend partly on the wage differentials created between sectors. Simple analysis predicts a rise in relative wages in tradables, but wage shifts are also caused by employment shifts and thus will tend to level out over time. Relative wages in different sectors are also mediated by the tradables to non-tradables composition of the consumption basket of workers in these sectors. In the longer term, there may be substitution in consumption of cheaper, locally marketed – or even home-produced – goods, for imported goods.[9] It is often women, as household managers, who bear the brunt of these substitutions in consumption in terms of increased time costs and physical effort.

Structural adjustment programmes (SAPs) are generally associated with labour shedding in formal and especially government sectors. There is a tendency for labour to move into sectors with flexible entry – such as the informal sector and agriculture. Labour crowding may then have the effect of depressing relative wages in these sectors. In non-tradables (commerce, services), wages are depressed both directly (through exchange rate changes) and indirectly (through labour crowding). In tradables (agriculture), the effect could go either way depending on the relative magnitude of the opposing income (rising wages due to devaluation) and substitution (labour crowding) effects (Bourguignon and Morrisson, 1992).

The concept of the informal sector, its composition in terms of activities and its relationship to the formal sector through both product and labour markets, remains an area of controversy.[10] One type of analysis – particularly popular in Latin America – sees the informal sector in developing economies primarily as soaking up the under- and unemployed (given a 'structural surplus of labour' and lack of comprehensive social security) and as comprising mainly low-return, low-productivity activities catering to low-income consumers (Tokman, 1991; Roberts, 1991). This accords with the view that, primarily as a result of recession rather than adjustment, the informal sector will increasingly become a refuge for the under- and unemployed, and suffer from labour crowding as well as reduced demand, thus depressing incomes (Bourguignon and Morrisson, 1992). Another view is that the informal sector has much potential for dynamic growth but has been held back by distortions favouring formal sector industry (such as restrictions on credit) so that what is needed is further deregulation under adjustment programmes, to increase the supply of labour and other inputs, such as credit, to the sector (Riveros, 1990).

Under recession and adjustment, some areas of informal sector activity may become closely allied to the formal sector, through processes of privatization (contracting out) and subcontracting by private industry to small-scale producers and units, including homeworkers, in order to cut costs (Standing, 1991). Some dispute that this is an important trend in developing countries (Tokman, 1991; Roberts, 1991). Other possible trends are that small firms may be driven into informality (or illegality) in order to survive recession (Roberts, 1991). The nature of employment also may become increasingly casual, unregulated and unprotected in order to reduce costs and make lay-offs easier. Further, 'autonomous' informal sector activities may increase (Judisman and Moreno, 1990).

Informal sector activity is highly heterogeneous, and not all 'free-entry', as some analyses imply. Certain informal sector activities require considerable physical or human capital and thus are unlikely to be taken up by unskilled, low-income workers, among whom women are over-represented (Weekes-Vagliani, 1992).

Given the heterogeneity of the informal sector, there is no clear coincidence between informality and non-tradability (Standing, 1991). However, certain kinds of activity in the informal sector, such as petty commerce and personal services – which tend to be where women predominate – may fall into the category of non-tradables. More detailed disaggregations of informal sector activity are needed, which look at type of activity, occupational status, levels of protection/regulation, and tradability as well as the gender, life cycle and other characteristics of informal sector workers.

Palmer (1991) distinguishes between three factors which influence the outcome of adjustment on the level of activity and employment in the informal sector. They are:

- whether informal sector demand increases or decreases (which depends on the relative importance of income and substitution effects);
- the share of tradables in the informal sector – and the effect of devaluation and trade liberalization on domestic demand for these;
- the impact of market deregulation on removing discrimination between the formal and the informal sector, particularly in factor markets (such as credit).

In the rural sector, the effects of adjustment should in theory be favourable or neutral, due to increases in relative prices of agricultural output to producers (through devaluation, market deregulation and trade liberalization). Nevertheless, exogenous factors may outweigh the impact of adjustment measures either positively (e.g. good rainfall) or negatively (e.g. drought; falling international prices). In theory, demand for labour will not fall and the slower growth of the labour force in rural areas – due to rural-urban migration – also limits the increase in labour supply. However, the decline in employment opportunities in urban areas may be leading to a slow-down or even a reversal in rural-urban migration in some countries (Bourguignon and Morrisson, 1992).

The effect of adjustment on agricultural incomes should in theory be less negative (or more positive) compared to incomes in the formal or informal urban sectors, because of increased incentives to agricultural production and because measures which are directly employment/income reducing, such as cuts in public sector expenditure, tend to have a more limited effect in rural areas. However, some measures, such as the removal of subsidies on inputs or consumption goods may have a countervailing effect on the incomes particularly of small producers or net food buyers. Further, a substantial proportion of rural incomes – particularly of those with smallholdings – may come from off-farm sources such as remittances or petty trade and other services. To the extent that these are dependent on urban incomes they will tend to be falling (Bourguignon and Morrisson, 1992).

The direct benefits of the growth of agricultural exports under trade liberalization – assuming that international prices are stable – will tend to be captured mainly by larger producers, unless a high proportion of small and medium farmers are engaged in export crop production. However, this expansion may indirectly benefit producers of locally traded foods (who may be predominantly women in the sub-Saharan African context) responding to increased demand and prices as agricultural incomes rise (Joekes, 1991b). There are also possibilities for growth in rural wage employment associated with the expansion of export crop production, but this may be limited by technological change factors such as mechanization (Bourguignon and Morrisson, 1992). Those who are unlikely to benefit at all, or to lose out, are food-deficit households, which will be forced to purchase their additional requirements at rising prices.

Another crucial and often neglected aspect of stabilization and adjustment, mediated partly through labour market shifts, is the long-term impact on human capital investment, which may be affected both by unemployment and by sectoral shifts in employment (Horton *et al.*, 1991). There is evidence that in Latin America teenagers who would otherwise be in school have entered the labour market in significant numbers as 'secondary workers' under conditions of recession. The relative effects of this labour market response on teenage girls and boys are not clear (Gindling and Berry, 1992; Benería, 1991). Moser (1992) suggests that the increased reproductive burden as more women enter the labour force is being transferred to older daughters, often with prejudice to their school attendance or performance (cited in Humphrey *et al.*, 1993).

A related issue possibly more pertinent to sub-Saharan Africa is the diversion of skilled and professional labour from public sector employment to the informal sector (see evidence in section below on the urban informal sector). Women (and men) are known to be leaving occupations such as teaching and nursing to engage in potentially more lucrative informal sector activities, implying a considerable erosion of the professional skills base over the longer term. Others are maintaining their foothold in the public sector, but simultaneously engaging in other activities, with negative implications for the efficiency and quality of public sector service provision.

Declines in public investment in education, resulting in increased private costs of schooling under adjustment programmes, are also acting as a disincentive to the education of children, with possibly a greater negative impact on girls' education. Given the apparent premium on education for girls entering the formal labour market, this can only reinforce a vicious circle of women's involvement in low productivity and low-paid work.

Assessments of the impact of recession and adjustment on labour in developing economies

Changes in levels and structure of employment

Latin America and the Caribbean The slow growth of the Latin American and Caribbean economies, especially in the early 1980s, resulted in a slow-down in job creation and increases in open unemployment, particularly in the smaller Caribbean and Central American countries and particularly among youth and women. Whilst private sector formal employment, especially in large enterprises, declined during the early 1980s recession and did not increase during the post-1984 recovery (large private enterprise employment fell from 59 per cent of non-agricultural employment in 1980 to 54 per cent in 1990), public sector employment continued to grow in the early 1980s (at 4.5 per cent per annum, 1980–85) rising from 15.8 to 16.8 per cent of non-agricultural employment. This compensated somewhat for the shortfall in the private sector. However, later in the decade, public sector employment growth also slowed – in Chile, for example, it declined by 15 per cent between 1985 and 1990 (ILO, 1992, 1993).

There have been reports (ILO, 1992, 1993) of a significant expansion in urban informal sector employment in Latin America. If domestic service is included, informal sector employment doubled in the 1980s.

This expansion was mainly concentrated in the growth of small enterprises and in low productivity services (ILO, 1992, 1993).

In a differing interpretation, Riveros (1990) argues that the urban informal sector in Latin America has not expanded as rapidly as might have been expected under recession and adjustment, in spite of increased unemployment and declines in formal sector wages. He suggests that further deregulation of labour markets and adjustment of relative wage levels may be required to encourage the movement of unemployed workers into the informal sector.

Levels of underemployment in Latin America also rose over the 1980s, particularly in the informal sector. Furthermore, there has been a growth in the number of casual workers in agricultural labour in the export sector. In Chile, the number of casual workers in this sector increased by 52 per cent between 1976 and 1986 (ILO, 1993). Open unemployment levels have fallen slightly overall in Latin America since the mid-1980s, but have remained constant in the Caribbean. Young people and women in particular, however, continue to experience disproportionately high rates of unemployment.

The mean unemployment rate across 12 Commonwealth Caribbean countries in the mid- to late 1970s was 17.5 per cent, with rates ranging between 2 and 44 per cent. The economic performance of some Latin American countries had begun to improve in the late 1980s in terms of growth, although poverty is still on the increase. In the Caribbean the prospects are not as good (ILO, 1992, 1993).

Sub-Saharan Africa   The protracted economic crisis in sub-Saharan Africa has been characterized by a sharp deterioration in the employment situation, and dramatic declines in real wages. The rate of modern sector employment growth has declined as a result of recession and adjustment, particularly in the industrial sector, marking a process of deindustrialization. In the early 1990s the modern sector employed around 8 per cent of the labour force, compared with 10 per cent in 1980 (ILO, 1993; Vandermoortele, 1991).

Much of the slow-down of employment creation in the modern sector is due to a decline in the rate of growth of public sector employment since the early 1980s, which represents a high proportion (over half) of total non-agricultural employment. Prior to this, public sector employment had been expanding rapidly in many countries and had tended to act as an employer of last resort.

On the other hand, the informal sector in sub-Saharan Africa has grown rapidly (6.7 per cent per year, 1980–85) and is now absorbing the majority of new labour recruits. In the early 1990s, it was believed to employ 62.5 per cent of the urban labour force in the region.[11] Much of it was in commerce, and microenterprises tended to dominate. The sector is increasingly characterized by underemployment, low productivity and low wages.

Open unemployment in sub-Saharan Africa is rising, particularly in urban areas and among youth, women (young and adult) and the educated (particularly secondary school-leavers). Average urban unemployment in the mid-1980s was 18 per cent compared with 10 per cent in the mid-1970s, and the rising trend is projected to continue (ILO, 1992).

Wage trends

The general picture of wage trends under recession and adjustment is one of falling real wages, such as in sub-Saharan Africa and to some extent in Latin America. Toye (1995), in his analysis of structural adjustment, wages and employment in Chile and Indonesia, observes that if a general impact of adjustment policies is a reduction in the real wage, then, without considerable expansion in employment, income distribution is likely to worsen.

Average real wages fell by 30 per cent for all modern sector workers in sub-Saharan Africa between 1980 and 1986 with public sector pay falling most. However, the decline in real wages in sub-Saharan Africa predates the economic downturn starting in 1980. For instance, during the 1970s real wages fell by an average of about 2.9 per cent annually; the decline intensified in the 1980s under adjustment. Minimum wage levels also declined considerably in the early 1980s, but have since stabilized, though at levels where they cannot meet an individual's, let alone a family's, basic needs in many countries (ILO, 1992; Colclough, 1991; Vandermootele, 1991).

Real wages in Latin America have declined considerably since 1980. There has been considerable variation between countries, however, with wage levels holding up relatively well in some places (at least up to 1988) and falling dramatically in others. In Bolivia, Ecuador, Mexico, Paraguay and Peru, in 1990, minimum wages were between 15 and 40 per cent of their 1980 value.

The decline in real wages in the region is attributed in general to high inflation, to increased unemployment and to the growth of employment in low-productivity sectors, which has weakened the bargaining power of organized wage-earners. Adjustment policies implemented in the majority of countries in the region may have also led to real wage declines (ECLAC, 1992; ILO, 1993).

Relative wages

Horton *et al.* (1991) provide some information on relative wage shifts between economic sectors in nine countries studied. In several countries (Chile, Egypt, Malaysia), wages in manufacturing rose during recession and/or adjustment (partly due to the shedding of lower-paid labour), but fell in Bolivia where there were tariff cuts. Agricultural wages also increased in relative terms in several countries (Egypt, Ghana, Malaysia), but in the last case these gains were subsequently reversed during the recession. Wages in commerce and service sectors were falling in the one or two cases where this is mentioned.

In Latin America, workers in formal sector employment in the public sector and agriculture have been particularly hard hit, suffering wage declines of around 30 per cent.

In sub-Saharan Africa, in the 1980s, there has been not just an erosion but also a compression of wage levels, demonstrated by narrowing differentials between occupational groups, particularly in the public sector. In the period 1975–85, real salaries fell by 36 per cent in the lowest public sector grades and by 58 per cent in the highest grades.

There is some evidence that public and private sector wages have moved in different directions in the 1980s. Horton *et al.* (1991) report that public sector wages fell almost universally (although possibly with different trends in public service employment and parastatals), or did not rise as rapidly as in other sectors. In the private sector, real wages have tended not to fall, or at least not so rapidly as public sector wages.

The impact of recession and adjustment on women's work

Gender analysis of recession and women's work

Despite women's rising economic activity rates, particularly in the 25–44 age group, in most regions of the developing world except for sub-Saharan Africa, and declining rates for men over the past two decades, the gender gap in recorded activity rates remains wide. The effects of recession have to be seen against this background.

Most of the literature to date, which relates mainly to developed countries, argues that women's employment is less affected than men's in periods of recession. Women tend to be concentrated in areas of economic activity which are less cyclically affected, such as in finance, commerce and services, rather than manufacturing. Where women do work in manufacturing, it may tend to be in final goods consumption industries such as food, beverages, tobacco and pharmaceuticals, the products of which have low-income elasticity, rather than, say, consumer durables manufacturing. This may also be the case for formal sector employment in developing countries (Judisman and Moreno, 1990). However, where recession is protracted, or where structural adjustment programmes are implemented, women's employment may be seriously affected at a later stage, for example by policies of trade liberalization (leading to competition from imports), industrial restructuring and reductions in public sector financing. Judisman and Moreno (1990) suggest that this was the case for Mexico, where women's employment began to be affected seriously after 1988.

Another relevant issue is whether women's employment behaves pro- or counter-cyclically, i.e. whether it continues to rise during recession – or rises at an increased rate – or whether it declines. The reduction of household incomes under recession may lead to an 'added worker' effect, whereby the supply of female labour increases to compensate for loss of real income at household level as male real wages fall and unemployment rises; and, possibly, men are replaced by women in certain areas of employment to reduce costs. An alternative hypothesis is that the reduction in employment opportunities may lead to a 'discouraged worker' effect on women's labour participation; this kind of analysis also tends to view women's position in the labour market as a reserve army of labour, which will be shed as contraction gets under way. A third approach, that of 'job segregation', predicts that rigid sex typing of employment means that women's employment in recession is not closely related to cyclical factors, but more to secular trends in sectoral and occupational structures. These different approaches are, however, not necessarily competing interpretations (ICRW, 1986; Rubery, 1988).

Both 'added' and 'discouraged' worker effects can operate simultaneously, depending on the income group under consideration (Dessing, 1990b). Hence the overall effect on women's labour force participation depends, in part, on the relative importance of different income groups in the population. The International Centre for Research on Women (ICRW) also finds that 'changes in women's economic behaviour in response to employment contractions and declines in household income vary with household income and with women's ages and skill levels' (ICRW, 1986, p. 5). The added worker effect seems to apply particularly to low-income groups in developing countries.[12] Middle-income women may adopt strategies of reducing household consumption rather than entering the depressed employment market. Older, less-skilled women may also withdraw from the labour market (ICRW, 1986).

On the demand side, sectors may vary in their capacity to absorb or retain labour during downturns. In previous developed economy recessions – although less so in the early 1990s – women's concentration in

the retail sector and services has
contraction. However, the nature of
and the Caribbean, with the prevalenc
services provided by women in the inform
of the public sector, has meant that it has
cession and, latterly, adjustment policies squeez
As in developed countries, women employed in m
the first to be laid off during recession, i.e. women
manufacturing may be pro-cyclical (ICRW, 1986).

Overall, empirical data for Latin America and the Carib
1970s and early 1980s show continued rises in female labour
tion (although longer-term trends would have to be examined to
a counter-cyclical dimension to this), even where male rates are stag
ing or declining and rises in female open unemployment are greater
than those for men. However, the causality behind rising female open
unemployment levels under recession is not clear – to what extent is
this due to increased participation and to what extent to a reduction in
employment opportunities? (ICRW, 1986).

Humphrey *et al.* (1993) cast doubts on whether women's participation rates overall were pushed up by recession. On the other hand,
Judisman and Moreno (1990) find that up to two-thirds of the increase
in female participation in the period 1983–89 in Mexico City could be
explained in relation to male involuntary unemployment, which strongly
supports the 'added worker' thesis.

A study by Francke (1992) of the effects of recession on women's
work in Lima, Peru, finds a slow but continued expansion in female
labour participation, an expansion of underemployment, and a growth
of the informal sector (the latter not necessarily being synonymous with
the former). Among the various reasons are that: women are active in
market segments that serve as 'buffers' to unemployment, particularly
the informal sector; women industrial workers are concentrated in a few
branches where their skills are not easily replaced; and women are employed in areas that are not sensitive to recession, such as the public
sector, where employment was expanded under recession and heterodox adjustment, largely for political reasons (although this has changed
since the latter half of the 1980s). There is an added worker effect of
adult women and then children entering the labour force in order to
compensate for falling real incomes, but this does not explain the whole
rise. A closer analysis of the different phases of recession in Peru
reveals that female labour force participation behaves counter-cyclically
in a recession but does not closely follow GDP; rather it tends to be
negatively correlated with wages with a one-year lag. This implies that

cushioned them from employment
he service sector in Latin America
of income- sensitive personal
al sector and the dominance
een badly affected by re-
g public employment.
anufacturing may be
's participation in

bean in the
participa-
isolate

s; if this is unsus-
ly, there is a close
nt and the growth
ay) such that as
ed to work longer
expands with the
articipation in this

cts on men and
of São Paulo of
tion (1984-86) in
npact by gender,
marital status.

amework for the
ing on their paid
......udies is that the
impact of adjustment on women, particularly poor women, is negative. However, these works have tended to rely heavily on a priori arguments, rather than on rigorous empirical study. Moreover, little if any attempt is made to distinguish the effects of recession or longer-term trends from adjustment.

The basic argument is that adjustment intensifies the trade-off between women's producer and non-producer roles (Commonwealth Secretariat, 1991, p. 401), or, in stronger terms, that 'the crisis of social disinvestment (under adjustment) is financed from a "social fund" provided by the superhuman efforts of poor women' (UNICEF, 1989). Women are increasingly pushed into the labour force, often on highly disadvantageous terms, due to the lowering of household incomes as real wages fall and/or unemployment rises under adjustment. The removal of subsidies on basic goods and services and the introduction of charges for health and education under adjustment programmes may lead to the increased participation of women in paid employment, particularly in the informal sector, as they are forced to meet these increased expenditures (Moser, 1992; Weekes-Vagliani, 1992). At the same time, the burden of household and other unpaid work also increases under the pressure to reduce expenditures and as social support is eroded by cut-backs in public expenditure programmes, leading to a 'pincer' effect (Joekes, 1991b). The Commonwealth Secretariat (1989, 1991) disaggregates the impact of adjustment on women in terms of four major roles (producers, mothers, household managers, community organizers), emphasizing the pressures on women's time and energy brought about under adjustment as they strive to continue fulfilling these roles with reduced incomes and support. Various strategies, some detrimental to women's or other household members' welfare (e.g. reduced feeding, withdrawal of girls from school), some in the nature of collective self-help initiatives (e.g. communal kitchens, savings and loan associations), are deployed by women to deal with the effects of adjustment at household and community levels.

Moser (1992) differentiates women's responses to the pressures of adjustment within a low-income community in Guayaquil, Ecuador, and finds that factors such as the number of persons in the household in productive work, the stage in the household life cycle and the number of other females (particularly daughters) involved in reproductive work, are important in determining which women enter the labour force. She also finds that women are working longer hours than a decade previously in order to maintain the same income, and beginning work earlier in relation to the age of their children.

A summary of case-studies produced by the Commonwealth Secretariat (1991) concludes that, overall, the negative a priori arguments are borne out by the limited evidence. Under adjustment, female open unemployment tends to rise (having started from a higher baseline than men's); women's involvement in informal sector work increases, with a deterioration in the position of women working in this sector; there is an increase in women's unpaid family labour in agriculture; and the small scale of women's independent operations (in agriculture and the informal sector) limits their ability to take advantage of new incentives. On the other hand, there is no clear evidence that women suffer more than men from retrenchment in the public or private formal sectors; and women are the main beneficiaries of expansion of export processing employment where this occurs under adjustment.

The stress placed on women's time and energy use is perhaps the most salient feature of these approaches, which is often overlooked in other more conventional economic studies. There is a need to analyse not just changes in incomes and employment, but also trends in working hours and in the intensity of work, from a gender perspective. Time-use data, where available, can illuminate the former point, but as yet no method of measuring work intensity has been devised within the standard range of data collection methods (Joekes, 1991b).

Other studies of gender and adjustment have taken a different approach, which does not view the impact of adjustment on women as necessarily negative. This approach takes as a starting-point women's sectoral representation and emphasizes the problem of gender-based constraints to women's labour mobility as potentially undermining the effectiveness of adjustment programmes, by preventing women from moving into expanding (tradables) sectors out of non-tradables, or by preventing women in tradables sectors from expanding their output. Constraints on women's flexibility hinder success of adjustment in each case. Typically, the constraints on women's labour re-allocation cited include labour market discrimination, lack of education, limited access to credit or other inputs, and reproductive responsibilities. Thus, it is argued that countervailing policies are needed to facilitate the optimal allocation of women's labour (from an efficiency perspective) under adjustment (e.g. Haddad, 1992; Palmer, 1991).

However, not all such constraints or 'gender distortions' may be amenable to policy interventions. The appropriation of household income by men, for example, which creates a disincentive for increased women's labour supply in household-based enterprises, cannot easily be addressed. Moreover, if the arguments reviewed above are considered, it is likely that some consequences of adjustment policies may themselves intensify the constraints to women's labour mobility, by increasing their reproductive responsibilities and/or limiting their access to education (Elson, 1991; Lockwood, 1992).

Formal sector employment

Overall trends and impact on women
The formal sector tends to be the first to be hit under adjustment by the effects of demand restraint, leading to employment losses and wage declines in this area, particularly in public sector employment and in previously protected industries, following trade liberalization. However, the relative importance of the formal sector in employment, and its composition in terms of ownership, economic sector, tradables or non-tradables, varies considerably between regions and countries. Also, the gender composition of employment in the formal sector, and subdivisions thereof, is highly variable between countries. Country studies are needed which rigorously disaggregate formal sector employment by gender, but also according to ownership, economic sector and tradability (including levels of protection and import content).

In Latin America and the Caribbean in the 1980s, 62 per cent of women, as opposed to 56 per cent of men, were wage-earners, although the relative proportion of women wage-earners may be declining under adjustment. In sub-Saharan Africa, women form a significantly lower proportion of wage-earners than men (UN, 1991). The formal sector here has always been a limited source of employment and under recession and adjustment in the 1980s has shrunk even further, from 10 to around 8 per cent of the labour force.

In Latin America, the formal sector is a larger source of employment, providing around two-thirds of non-agricultural employment, and within it, the public sector is relatively less important, comprising around one-quarter of formal sector jobs. Over the 1970s and continuing in the 1980s, there was an expansion of employment in the services sector (finance, commerce, retail) in many Latin American economies, with women taking a major share of these jobs. In the 1980s, services employed around 70 per cent of economically active women in Latin America and the Caribbean (UN, 1991). Whilst manufacturing employment declined after the mid-1970s in some countries (e.g. Argentina), there has been a major growth in export-oriented manufacturing employment in others, particularly in the 1980s (e.g. Jamaica, Mexico), and women have also been the beneficiaries of a high proportion of these new jobs[13] (ECLAC, 1992).

However, the formal sector share of non-agricultural employment in Latin America fell from 73.9 per cent in 1980 to 69.3 per cent in 1985, with particularly sharp declines in Brazil and Mexico. The formal sector decline was largely concentrated in a decline in private sector employment in large enterprises. Small enterprises and public sector employment shares increased (Humphrey *et al.*, 1993). Although there is no detailed evidence, this would appear to imply that across the formal sector as a whole, women's employment (more likely to be in small enterprises and the public sector) has been relatively protected during the recession. On the other hand, women may have lost out more in labour-shedding from large enterprises (see below).

In sub-Saharan Africa, women employed in the formal sector are much more likely to be in public sector employment than in the private sector. Where, as in much of sub-Saharan Africa, the public sector has suffered considerable losses in both employment[14] and real wage levels, which have not been compensated by private sector growth, the share of formal sector employment in female employment must be shrinking. Across all spheres of formal employment, women tend to be concentrated at lower skill and occupational levels than men. This suggests that women may have less employment security and be more vulnerable to retrenchment in both public and private sectors, even though they may be less affected in aggregate than men because of their lower representation in the formal sector.

There is some evidence that women are discriminated against in developing country formal sector labour markets. Appleton *et al.* (1990) found that 'credentialism' operated against women in labour markets in Côte d'Ivoire, whereby education was used as an entry barrier for women trying to get formal sector jobs, particularly in the private sector. Similarly, Gindling (1993) found that the education levels of employed women were higher than those of employed men. Minujin (1990) also suggests that one effect of recession in Argentina is to reduce the upward mobility of female employees, for example from domestic service into public sector jobs. The effects of recession and adjustment on these processes of discrimination deserve further investigation.

Public sector employment

Within the formal sector, the public sector represents 54 per cent of employment in sub-Saharan Africa and 27 per cent in Latin America (Vandermoortele, 1991). In the developing regions, the female share of public sector employment is highest in Latin America and the Caribbean.

The decline and compression in public sector employment has been largely policy induced. In sub-Saharan Africa at least, compression in the public sector has tended to occur in several stages, beginning with a wage freeze, then the elimination of temporary or 'ghost' workers, followed by a recruitment freeze, and lastly by dismissals. Retrenchments in the public sector have occurred on a considerable scale where other measures have failed to produce sufficient savings. In sub-Saharan Africa, public sector recruitment has been limited or frozen by halting policies of guaranteed employment for secondary school-leavers and/or graduates from tertiary institutions (e.g. Central African Republic, Mali, Sudan, Togo). Selection is now being carried out by competitive examination in some cases. Whilst there is no information about how this is affecting the gender distribution of recruitment, it does introduce the possibility of a bias in selection.

The relative effects of the decline in public sector employment on men and women are not clear. The generally higher representation of men in public sector employment (though this is variable) would suggest that the cut-backs have had a greater impact on them. On the other hand, women tend to be concentrated in lower-grade jobs and therefore may be more vulnerable to retrenchment. In some countries in sub-Saharan Africa – such as Gambia, Zambia – actual dismissals in the public sector have been concentrated among temporary workers, since these are less costly and difficult to make redundant (Collier, 1988).

Whilst the loss of women's employment in the public sector may not be as great as that of men in absolute terms, it has been argued that it has an overall negative effect on women's bargaining power in labour markets, because public sector employment is relatively free from discriminatory practices compared to the private sector (Elson, 1991).

In general, the female share of public service employment in developing countries is stable or rising slowly. In Botswana, there has been a dramatic rise in the share of female employment, although this is probably one of the countries in sub-Saharan Africa least affected by recession and adjustment. In Kenya, women's share of public sector employment has increased consistently over the period 1970–90, with a jump from 21 to 26 per cent between 1985 and 1990, whereas the female share of private sector waged employment did not expand significantly between 1985 and 1990 (Joekes, 1991a). However, in Latin America, public sector employment was affected by adjustment only in the latter half of the 1980s, and even in sub-Saharan Africa, retrenchment (as opposed to freezes in recruitment or wages) has tended to come later rather than earlier in the adjustment process, so that these effects may not be captured in this series.

In Cameroon, by 1991, 30,000 people had been retrenched from parastatals. In Ghana, by the end of 1991, 50,000 people had been retrenched from the civil service and education sectors. Although no gender breakdown is given in these cases, in Benin it was found that whilst women represented only 6 per cent of those in private formal and parastatal employment, they represented 21 per cent among those retrenched (ILO, 1993).

In Jamaica, there was a fall in female employment in the public sector of 14,100 between 1981 and 1985 (the adjustment programme began in 1982). No comparison with men is given. The participation of women in public sector employment declined from 19.3 to 13.4 per cent in this period (Safa and Antrobus, 1992).

It is also important to look at the conditions under which public sector retrenchments are taking place. Programmes for retraining or assisting retrenched employees to set up in business have been introduced in many sub-Saharan African countries, along with other 'compensatory' schemes designed to mitigate the 'social costs of adjustment'. There is some evidence that women may receive less attention than men in such programmes, either directly because they are not included as a target group, or indirectly because of the way programmes are designed. (See section on compensatory programmes, pp. 55–56.)

Public sector pay has tended to fall faster than private sector pay, implying a relative decline in women's wages, if it is assumed that there is a greater concentration of women in public than in private sector employment. On the other hand, the compression of wage differentials across occupational groups *within* the public sector under adjustment (at least in sub-Saharan Africa) may have narrowed male-female pay differentials. However, in Costa Rica, in the period of stabilization 1982–83 following recession in the early 1980s, '... the increase in the male-female wage differential during the period of stabilization was due to a large increase in public sector employment which was disproportionately male. The evidence is that public sector hiring in this period was discriminatory' (Gindling, 1993, p. 291). Clearly, it cannot be assumed that discriminatory practices do not occur in public sector employment, particularly in periods of recession and adjustment.

There is some suggestive evidence that women – as well as men – have been 'voluntarily' leaving public sector employment due to the sharp falls in real wages to set up businesses in the informal sector, where there is some potential for higher earnings (Tripp, 1992; Commonwealth Secretariat, 1991).

Manufacturing

Overall, women are under-represented in manufacturing industry worldwide, including in developing regions. In Latin America and the Caribbean, 16 to 17 per cent of economically active women were employed in manufacturing in 1991; in sub-Saharan Africa the proportion was even lower, at around 6 per cent (UN, 1991). Where women are employed in manufacturing, they tend to be concentrated in specific industries (such as garments, electronics) and in relatively unskilled occupations.

The implicit assumption about the effects of adjustment on manufacturing industry is usually that where protective tariffs are removed there will be a decline in import-substituting industry with a high proportion of male employment. On the other hand, export-oriented industries, where a much higher proportion of women are employed, will tend to expand as a result of devaluation. Thus, it is assumed that women will lose less, or gain more, than men. However, Palmer (1991) points out that the picture is much more complex than this, depending on changes in protective tariff levels, different degrees of import content and the extent of demand contraction. Moreover, the same industry could be import-substituting in one context and partly export-oriented in another and with differing import contents. Thus, detailed case-studies are needed to get beyond such general statements. Given the more limited industrial base in sub-Saharan Africa and the general process of deindustrialization occurring under recession and adjustment, the potential expansion of export-oriented industries and the possible benefits of this for women's employment are much less relevant in this case.

There is little exact empirical evidence on the impact of recession and adjustment on women's employment in manufacturing. There is some evidence, particularly in Latin America and the Caribbean, of a shift of manufacturing industry in the 1980s from large to small enterprises and of increases in subcontracting, homeworking and other forms of unprotected employment. This may imply a growth in women's employment in manufacturing but probably under unfavourable conditions (see section on the informal sector, pp. 49–52). In other instances, the development of large-scale industries and trade liberalization accompanying adjustment have led to the displacement of women employed in small-scale, craft-based industries (Jayaweera, 1993).

Hirata and Humphrey's (1990) study of the impact of recession on male and female industrial workers in São Paulo found that, on the whole, women, having lost jobs in industry, were unable to recover their position in the labour market even following recuperation, whereas for men the impact was not so lasting. Unskilled and married women particularly were unable to improve their position in the recovery and remained in the informal sector.

This process of renewal of the labour force (such as older workers' jobs being taken by younger workers) affected a minority of the male labour force. In the case of women, it had a much broader effect. Unskilled production workers (predominantly women) were disproportionately laid off during the recession. These workers were the least likely to be re-hired. The older women would be forced into inactivity, domestic service or service sector waged employment while the companies would look to younger women when expanding their labour forces again (Hirata and Humphrey, 1990).

In some countries, particularly in Latin America, the Caribbean and Asia, there has been a rapid expansion of female employment in export processing manufacturing industries, even during the 1980s period of recession and adjustment. In Mexico, for example, employment in the export (*maquiladora*) sector and in-bond toll manufacturing industries grew by 14.5 per cent annually between 1980 and 1989, taking up a large – but falling – proportion of female labour (Judisman and Moreno, 1990). One possible explanation of the falling share of female labour in the sector is a shift in the skills requirements of export industries over time as technological upgrading occurs. This demonstrates that the gains to women's employment of the expansion of export-oriented industries may not be permanent.

Wage levels in (female-dominated) export processing industries are not systematically higher or lower compared to other manufacturing industry (which tends to be male-dominated). There is some evidence to support the idea of a 'salary life-cycle', whereby early in the development of export processing industries wages are relatively high and draw on a comparatively educated female labour force, but over time they fall relative to other employment (Baden and Joekes, 1993).

Services

There is little information about women's employment in services in developing countries, particularly sub-Saharan Africa, or about shifts taking place in this sector. A high proportion of women's employment in services – especially in sub-Saharan Africa – takes place within either the public (see pp. 43–45) or the informal sector (particularly personal services – see pp. 55–56), which may explain the lack of attention to this area.

There is a high and rising proportion of women in the service sector in Latin America, particularly office and shop workers and domestic servants, although the number of women in domestic service appears to be falling in some countries (e.g. Peru, see Francke, 1992). Even during the recession and adjustment, some areas of service employment continued to expand, suggesting an increase in employment opportunities for women. For example, in Mexico, employment in financial services, real estate and insurance expanded by 6.5 per cent yearly between 1981 and 1984 (Judisman and Moreno, 1990). Another area of service employment which might be expected to expand under adjustment, and to employ a high proportion of women, is tourism.

In Moser's study in Ecuador, the greatest increase in women's employment was in professional (mainly teachers and nursing auxiliaries) and office jobs, in which the share of women in the sample had risen from 2 per cent in 1978 to 10.2 per cent in 1988 (it is not clear whether these are mainly public sector jobs or include private sector employment), reflecting a process of differentiation in this community. She also found that: 'Of those households with working daughters, the largest number were employed as shop workers (36 per cent). Although the majority of them had completed secondary school, they were either on short-term contracts or selling on commission. A further 15 per cent were in professional and office jobs and over 20 per cent were in domestic service' (Moser, 1992, pp. 98–99).

According to some sources, although women's employment in services is expanding, even under conditions of recession and adjustment, wages in this sector are falling (ECLAC, 1992; UNICEF, 1989). Moser (1992, p. 98) concludes that: 'Although gender segregation in the labour market has protected women's employment in the service sector, this has only been achieved at lower rates of pay.'

Impact of recession and adjustment on male-female wage differentials

Little work has been done on male-female earnings differentials under recession and adjustment. Increased earnings differentials are not necessarily due to employer discrimination *per se*: it could be that human capital, skill or seniority factors (which in standard approaches are often seen as independent from gender *per se*) come into play. For example, it is likely that in a recession (or under adjustment) employers may initially shed the least skilled labour and retain workers with more skills. At the same time, more (lower skill) women may be entering the labour force to meet increased living costs, thus bringing down the mean human capital level of women workers. Thus, it is argued, the male-female earnings differential could increase on the basis of widening endowment levels rather than discrimination (Gindling and Berry, 1992).

Consistent with the downward pressure on real wages (see above) and the informalization of many developing economies under recession and adjustment (see next section), there is evidence that informal sector incomes form an increasing proportion of household income. In urban United Republic of Tanzania, by 1988 wage income constituted only 10 per cent of household income – the rest came from informal sources (Tripp, 1992).

Urban informal sector employment

The conceptual and empirical measurement problems that beset analysis of the informal sector are further complicated when looking at women's participation in the sector, where much labour takes place within the home and in many cases is unpaid.

Francke (1992) stresses the fluidity between formal and informal sectors, such that in recession, formal enterprises will subcontract work or deregulate and partially enter the informal sector; in periods of growth small enterprises will expand and become regularized, or register in order to obtain loans and benefits. The shifting participation of men and women in the sector has to be seen in this context.

Women are not generally more numerous than men in informal sector employment. For example, the female share of informal sector employment in the Congo in 1990 was 25 per cent and in Kenya 37 per cent. However, a greater proportion of the female than the male labour force tends to be represented in this sector (Palmer, 1991).

On the whole – but not exclusively – women tend to be concentrated in the small-scale production and personal services end of informal sector activity (which is more likely to be non-tradable) and thus are vulnerable to both falling incomes (due to demand restraint) and crowding effects (because of ease of entry) of recession and adjustment.

Women in the informal sector may be hit by income declines among not only low-income but also higher-income groups, for example through a reduction in demand for domestic 'servants' (employees). These effects may be offset to some extent by substitution towards cheaper informal sector goods as downward pressure on incomes takes hold. Overall, however, it seems likely that the net effect of demand restraint and labour crowding will lead to a decline in women's informal sector earnings.

There is little information on women's and men's relative positions in the informal sector, except that women tend to be concentrated in the small-scale, undercapitalized, low-productivity end of informal sector activities (Palmer, 1991; Weekes-Vagliani, 1992). Women's participation in the sector is characterized not only by 'tertiarization' but also by 'overconcentration', in a few lines of work – whereas men have a greater occupational spread in this sector (Francke, 1992). In Guayaquil, they are in selling, dressmaking and personal services, whereas men are in selling, tailoring, carpentry, personal services and mechanics (Moser, 1992). Similarly, in Kenya, Joekes (1991a) shows that over 80 per cent of self-employed women are in agriculture and sales compared with only 50 per cent of men, with men engaging in a range of other informal sector activities.

In Latin America, particularly, there appear to be life-cycle factors associated with informal sector participation for both women and men, but particularly for women. Younger women are more likely to be employed in low-wage white-collar work, whilst older married women, and especially female heads of household, are most likely to be employed in the informal sector. Conversely, age and marital status may be negatively associated with the informal sector participation of men (Roberts, 1991; Moser, 1992). Moser's study shows that between 1978 and 1988 the proportion of women in typical informal sector occupations did not alter markedly over the ten-year period, although there was a significant rise in female participation rates from 40 per cent in 1978 to 52 per cent in 1988, reflecting both the increasing unreliability of male incomes and increases in prices faced by households.

Jamaica saw a considerable growth in self-employment in the period 1980–87: women's self-employment rose from 91,200 to 114,000; men's rose from 208,000 to 238,900. (This represents a growth of 25 per cent in female self-employment, compared to 15 per cent in male self-employment.) The growth of informal sector employment was partly stimulated by government seed-capital programmes and partly by de-regulation.

In sub-Saharan Africa official figures show that, since 1985, there has been a slow-down in women's entry into the informal sector, probably due to increased competition and crowding, especially in trading, which occupies around 80 per cent of female informal sector workers. Whereas between 1980 and 1985, women's participation in the informal sector rose by 6 per cent per year, between 1985 and 1990 this slowed to 2 per cent per year (ILO, 1993).

A study of the impact of adjustment on women in Zimbabwe in mid-1991 found that, in one particular district of Harare, the majority of women surveyed were engaged in some form of informal sector activity. Self-employment was also highly gender segregated, with men commonly working as taxi drivers, whilst women worked mainly as seamstresses and knitters, and vendors of agricultural produce. Gender differentials in earnings did not appear to be particularly marked; however, most of the women who identified themselves as 'housewives' were in fact engaging in regular or irregular income-generating activities (Kanji and Jazdowska, 1993).

In Ghana, the 1983 adjustment programme had the effect of cutting commercial margins and consequently the incomes of small vendors, who are usually women, reducing this overdeveloped (because of prior rapid growth in the 1970s) sector in favour of directly productive activities (Bourguignon and Morrisson, 1992). A study by Clark and Manuh (1991, cited in BRIDGE, 1993b) of female traders working under adjustment in Accra and Kumasi found that the women reported a crowding of the sector with new entrants. These newcomers included men, some of whom had begun to move into areas of trade traditionally associated with females.

In the United Republic of Tanzania, there has been a very large increase in self-employment amongst women (Tripp, 1992). Nevertheless, more men than women were engaged in informal work full time, but a high proportion of women combined informal work with farming (45 per cent of women versus 17 per cent of men). Sixty per cent of women reported that children were helping them in informal sector activities and 44 per cent of women got their starting capital from husbands (it is not specified where the other 56 per cent obtained their capital, although rotating credit societies had expanded dramatically and were perhaps an alternative source).

Some of these women's activities were proving very lucrative: an example is given of a woman who started a 'project' with her husband's capital. One year later the income from the 'project' was 26 times his wage! A common pattern seemed to be men maintaining their formal employment – possibly as a source of income security, access to other benefits, reserve funds in case of business failure, or sources of information and contacts – whilst women engaged in informal sector activities where they could potentially earn much higher incomes than their husbands. Many of the women working in the informal sector had themselves left low-paying jobs in the formal sector to become self-employed. Whilst there had been a considerable lowering of differentials in formal sector wages, there was evidence of rising income differentials among informal sector activities. The upper- and middle-income groups of women working in this sector were earning up to 10 times the amount that lower-income women were able to earn (Tripp, 1992).

Weekes-Vagliani (1992) found that in Côte d'Ivoire there was a wide spread of income groups operating in the informal sector. One-quarter of the men and nearly one-third of the women in the informal sector in Abidjan were from higher-income groups; in other cities one-third of the men and over half of the women were from higher-income groups. Nevertheless, the proportion of middle-income and poor informal sector workers was higher in each case.

Agricultural employment

Much of the literature relating to adjustment and the agricultural sector, and more particularly that with a gender focus, relates to sub-Saharan Africa. Typically, the model presented of gender and agricultural production in sub-Saharan Africa is one of women predominantly producing food for subsistence and/or working as unpaid family labour on men's cash-crop fields. However, as Palmer (1991) points out, this is a simplistic generalization and there are considerable regional variations.

In theory the overall impact of adjustment on agricultural output, prices and incomes should be more positive (or at least less negative) than for other sectors, because of improved rural-urban terms of trade brought about by devaluation and price deregulation. However, there is some evidence that both the extent and the impact (in terms of output and incomes) of price shifts under adjustment may not be as significant as advocates predicted. There is a need to disaggregate the impact of adjustment on the rural sector in order to examine both inter- and intra-household differentiation, both of which have a gender dimension.

Both the intention, and in some cases the effect, of adjustment policies in agriculture is to increase incentives to cash-crop production and thus to increase agricultural output and incomes. Improved price incentives lead to increased acreages planted and to increases in demand for labour, which may be met from intra- or extra-household sources. There is evidence to suggest that women's labour is an important component of both these sources.

Sarris and Shams (1991) find that in Ghana one effect of adjustment on the agricultural sector is increasing agricultural wage rates. This has created a strong incentive for the substitution of hired labour with family labour among traditional technology farmers, even though the returns to intensified family (i.e. particularly female) labour are low.

Evans (cited in Humphrey *et al.*, 1993) finds an increase in the supply of male labour to hybrid maize production. The most successful households were those (usually joint-headed households) with sufficient labour, land and finance (often from off-farm sources) to cover the costs of credit and hiring seasonal labour. Wives often apportioned some of their household labour responsibilities to other women, adopted labour-saving practices (e.g. cutting down on meal preparation time) or cut down on leisure. Women-headed households were the least able to benefit from new incentives, mainly because of their labour constraints. They tended to concentrate on activities which required minimal male labour, and which tended to have low returns. The expansion of commercial maize production had also led to an increased demand for casual labour, which was being met primarily by female heads of household or women from mainly subsistence households, with wages often paid in kind. Again, a growing differentiation is noted between successful commercial farming households and less successful subsistence, trading and labouring households, i.e. between net food sellers and net food buyers. Female-headed households, which comprise a significant and possibly growing (25–35 per cent) proportion of rural households in sub-Saharan Africa, are likely to be over-represented among net food buying households (Gladwin, 1993).

Various factors have been isolated that tend to lead to households becoming successful adopters of cash crops under adjustment, i.e. larger holdings, access to labour (including wives) and to off-farm income. All these factors suggest that men, rather than women farming on their own account, are more likely to benefit from incentives under expanded commercial agriculture. Poorer households, and particularly female-headed households, are likely to have smaller holdings, and to lack access to off-farm income or credit to purchase inputs.

Women farmers are further constrained by lack of access to labour, which limits their ability to expand production even where land is available. Since women in sub-Saharan Africa bear a major responsibility for producing food for consumption, as well as for domestic labour, they are constrained in their ability to reallocate their own labour to cash-crop production. Also, they lack command over other adult (particularly men's) labour, although they may be able to mobilize child labour (with possibly negative implications for school attendance). Where men intensify their own labour inputs into cash cropping, as illustrated above, the responsibility for household food provisioning may become even greater for women, as noted by Sarris and Shams (1991) for Ghana. An example from Malawi shows how men are able to capture the benefits of structural adjustment programme (SAP) incentives, whereas women's response is constrained, even where incentives are strong (Gladwin, 1993).

SAPs can lead to competing demands over land and labour, which act to the detriment of women's autonomous production and incomes. The increased profitability of farming under SAPs is tending to lead to rising land values and at least localized land pressure, which may further weaken women's land entitlements.

Where women have successfully responded to SAP-induced incentives, it tends to be where they are able to market surplus produce from traditional food or cash crops (e.g. root crops or groundnuts). This may be partly as a result of favourable price changes, but also requires access to sufficient land, labour and markets, as well as prior investment in improving productivity (Gladwin, 1993; Elson, 1991).

Another area where women are being affected by SAPs is the transportation and marketing of agricultural produce. In some areas (e.g. Ghana and the United Republic of Tanzania), rises in transport costs (e.g. imported bicycles, vehicles and fuel) and the deterioration of road systems (due to declining public investment) may have led to an intensification of headloading by women, a highly labour-intensive and physically arduous task (Sarris and Shams, 1991; Gladwin, 1993). On the other hand, in West Africa particularly, where women form a high proportion of traders (over 80 per cent in Ghana), the liberalization of agricultural marketing and increased prices may have enabled a small proportion of women to increase incomes and expand operations. Ironically, this may work against women farmers, since they tend to sell produce to such traders at the farm gate at depressed prices. However, only a very small proportion of women traders (1 per cent) are in the wholesale/export trade, where sizeable profits can be made (Sarris and Shams, 1991).

In the longer term, SAPs may indirectly induce technological change, which leads to labour displacement from some activities and labour intensification in others. Such trends would have to be examined against the (changing) gender division of labour in agriculture in specific localities in order to draw out the implications for women's agricultural employment. There is little information about the impact of SAPs on agriculture, and particularly agricultural employment, in Latin America and the Caribbean. There is some evidence that increasing numbers of women, as well as men, are engaging in casual (including day) labour in the agro-export sector (Bourguignon and Morrisson, 1992). In Jamaica, Safa and Antrobus (1992) show women's employment in agriculture rising by 1 percentage point (8,000) between 1981 and 1985. However, another study on Jamaica (Commonwealth Secretariat, 1991) records a decline in female agricultural employment after 1985, with over 8,000 leaving the sector between 1985 and 1987. The divestment or closure of large state-controlled sugar- and banana-producing estates under adjustment may have been partially responsible for loss of employment after 1985. Women workers are a minority in the sugar industry (25 per cent), being mainly temporary workers. They therefore received little or no compensation. Workers were also displaced from the privatized banana industry, which employs predominantly (90 per cent) female labour. It is not clear that the privatized and diversified agricultural sector has been able to soak up any of this surplus (female) labour (Commonwealth Secretariat, 1991).

Unemployment and underemployment

Historically, female open unemployment rates in sub-Saharan Africa and Latin America and the Caribbean have been considerably higher than male rates, and this trend persists (ILO, 1989). Recession has led to increases in female (as well as male) open unemployment in most Latin American, Caribbean and African economies, through a combination of the 'added-worker' effect, whereby female participation rates are rising, and a fall in demand for female labour in specific areas. The 'discouraged worker' effect seems to have been limited to middle-income women in Latin America (as noted earlier).

The failure of adjustment to bring about significant employment creation in most countries means that unemployment rates, including those of women, have persisted at relatively high levels, even when recovery has set in (as in some Latin American countries). Open unemployment rates are rising rapidly in urban Africa. On average they doubled between 1975 and 1990 from around 10 per cent to 20 per cent. Women are particularly vulnerable to unemployment: rates are usually twice those for men (Vandermoortele, 1991).

Compensatory programmes and women's employment

In general the employment or social action programmes (such as PAMSCAD in Ghana, ESF in Bolivia) introduced to alleviate the effects of recession and adjustment have a poor record with respect to employment creation. They have tended to target certain groups (primarily male, urban, retrenched workers) for political reasons rather than on the basis of need (Commonwealth Secretariat, 1993; BRIDGE,

1993b). The generally much higher rates of female unemployment suggest that far more attention is needed to targeting and adapting employment and related programmes to women's labour market situation.

Vandermoortele (1991) notes the failure of special employment programmes in sub-Saharan Africa to address female unemployment. They predominantly enrol males, and the limited range of activities often leads to implicit discrimination against women workers. He suggests that there is a need to make an explicit distinction between programmes aimed at male and female youth because of the very different labour market situations they face. Horton *et al.* (1991) find evidence of male bias in emergency employment programmes in Latin America.

While some observations can be made, limitations of available evidence, and regional variations in experience, hinder to some extent the drawing of very firm conclusions regarding the impact of recession and adjustment on women's work in developing countries. Moreover, there are conceptual and methodological problems in separating out the effects of recession from those of adjustment, and in distinguishing these from longer-term trends towards increased female labour-force participation in most regions, and shifts in the sectoral composition of female labour.

Notes

1. This is an abridged version of a longer document.

2. Among the few is G. Mhone, 'African women workers, economic reforms ...', ILO, Geneva, IDP Women/WP-23., 1995.

3. Early adjustment has enabled some countries to compensate for the effects of recession, e.g. in Costa Rica, through the expansion of public sector employment; in Malaysia, through increases in health and education expenditure (Bourguignon and Morrisson, 1992). In other countries (particularly in sub-Saharan Africa) delays in implementing adjustment have arguably made the process much more painful.

4. Whilst stabilization policies are generally associated with short-term demand restraint to correct external imbalances, and structural adjustment with longer-term changes in the incentive and institutional structures, it is difficult to separate analytically the effects of these and in practice the first is usually a precondition for the second, where external financing is involved. Here 'adjustment' is taken to cover both stabilization and structural adjustment policies, unless otherwise specified.

5. One interpretation of the varied country experiences under adjustment is that better-off countries which already have a relatively developed industrial base and international markets (e.g. Thailand, Turkey) are much more likely to respond to conventional adjustment packages. On the other hand, less developed countries that have undergone protracted economic crises, as have many in sub-Saharan Africa, are unlikely to respond because of structural features of their economies and severely weakened economic bases. It is argued that in such cases conventional SAPs may lead to further decline; it is therefore more appropriate to rehabilitate existing industry and infrastructure (Mosley *et al.*, 1991).

6. However, this is not straightforward either, since sectoral shifts themselves involve employment losses in declining areas. In theory, given sufficient incentives and labour mobility, these will be offset to a greater or lesser degree by gains in employment elsewhere, but there will be lags in this process leading to at least temporary unemployment for some. Furthermore, reductions in public sector employment and/or wages have been a central feature of adjustment programmes as a consequence of public expenditure reductions, privatization and public enterprise reforms.

7. Expansion of the informal sector is not necessarily associated with a worsening of the employment situation. Dessing (1990b) has pointed out that the informal sector has 'involutionary' and 'evolutionary segments', expansion of which could be associated with falling or rising wages respectively.

8. De-indexation of wages refers to a system whereby the minimum wage is no longer adjusted automatically to the level of prices or to the actual wages paid.

9. This implies that some types of goods that were previously not tradable are becoming so under adjustment, i.e. where they are being substituted for previously imported goods, further emphasizing the fluidity of the concept of tradability and its limitations in empirical assessment.

10. Given that what defines the informal sector is largely the extent of regulation, rather than type of activity, certain kinds of employment may shift across the informal/formal sector boundary depending on changes in employment practices generally (especially increasing casualization in the formal sector), overall economic conditions, government policies and the way in which data is collected (Francke, 1992; Roberts, 1991).

11. However, the informal sector had also expanded rapidly in the 1970s in some African countries: e.g. in Côte d'Ivoire from 1975 to 1980, half of the jobs created were in the informal sector; in Ghana the informal sector also expanded rapidly in the 1970s (although this is a rather special case due to the extensive system of price controls – such that the informal sector has become overextended) (Bourguignon and Morrisson, 1992, p.37; Weekes-Vagliani, 1992, p.136). Whereas the process of informalization in sub-Saharan Africa seems to have been associated with increased participation of women since the 1970s, there is some evidence that informalization in Latin America, at least until the early 1980s, was a predominantly male phenomenon, with women moving into low-wage service and white-collar jobs in the formal sector during the 1970s (ECLAC, 1992, p.72).

12. ICRW (1986) finds that the 'added worker' effect is limited to low-income women. Judisman and Moreno (1990) find that the number of female income-earners in middle-income groups does not rise in Mexico. On the other hand, Minujin (1990, p.3) finds that the participation rates of non-poor women in Argentina rise more than those of poor women.

13. As a proportion of total manufacturing employment and/or total female employment, these jobs may be limited in number, however. Lim (1990) argues that the importance of EPZ (export processing zone) employment for women is overstated by lack of comparison with the aggregate context.

14. Accurate figures on net formal sector job losses in sub-Saharan Africa are not readily available. Retrenchment figures may exaggerate actual job losses due to the prevalence of 'ghost workers'; moreover, some of those retrenched from the public sector may later be re-employed in different public sector jobs, as suggested for Ghana (BRIDGE, 1993b).

References

Afshar, H. and C. Dennis (eds) (1992) *Women and adjustment policies in the third world*, London, Macmillan.

Appleton, S. *et al.* (1990) 'Gender, education and employment in Côte d'Ivoire', in *Social dimensions of adjustment*, Working Paper No. 8, Washington, World Bank.

Baden, S. and S. Joekes (1993) 'Gender issues in the development of special economic zones and open areas in the People's Republic of China', paper prepared for presentation at the seminar, Women's Participation in Economic Development, Fudan University, Shanghai, China, 15 April.

Benería, L. (1991) 'Structural adjustment, the labour market and the household: The case of Mexico', in Standing and Tokman (eds.), 1991.

— (1992) 'Accounting for women's work: The progress of two decades', in *World Development*, Vol. 20, No. 11.

— and S. Feldmann (eds) (1992) *Unequal burden: Economic crises, persistent poverty, and women's work*, Westview, Boulder, Colo.

Bourguignon, F. and C. Morrisson (1992) *Adjustment and equity in developing countries: A new approach*, Development Centre, Organization of Economic Co-operation and Development, Paris.

BRIDGE (1993a) 'Gender and adjustment in sub-Saharan Africa', report for the Commission for the European Communities, Brighton, Institute of Development Studies.

— (1993b) 'Gender and development in Ghana', background paper prepared for West and North Africa Development Division, Overseas Development Administration, Brighton, Institute of Development Studies.

Colclough, C. (1991) 'Wage flexibility in sub-Saharan Africa: Trends and explanations', in Standing and Tokman (eds).

Collier, P. (1988) 'African public sector retrenchment: An analytical survey', in *Labour Market Analysis and Employment Planning Working Paper No. 27*, Geneva, ILO World Employment Programme.

Commonwealth Secretariat (1989) *Engendering adjustment for the 1990s*, London.

— (1991) 'Women and structural adjustment: Selected case-studies commissioned for a Commonwealth group of experts', in *Commonwealth Economic Papers No. 22*, London.

Corbo, V. *et al.* (eds) (1992) *Adjustment lending revisited: Policies to restore growth*, Washington, World Bank.

Deere, C.D. *et al.* (1991) *In the shadows of the sun: Caribbean development alternatives and US policy*, San Francisco, Westview Press.

Dessing, M. (1990a) 'Implications for minimum wage policies of an S-shaped labor supply curve', unpublished paper, Harvard University, Cambridge, Mass.

— (1990b) 'The urban informal sector in developing countries: Labour supply and the family', Ph.D dissertation, Graduate Institute of International Studies, University of Geneva.

ECLAC (Economic Commission for Latin America and the Caribbean) (1992) *Major changes and crisis: The impact on women in Latin America and the Caribbean*, Santiago, Chile.

Elson, D. (1991) 'Gender and adjustment in the 1990s: An update on evidence and strategies', background paper for the Interregional Meeting on Economic Distress, Structural Adjustment and Women, June, Commonwealth Secretariat, London.

Fallon, P.R. and L.A. Riveros (1989) 'Adjustment and the labour market', in *Policy, Planning and Research Working Paper Series No. 214*, Washington, DC, Country Economics Department, World Bank.

Francke, M. (1992) *Women and the labour market in Lima, Peru: Weathering economic crisis*, International Centre for Research on Women.

Gindling, T.H. (1993) 'Women's wages and economic crisis in Costa Rica', in *Economic Development and Cultural Change*, Vol. 41, No. 2.

Gindling, T.H. and A. Berry (1992) 'The performance of the labour market during recession and structural adjustment: Costa Rica in the 1980s', in *World Development*, Vol. 20, No. 11.

Gladwin, C. (1993) 'Women and structural adjustment in a global economy', in R. Gallin et al. (eds), *The Women and International Development Annual*, Vol. 3, San Francisco, Westview Press.

Haddad, L. (1992) 'Gender and adjustment: Theory and evidence to date', paper presented at the Workshop on the Effects of Policies and Programmes on Women, International Food Policy Research Institute, 16 January.

Hirata, H. and J. Humphrey (1990) 'Male and female workers and economic recession in Brazil, mimeographed paper prepared for ICRW project, 'Weathering economic crises: Women's economic responses to recession in Latin America and the Caribbean'.

Horton, S. *et al.* (1991) 'Labour markets in an era of adjustment: An overview', in *Policy, Research and External Working Papers, No. 694*, Washington, DC, Economic Development Institute, World Bank.

Humphrey, J. *et al.* (1993) 'Gender and households as factors in adjusting to macroeconomic change', in *World Employment Programme Discussion Paper*, Geneva, ILO.

ICRW (International Centre for Research on Women) (1986) 'Weathering economic crises: Women's responses to the recession in Latin America and the Caribbean', a proposal submitted to the Ford Foundation.

ILO (1989) *World labour report 1989*, Geneva.

— (1992) *World labour report 1992*, Geneva.

— (1993) *World labour report 1993*, Geneva.

Jayaweera, S. (1993) 'The impact of structural adjustment on women in Asia', paper presented at the Commonwealth Secretariat Asian Regional Seminar on Structural Adjustment, Economic Change and Women, 5–8 January.

Joekes, S. (1991a) *Kenya: Report of an ILO exploratory mission on women's employment, with recommendations for follow up*, Geneva, Employment and Development Department, ILO.

— (1991b) 'Women and structural adjustment: Operational implications for the JCGP member agencies', mimeographed document.

Judisman, C. and A. Moreno (1990) 'Women, labour and crisis: Mexico', paper prepared for ICRW project 'Weathering economic crises: Women's economic responses to recession in Latin America and the Caribbean'.

Kanji, N. and N. Jazdowska (1993) 'Structural adjustment and women in Zimbabwe', in *Review of African Political Economy*, No. 56.

Lim, L.Y. (1990) 'Women's work in export factories: The politics of a cause', in Tinker (ed.), 1990.

Lockwood, M. (1992) 'Engendering adjustment or adjusting gender: Some new approaches to women and development in Africa', in *IDS Discussion Paper*, Brighton, Institute of Development Studies.

Minujin, A. (1990) 'From 'secondary workers' to breadwinners: Poor and non-poor women facing the crisis', paper prepared for the ICRW project, 'Weathering economic crises: Women's economic responses to recession in Latin America and the Caribbean'.

Moser, C. (1992) 'Adjustment from below: Low-income women, time and the triple role in Guayaquil, Ecuador', in Afshar and Dennis (eds), 1992.

Mosley, P. *et al.* (1991) *Aid and power: The World Bank and policy-based lending*, 2 vols, London, Routledge.

Palmer, I. (1991) 'Gender and population in the adjustment of African economies: Planning for change', in *Women, Work and Development Series No. 19*, Geneva, ILO.

Riveros, L. (1990) 'Recession, adjustment and the performance of urban labour markets in Latin America', in *Canadian Journal of Development Studies*, Vol. XI, No. 1.

Roberts, B. (1991) 'The changing nature of informal employment: The case of Mexico', in Standing and Tokman (eds), 1991.

Rubery, J. (1988) *Women and Recession*, London, Routledge and Kegan Paul.

Safa, H. and P. Antrobus (1992) 'Women and the economic crisis in the Caribbean', in Benería and Feldman (eds), 1992.

Sarris, A. and H. Shams (1991) 'Ghana under structural adjustment: The impact on agriculture and the rural poor', in *IFAD Studies in Rural Poverty No. 2*, New York, New York University Press.

Standing, G. (1991) 'Structural adjustment and labour market policies: Towards social adjustment?', in Standing and Tokman (eds), 1991.

— and V. Tokman (eds) (1991) *Towards social adjustment: Labour market issues in structural adjustment*, Geneva, ILO.

Tinker, I. (ed.) (1990) *Persistent inequalities*, Oxford University Press.

Tokman, V. (1991) 'The informal sector in Latin America: From underground to legality', in Standing and Tokman (eds), 1991.

Toye, J. (1995) *Structural adjustment and employment policy: Issues and experience*, Geneva, ILO.

Tripp, A.M. (1992) *The impact of crisis and economic reform on women in urban Tanzania*, in Benería and Feldman (eds), 1992.

UN (1991) *The world's women: Trends and statistics, 1970–1990*, New York.

UNICEF (1987) *Adjustment with a human face*, Vol. I, Clarendon Press.

— (1989) *Invisible adjustment: Poor women and the economic crisis*, Santiago, Chile.

Vandemoortele, J. (1991) 'Labour market informalization in sub-Saharan Africa', in Standing and Tokman (eds), 1991.

Weekes-Vagliani, W. (1992) 'Structural adjustment and gender in Côte d'Ivoire', in Afshar and Dennis (eds), 1992.

3
The impact of the transition from centrally planned to market-based economies on women's employment in East Central Europe

BARBARA EINHORN

Introduction

Two central issues in the transition from a centrally planned to a market economy in East Central Europe are its effects on women's labour force participation and on the overall structure of employment. This chapter examines the empirical evidence on these two policy issues. It also explores some theoretical questions about the nature of the transition and accompanying labour market trends. This dual-level analysis provides the basis for speculation on possible longer-term implications for women's role in the economy as compared with the relatively short-term data presently available.

Section two briefly outlines the level and structure of women's employment in the centrally planned economies of East Central Europe prior to 1989. It highlights inequalities and discriminatory tendencies which persisted despite the state socialist paradigm in which women's labour force participation was both 'a political aim and an economic necessity' (Maier, 1993, p. 268).

Section three examines the gender-biased effects of the transition to the market, at least in the short term, in the light of empirical evidence about unemployment, re-employment, retraining and social policy constraints. In dealing with the latter, this section also draws on surveys that address the need to consult women in these countries themselves about their priorities in terms of employment opportunities, so that both much-needed retraining programmes, and the organization of work in the newly privatized industries and the service sector, for example, can take women's own needs and aspirations into account.

Section four is more discursive, relating the empirical evidence to theoretical debates about the longer-term effects of economic transformation on women's employment opportunities. It refers specifically to the introduction of new technology and the process of privatization as decisive factors in influencing women's employment opportunities. It also discusses the shift in sectoral emphasis towards services inherent in the transition to the market and the probable impact of this shift on women's employment, looking briefly at evidence from the finance, banking and insurance sector.

The concluding section sums up both evidence and arguments. Although in the short term it can be said that women are undoubtedly disproportionately disadvantaged by the transition to the market, the longer-term prognosis is less clear. Much has been written on the politics of the transition, and there has been large-scale intervention from the West in terms of economic policy models. At the analytical level, however, with regard to equal opportunities for women in employment, there is a dearth of analyses which could provide or inform policy perspectives. Most of the existing research consists of single-country studies (e.g. Maier, 1993; Paukert, 1991), or collections of country studies (UN, 1992; Moghadam 1993). There is an urgent need for more detailed and desegregated empirical data on a sectoral basis. Beyond these, there are disappointingly few comparative analyses that outline trends applicable in varying degrees to all the East Central European countries undergoing transition to the market, trends from which policy initiatives with regard to equal opportunities for women in employment could be drawn (Einhorn, 1993, Chapter 4; Einhorn and Mitter, 1992; Fong and Paull, 1992; Hübner, Maier and Rudolph, 1991; Kroupová, 1990; UN, 1992). Much more work needs to be done in this area.

Women's employment in the centrally planned economies of East Central Europe

Women's labour force participation in the centrally planned economies of East Central Europe was dictated by both political principle and economic expediency. On the one hand, the state socialist paradigm saw labour market involvement as providing women with both economic independence from men and an enhanced self-esteem, the essential ingredients, as state socialist theorists viewed it, for what they termed women's 'emancipation'. On the other hand, the decimation of the male population during the Second World War, especially acute in the Soviet Union, Poland and East Germany, gave a material urgency to campaigns to draft women into the labour force.

State socialist definitions of women's 'emancipation' were drawn from a selective reading of the Marxist canon, which focused on women's labour force participation as the single sufficient condition rather than one of several necessary conditions for the achievement of this goal (see Einhorn, 1993, Chapter 1). The result was an exclusive focus on employment, on legislation for equal opportunities in employment, on education and vocational training to enhance women's status in employment, and on social policies which underwrote women's role as workers. The obverse side of this policy was a failure to address gender-based inequalities within the family, such as those centring on the domestic division of labour. Legislation defined women as workers *and* mothers, yet the emphasis of social policy and affirmative action measures was on women's role in the economy rather than in the household. The pro-natalist policies introduced by several of the East European regimes in the late 1970s to combat the fall in the birthrate induced by women's dual role did not, in most countries, significantly lower the level of female labour force participation. Rather, it can be argued that it increased the pressures on women to combine motherhood with their working lives. In summary, it can be said that state socialist policies for women's 'emancipation' prioritized women's productive over their reproductive roles.

Levels of female labour force participation

The singular force of state socialist policies on women's economic role as the means to equality resulted in unprecedentedly high levels of female labour force participation, with women accounting for an average 45–61 per cent of the total labour force in 1988. The rate of growth in female employment, for example, in Czechoslovakia was much higher than that in OECD countries (Paukert, 1991). The same is true for the other centrally planned economies of East Central Europe. In the former German Democratic Republic (GDR), the female employment rate was more than 85 per cent of women of working age (91 per cent if students and those in vocational training were included) in 1989, as compared with 55 per cent in the FRG (West Germany). This meant that women in the GDR comprised 49 per cent of the total labour force (Maier, 1993, p. 268).

The East-West discrepancy in female shares of the labour force is compounded by the fact that the majority of women in East Central Europe worked full time, whilst the majority of those in Western Europe worked part-time.[1] As Paukert (1991, p. 619) has observed: 'The end result was that the social environment was transformed, in that full-time lifelong work for women became the established norm, to which family and social life gradually adapted itself'.

Social policies to facilitate women's employment

This level of labour force participation was underwritten by a far-reaching programme of education and training, and by a comprehensive network of child-care facilities and other social provisions designed to ease women's dual role as mothers and workers. The degree to which such social policies were implemented varied from country to country, as well as over time. It has been argued that in Poland, for instance, pro-natalist and pro-worker policies alternated over the postwar period, depending on whether the regime felt the country needed women's labour more as workers or as mothers. Child-care provision was never adequate (Heinen, 1990). In the former GDR, meanwhile, there were sufficient pre-school child-care places throughout the 1980s to meet demand.

The level of child-care provision in the former GDR meant that the pattern of employment for women there more closely resembled that of men in terms of unbroken service. In the GDR there was no difference in the employment rates of married and unmarried women, or of women with and without children, whereas only 20 per cent of West German mothers had an uninterrupted labour market attachment. Even after the introduction of extended child-care leave in the GDR in 1976 (the so-called 'baby year'), women there tended to stay out of the labour force for childbirth and child-rearing reasons for a far shorter period than the average six to eight years characteristic of women in the FRG, where there were creche places available for only 4 per cent of children under three (Maier, 1993: p. 273). Indeed the fact that women in West Germany still felt confronted to a degree by the old choice between career *or* family is illustrated in statistics showing that while almost 90 per cent of women in the GDR had at least one child, 26 per cent of women in the FRG remained childless (Maier, 1993, p. 272).

Distribution of female labour by sector and occupation

Despite the emphasis on policies to facilitate women's employment, the labour market in the centrally planned economies of East Central Europe manifested considerable gender-based segregation. Women workers were concentrated in light industry, and in the retail and service sectors. Within industry as a whole, women tended to be located in the administrative and clerical branches. Those industrial branches with a high concentration of female production workers were also lower-status and hence less well-paid branches, such as light industry – electronics, chemicals, pharmaceuticals, optics, lighting, textiles, clothing and the food industry. Even in female-dominated professions or branches of the service sector, women were located at the lower end of occupational and career hierarchies.

Although far more substantial numbers of women were employed in industry as compared with services than was the case in Western Europe,[2] they were concentrated in light industry, and in relatively low-paid clerical and administrative jobs within mining and heavy industry, sectors prioritized by the centrally planned economies in their postwar drive to industrialize. Hungarian economist Mária Ladó found that in Hungary during the 1980s, 80 per cent of all working women were in female-dominated jobs. In the mid-1980s, more than 90 per cent of workers in clerical and administrative occupations such as typists, accountants, payroll clerks, financial clerks, cashiers and ticket-office clerks were women (Ladó, 1992). Since the top-heavy clerical and administrative branches in public administration as well as in industry have been amongst the first to shed labour in massive proportions, this apparent inroad into the formerly male-dominated preserve of the industrial sector by female workers is ironically proving to be a major cause of the disproportionate unemployment suffered by women in the first stages of transition to the market.

Mária Ladó (1992) describes a vicious circle of occupational segregation in Hungary. Women tended to be over-represented in those sectors of the economy (light industry, administration, services, feminized professions such as teaching and health) which offered lower wages than those sectors (mining, metals, heavy manufacturing industry) which were prioritized by state socialist regimes. Conversely, as industrial sectors or occupations became female-dominated, their status and prestige tended to fall. This phenomenon was common to all the centrally planned economies.

Women were also under-represented at the top of career hierarchies, even in female-dominated professions. Pre-school facilities were exclusively staffed by women in the former GDR, but although 77 per cent of all teachers in 1985 were women, only 32 per cent of head teachers were women. Women accounted for almost half of all employees in higher education in the former GDR, yet scarcely 3 per cent of those in top positions, such as full professors, departmental heads or institute directors, were women. Despite the drift of women into higher education and research in Poland, as a result of which women accounted for 81 per cent of the workforce in education and science, they comprised only 13 per cent of full professors in 1987–88, and there was only one female university rector. In Hungary, 80 per cent of primary school teachers, 50 per cent of secondary level teachers and 33 per cent of university teaching staff were women in 1984. However, only 7 per cent of university rectors were women in 1991. A 1976 survey conducted by the then Karl Marx University of Economics in Budapest (now the Budapest University of Economics), found that although more than 50 per cent of instructors and 33 per cent of assistant professors were women, only 20 per cent of associate professors and 4 per cent of full professors were women (Einhorn, 1993, p. 124).

Women *did* make inroads into formerly male-dominated professions. This was especially true in medicine and law.[3] However, aside from the loss of status and remuneration which followed the feminization of these professions, other gender-based forms of segregation also survived. Thus in medicine, senior hospital consultants tended to be men, whilst in 1989 in the GDR, 95.5 per cent of trainee nurses were women. Amongst specializations, there was a stereotypical gender divide: surgery, neurology and psychiatry were heavily male-dominated, whilst gynaecology and paediatrics were female-dominated (Einhorn, 1993, pp. 124–5).

Even in female-dominated industries such as light industry, textiles and clothing, and food processing, although women made some inroads into middle management, top management was dominated by men. In 1989, only 14 per cent of the total female labour force in Czechoslovakia held management positions. Of those, 65 per cent were in lower-level management, 25 per cent in middle management, and only 10 per cent in top management. The number of women holding top management positions in Poland in 1988 was even lower at 4.5 per cent. In Hungary in 1980, only 12 per cent of managers of enterprises or directors of institutions were women. Even more telling perhaps, because of women's traditionally strong involvement in agricultural labour, only 5.6 per cent of directors of agricultural co-operatives were women in the same year. By 1991, only 5 per cent of large Hungarian companies were headed by women (Einhorn, 1993, p. 125).

Earnings differentials

Despite having introduced equal pay legislation comparatively early – in 1946 in East Germany (see Einhorn, 1989, p. 285) – the centrally planned economies of East Central Europe were characterized by a gender gap in income differing only in degree from that in Western Europe. Women earned on average 66–75 per cent of men's salary, across all branches of economic activity (see Einhorn, 1993, pp. 122–3; Paukert, 1991, p. 626). This gap in earning power could not easily be explained, as it often is in the West European case, by pre-market factors such as lack of vocational qualifications, since, at least in East Germany, the level of vocational training was equal for men and women (Maier, 1993, p. 272). Rather, the prioritization of heavy industry in the economic plans of the state socialist countries provides a structural explanation: the male blue-collar worker was glorified above the usually female white-collar employee. Even skilled women workers in female-dominated sectors such as light industry earned less than those in the male-dominated manufacturing industry and mining. Overall, then, a majority of women workers were concentrated in sectors of the economy and in occupations and professions which had lower status and lower remuneration than the majority of men.

The fact that women in East Central Europe possess unusually high educational and skill levels did not in the past overcome the structural perpetuation of gender-based wage differentials. Nor is it likely that their education and skills will protect them from discrimination in the operation of gender-segregated labour markets in the transition to a market economy.   Indeed, women are more likely than men to be disadvantaged by possessing the wrong skills, or having less access to retraining to adapt their qualifications to the demands of a market economy.

After 1989: women's employment opportunities in the market

A recent study by the Federal German Labour Ministry states un-equivocally that women are particularly adversely affected by the labour market developments following unification (Engelbrech, 1993). Obvi-ously the case of East Germany is a special one, in that the change to a market economy happened overnight, by treaty, due to unification, and not as a process of transition. Nevertheless, the fact that women are disproportionately disadvantaged by the transition process is also true of the other former centrally planned economies.

In a sense this is paradoxical. The fact that women formed almost half of the total labour force prior to 1989 and that they possessed high levels of education and vocational training suggests that it is not obvi-ous that they should suffer the results of the economy's need to shed labour more than men. Indeed the restructuring and modernization of the economy might suggest the opposite, namely more favourable em-ployment opportunities for women than for men employed in the crumbling heavy industry state sector.

Yet the empirical evidence shows that women form the majority of the unemployed in all the former state socialist countries except Hungary. They face discrimination when seeking re-employment, and suffer a lack of appropriate retraining opportunities which might help them find new jobs. Additionally their efforts to find alternative employment are hampered by the collapse of heavily subsidized state child-care and related social provision, and the re-emergence of a conservative social policy model predicated on the concept of the 'breadwinner' family, with women in the role of dependent wife and mother. This section concludes with an examination of the constraints these factors place on women's ability to seek full-time work, and of the mismatch between women's aspirations and the ability to fulfil them in the gender-segregated labour market under these new social and economic conditions.

Unemployment

Clearly the struggle to survive in the market, let alone compete in the global economy, accompanied by the pressures of the privatization process in East Germany, Poland, Hungary and the Czech and Slovak republics create an inexorable logic for the need to shed labour. The unproductive overemployment of the state socialist period has been well documented. So too have the archaic technological base and the poor infrastructure operating in these economies been much cited as barriers to foreign investment. Privatization, marketization more generally, and modernization with the introduction of new technology therefore combine to force high levels of redundancies and unemployment. Additional contributory factors have been the recession in East Central Europe, which intensified in 1991, partly driven by external factors such as the collapse of internal trade in the Eastern bloc, and the rise in energy prices as a result of the former Soviet Union adopting world prices for its energy exports. Price liberalization and the removal of state subsidies have led to a fall in real wages, rapid rises in inflation and increasing social inequalities, with the danger of young urban families, pensioners and single-parent families falling below the poverty line (Einhorn, 1993, pp. 137–8). The danger of poverty is particularly great for women who are unemployed. In Hungary in 1991, 79 per cent of unemployed women (and 55 per cent of unemployed men) received benefit lower than the official minimum wage, since unemployment benefit is calculated as a percentage of previous income, and women's incomes are usually lower than men's (Ladó, Adamik and Tóth, 1991, p. 13).

As enterprises streamline their workforces (such as through downsizing) to survive the process of fundamental restructuring in a recessionary context, it seems that women are the first to go. It is striking that in all of the former state socialist countries of East Central Europe with the exception of Hungary, they currently form the majority of the unemployed (OECD, 1992, p. 252, Chart 6.3; ILO, 1994b, p. 16). In the Czech Republic from May to December 1991, the female share of unemployment rose from 50.6 per cent to 57.4 per cent, and reached 60 per cent of an admittedly low overall unemployment rate by mid-1994 (Paukert, 1995). In Russia, women currently account for 70–75 per cent of those registered unemployed, plus the great majority of those unregistered (Posadskaya, 1993; Silovic, 1993; Khotkina, 1994, p. 98). In Romania in September 1990, a dramatic 85–90 per cent of registered unemployed were women, and in Albania around 60 per cent (Watson, 1993, p. 78). In Bulgaria in April 1991, women's share of unemployment was 62 per cent (Einhorn, 1993, p. 129).

The official unemployment rate for the new Federal states (former German Democratic Republic) was 15.9 per cent in October 1993. Marked regional differences meant that in the state of Sachsen-Anhalt, the total was 17.6 per cent (IAB, 1993). Women's unemployment rate as of January 1993 was officially quoted as 20 per cent as compared with 11 per cent for men. This made women's share of unemployment 64.9 per cent as of the end of 1992, or around two-thirds by June 1993 (Engelbrech, 1993; Maier, 1993, p. 274). Such high concentrations of female unemployment are also common in the other East Central European countries (Einhorn, 1993, pp. 128–31).

The high female shares of unemployment are particularly striking in the context where, prior to 1989, women made up between 45 per cent (Poland, see Watson, 1993, p. 78) and 51 per cent (former Soviet Union) of the workforce in most of the centrally planned economies. Given their high level of education and vocational qualifications, there was no a priori reason to suppose that women would be 'the first to go' as a result of the economy's need to shed unproductive labour from what has been called the 'overemployment' of state socialism in the transition to the market.

First responses to the high female share of unemployment might have interpreted it as in part an expression of choice. Women exhausted by their double burden as workers and mothers in the centrally planned economies might choose to reduce their stress by staying at home. However, both the material necessity of two or more incomes to provide for the family and the subjective attitudes to labour market involvement would tend to discount this explanation. The fact that women find it more difficult than men to find re-employment is cited by an OECD report as 'an additional factor that seems to indicate that high unemployment among women is not being driven by voluntary quits' (OECD, 1992, p. 253).

One of the reasons for high female unemployment has been the counter-intuitive pattern of job losses. As expected, there have been substantial falls in employment in mining, heavy industry and agriculture, but it was expected that job losses would exclusively affect men. However, women have been affected as a result of the female domination of top-heavy administrative and clerical branches within these industries (Einhorn, 1993). There have also been massive job losses in female-dominated branches of light industry, especially textiles and food processing, which some analysts had previously seen as 'possible sources of job creation in Central and Eastern Europe'. A factor influencing this collapse has been the import restrictions curtailing access to EU and other OECD markets (OECD, 1992, p. 245).

Young people are particularly badly affected by unemployment (OECD, 1992, p. 253). It seems that with the introduction of the market, traditional notions about women's interrupted labour market attachment are overriding the actual experience of the past 40+ years, in which women left the labour market for childbearing reasons for short periods only. As a result, more young women than young men are unemployed, for example female school-leavers previously guaranteed an apprenticeship or a place in tertiary education, who are finding it harder to gain such places than are young men (Knothe, 1993 on Poland; Maier, 1993, p. 277 on East Germany). Also disproportionately affected are single mothers affected by the lack of child-care places or less mobile than their male equivalents, many of whom in East Germany, for example, commute long-distance to West Germany in search of employment, and middle-aged women who are being classed in the so-called 'pre-retirement bracket' (Einhorn, 1993, pp. 137–9; on Russia, see Khotkina, 1994, p. 97; on Poland, see Pine 1994, p. 31).

A substantial source of unemployment for rural women is the land reprivatization programmes in several of the former state socialist countries (ILO, 1994b, p. 17). The percentage of women active on the land was substantial in these countries. They continue to represent 17 per cent of the total female labour force in Hungary, 28 per cent in Poland, 34 per cent in Romania, and 60 per cent in the still heavily rural Albania (Silovic, 1993, p. 8) in the early 1990s. In East Germany, where the number of those employed in agriculture has dropped by over 50 per cent since 1989, women previously made up 38 per cent of the workforce in this sector (Maier, 1993, p. 275).

Robert McIntyre has pointed to the striking lack of pressure for decollectivization since 1989 from co-operative or collective farmers in Eastern Europe and the former Soviet Union (McIntyre, 1993). The reasons for this, he points out, originate in the post-Stalinist social contract which provided local infrastructures in the rural areas (pre-school child-care, schools, housing, clinics, shops, cultural facilities, transport services), income stability, social support programmes, and regular working hours (with weekends and paid vacations). He argues that 'as a result of the quality-of-life effects of these programmes, which overlap with the effective evaporation of urban-rural income differentials, most of the active farm population came to be quite happy with collective agriculture' (McIntyre, 1993, p. 12). Certainly his conclusion was supported by this author's interview with a female co-operative farm president in Hungary in 1990, who expressed the anxiety of her members about the loss of health insurance and old-age pensions. In addition, the projected closure of small local clothing and bottling factories under market pressure would specifically affect the incomes of rural women who made up most of the workforce in these factories. In south-west Poland, such local branch industries employed mainly men, leaving rural women (in the largely uncollectivized Polish agricultural sector) carrying an even heavier load of farm and domestic labour than they had done traditionally. But as Frances Pine argues, 'there is little in the experience of women under capitalism which would indicate that a demand economy heralds the birth of a new era for rural women' (Pine, 1992, p. 73).

Re-employment

Women form the majority of the unemployed in most countries in East Central Europe. They also face considerably greater difficulty in finding new employment (ILO, 1994a; Paukert, 1993). A survey of the prospects of men and women unemployed workers in the new federal Länder in November 1990 showed that after one year, 45 per cent of men, but only 33 per cent of women, had found new jobs. This leads Maier (1993, p. 275) to speak of a 'quite substantial ... mismatch between jobs lost and jobs offered ... in the case of women' (see also OECD, 1992, pp. 253, 256).

Ironically, the very same social provisions that underwrote women's labour force participation in the centrally planned economies are now working against their chances of re-employment. An enterprise struggling to survive in the market is likely to shed as an 'optional extra' the child-care facilities that were previously its responsibility. Maternity and extended child-care provisions act together with protective legislation to deter potential employers from recruiting women workers, since they make women appear as relatively expensive labour. Women workers' frequent absences on paid leave to look after sick children tended even prior to 1989 to earn them the label of 'unreliable labour'. Thus many of the discriminatory hiring practices that have emerged since 1989 (Engelbrech, 1993, p. 18) can be attributed to prejudices against female labour originating in the social policies of the past regimes as well as renascent traditional beliefs. One of the many paradoxes adversely affecting women's re-employment prospects in the present, therefore, is that both the protective legislation and the positive discrimination enjoyed by them in the centrally planned economies are operating to their disadvantage in the new gender-segregated market conditions (Einhorn, 1993, p. 130; Knothe, 1993, p. 10; Paukert, 1991, p. 628; Standing, 1994, p. 30). Fong and Paull (1992) distinguish here between the real and the perceived cost of labour. Part of the solution lies in the need to build up an infrastructure of services and social welfare to take over functions previously performed by enterprises themselves (OECD, 1992, p. 243; Paukert, 1993).

A further impediment to women's re-employment prospects is that neither sex discrimination in employment opportunities, nor such issues as sexual harassment at work were on state socialism's gender-blind agenda. The result is that advertisements for jobs are often blatantly gender-specific. 'Men only' advertisements are widespread (Posadskaya, 1994, p. 171; Paukert, 1994a, p. 171). For example, in the Slovak Republic in February 1991, there were 7,563 vacancies, but only 29 per cent of them were for women. In Hungary in 1988 and 1989, between 65 per cent and 71 per cent of vacancies for manual jobs were for men only. Mária Ladó reported that the better the job offered, the more likely it is to specify men only. Foreign joint ventures openly prefer men to women in their job advertisements and many companies specify men for their higher managerial positions (Ladó, 1992; Paukert, 1993). Women in Poland reported that the length of skirt to be worn to interview or the shape of legs favoured for the job has been included in some advertisements. The state-run employment agency initially had different departments for men and women, which inevitably meant gender-specific job vacancy advertisements (Einhorn, 1993, p. 134).

Another problem is the requirement, often stated in job advertisements or by employment agencies, that a person seeking work be 'available' to take up a job at a moment's notice. In a situation where redundancy can mean the loss of entitlement to a child-care place or of the ability to pay massively increased child-care fees, women with young children are unlikely to be immediately available, and are therefore disadvantaged from the outset. Getting a job is predicated on having one's children placed, yet finding a child-care place is often dependent on having a job (Einhorn, 1993; Maier, 1993, p. 278; Pine, 1994, p. 38).

The result of such disadvantage is a marked gender imbalance in the relation of those unemployed to job vacancies. In January 1990 there were three unemployed women for every job offer in Poland, while the number of men who were unemployed was the same as the number of jobs available. By December 1990, there were 40 women, but only 14 men, for every job offer for their sex. In six regional districts, there were 100 women for every job opening. In one district, this figure had reached 1,398 women for one job. This was equivalent to there being no job offer for 97.3 per cent of registered unemployed women. By April 1991, there were 17 unemployed men for each vacancy for men, but 59 unemployed women for each vacancy for women. In this

WOMEN'S EMPLOYMENT IN EAST CENTRAL EUROPE / 71

situation, Fong and Paull calculated that the probability of obtaining new employment for a man in East Central Europe was over three times greater than for a woman (Einhorn, 1993, p. 134; Fong and Paull, 1992).

Retraining

One of the disturbing phenomena of the transition period is the lack of forward planning, particularly in relation to the specific employment needs of women. There has been no consciousness on the part of politicians that regional concentrations of high female unemployment, for example, or the widespread closure of child-care facilities, could have gender-specific implications for which one should plan in terms of retraining opportunities. Hence, retraining is haphazard and unfocused, and in most of these countries it seems to consist, as far as women are concerned, almost exclusively of computer training courses. This may represent a skilling process for secretarial, clerical or administrative workers previously working with archaic office equipment, but for highly skilled female industrial workers, fully qualified women engineers, or researchers, it must mean a level of deskilling. In addition, Hungarian data show that computer courses are gender divided, with men forming the majority of those retraining as technicians, while women form the (slight) majority of software engineers but the great majority of computer operators (Ladó, Adamik and Tóth, 1991).

Part of the problem lies in the fact that women workers' existing skills are often inappropriate to the requirements of a particular economic sector under market conditions. This is especially marked in the case of a sector such as banking and insurance, which played a minor role in the centrally planned economies (Nickel, 1993; Hübner, Maier and Rudolph, 1991). Where an industry such as textiles collapses, causing regional concentrations of unemployed women workers in several of these countries, there is little provision for the fact that they will never again be able to work in the industry or occupation for which they have qualifications (Khotkina, 1994, p. 93).

This mismatch between women's existing training and employment opportunities in the former centrally planned economies makes clear the need for retraining courses specifically geared to the needs of women workers (Khotkina, 1994, p. 98). Fong and Paull point out that 'policy-makers' neglect during transition of the particular employment needs and requirements of women ... would have negative consequences, not only for parity between men and women, but also for reform'. Fong and Paull therefore recommend a series of 'pro-active measures', including retraining programmes for women and the provision of child-care facilities (Fong and Paull, 1992).

In Hungary, empirical data show gender segregation in retraining programmes. In the first half of 1991, women formed the great majority of those retraining as shop assistants, and the total of aspiring supermarket cashiers. Retraining courses in both industry and services were totally gender divided, dressmakers being exclusively female, while welders and bricklayers were exclusively male; florists, domestic help and home economics trainees being exclusively female, while building maintenance trainees, painters and glaziers were exclusively male (Ladó, Adamik and Tóth, 1991, pp. 50–51).

At the end of 1992 in the new Federal Länder in Germany, women made up 60 per cent of those on retraining courses. However, as Maier points out, many of them (19 per cent of all women and only 7.6 per cent of all men) were involved in training that was inappropriate in that it was short term, introductory, or based in vocational schools. In contrast, more men (26 per cent of all men, but only 11 per cent of all women) undergo longer-term in-firm training, which offers better employment prospects (Maier, 1993, p. 276). Obviously there is a need for more gender- and occupation-specific retraining. At present the need for affirmative action on behalf of women in the labour market in East Central Europe is not being adequately addressed. On the contrary, some politicians have suggested that East European women workers have 'unrealistic' expectations based on the earlier high levels of labour force participation, and that many of them will never work again. Rather they should accustom themselves to the much lower female economic activity rate characteristic of Western Europe.[4]

Social policy constraints

Women's high unemployment and difficulties in finding new employment in the former state socialist countries are occurring within an altered social context. A loss of former social provision is compounded by inadequately established new social networks and forms of social insurance (OECD, 1992). Legislation that underwrote women's labour market involvement has changed (such as in the case of the former GDR; for Russia, see Khotkina, 1994, p. 100), or is being ignored or is acting against the interests of women workers in many of the countries. Most fundamental, however, is the emergence of an altered social policy paradigm based on the notion of a single breadwinner family with women as dependent wives and mothers (for further discussion, see Einhorn, 1993, pp. 42–44; Engelbrech, 1991). Partly this is ideologically driven and conflicts with the material need for two or more incomes to provide for the family. In part, it parallels the economy's need to shed labour by defining women as a secondary labour force in a time of recession (Mezentseva, 1994).

Perhaps the most extreme case of diminution in social provision, although not untypical, is that faced by women in East Germany after German unification. Whereas child-care for pre-school children was sufficient to meet demand in the former GDR, the FRG provided nursery places for only 4 per cent of children under three (as compared with 80.2 per cent in the GDR). Most child-care facilities in the FRG were open half-days only, militating against full-time work on the part of working mothers. In many of the other countries of East Central Europe, child-care facilities are being closed or priced out of reach. Legislation that is still legally valid, such as the right to return to one's job after extended child-care leave, is in practice being 'violated all the time' in Russia, maintains Anastasia Posadskaya, Director of the Institute for Gender Studies at the Russian Academy of Sciences, 'because either the job doesn't exist any more, or the enterprise has been privatized and the new owners feel no responsibility to take women back'. Likewise, pay differentials operate against women. Polish sources claim that employers will tend to try to protect the 'main provider' for the family, which almost inevitably, as a result of his higher income, is thought to be the man (Einhorn, 1993, p. 130). In the case of the former GDR, legislation such as the 'baby year' and the right to paid leave to look after sick children has disappeared in favour of far less generous West German social provision (Einhorn, 1993).

Even prior to 1989, ideologues in many East Central European countries were subscribing publicly to the view that juvenile delinquency, alcoholism and other social problems were the result of women's labour market participation (Pine, 1994, p. 34). This trend has contributed to the currently emerging notion that women should return home and assume primary responsibility for the family, for social cohesion and the preservation of moral and cultural values. In the short term, some women have welcomed this trend as respite from the rigours of the double burden. In so far as voluntary exit from the labour market is a factor at all, some women when made redundant welcome 'the chance to spend a few years at home with the children'. Such women have no experience that would suggest that the 'few years' may well become long-term unemployment (Mezentseva, 1994, p. 78; Paukert, 1995, p. 12) with the skills acquired under the previous system becoming ever more inadequate, since previously, extended child-care leave (up to the child's third birthday in Poland and Hungary) was universally linked with the right to the same job or an equivalent position being made available when the woman returned to work.

The 'new' conservative family and social policy model, together with the withdrawal of welfare services formerly provided by the state, construes women as the providers as well as the consumers of informal welfare. It also implies that any labour market involvement by them will be part time, to fit in with their role as mothers. It is significant in this context that this change is reflected in German terminology referring to women's economic involvement. The term used in the former GDR was *Berufstätigkeit* built on the word for career *(Beruf)*. This has given way to the West German *Erwerbstätigkeit* which merely describes earning activities. This apparently inconsequential shift in terminology in fact represents a substantive change, from every woman's right to a career, to the notion of minor or low-level employment in the context of the breadwinner marriage (see Pfau-Effinger and Geissler, 1992).

A German Institute for Economic Research report, cited by Nickel (1993, p. 6), comments on the way that the legislative and social changes described, and the social policy model underlying them, fundamentally alter East German women's employment and life prospects, when it remarks: 'Underlying these measures we find a family policy which makes looking after small children primarily the task of their mothers. In practice, it means that these mothers give up their paid employment substantially or totally, which leads to a "family phase" lasting several years. This legislation on women's non-employment has been extended to the new Federal states ...'. This is presumably contributing to the process whereby the biographies of a great many women in East Germany (must) adapt to the West German pattern, a process that is reinforcing the existing displacement of women on the labour market. The implied notion that women's biographies and life courses need to undergo fundamental change to adapt to the new situation can also be applied to the other East Central European countries.

There appears to be a major mismatch and potential conflict between this new family model, with its emphasis on women's role as mothers, and their own aspirations in terms of their role as workers. Despite the difficulties of working in both the old and the new labour market conditions, recent opinion surveys make it clear that women in the former state socialist countries got more out of their labour force involvement than relative economic independence. In the Czech Republic, an ILO survey showed that only 28 per cent of married women would like to stay at home if their husbands earned enough for them to do so, but a substantial 40 per cent expressed a definite wish to continue working even if this were not financially necessary (Paukert, 1995). As Liba Paukert suggests, 'the professional activity of women has now become so much a part of the social norm in Czechoslovakia that a change might be difficult to accept' (Paukert, 1991, p. 621).

Surveys conducted in several other East Central European countries support the notion that after more than 40 years in which it was the norm, labour force participation has become an integral part of women's self-perception and sense of identity. Although economic necessity certainly played an important role in women's labour force participation prior to 1989 (Paukert, 1991), many also felt that their work collective was their most important social network. Polish young people of both sexes regard women's labour market activity as the norm (Paukert, 1995, p. 7).

A survey of East German women's attitudes to employment conducted in autumn 1991 found only 10 per cent of women in the new federal states who would definitely give up work if they no longer needed the money. A further 20 per cent expressed uncertainty, but 70 per cent were convinced they would still wish to work, even if it were not a material necessity. Nor had their attitudes changed one year after an earlier survey in autumn 1990. (For analyses of the surveys, see Beer and Müller, 1993, pp. 288–91; DIW, 1992; Engelbrech, 1993; Maier, 1993, pp. 277–8.) The surveys established no 'voluntary' withdrawal from the labour market amongst the younger and middle generations of women. There is also no evidence to support the view (Pfau-Effinger and Geissler, 1992) that women in the former state socialist countries might actually prefer part-time work as an optimal mode of reconciling their aspirations for family *and* career. Indeed, a survey of women's desired work patterns established that three-quarters of all married women currently working, four-fifths of working single mothers, and even a narrow majority of currently non-working mothers would prefer full-time to part-time work for the future.

The results of these various attitudinal surveys suggest that the concept of the 'breadwinner family', which forms the basis of West German social policy, or the 'family wage' policy, espoused at least in theory by former Polish President Lech Walesa, are out of tune with the aspirations of women in the new market economies.

Possible labour market trends

In all of the former state socialist countries, there is a simultaneous double transformation occurring, in which the transition from a centrally planned to a market-based economy is accompanied by a process of restructuring. This involves a shift away from state socialist prioritization of heavy industry to a focus on light industry, with a special emphasis on the introduction of new and microtechnology, consumer goods production, and expansion of the service sector (ILO, 1994b, p. 17).

The idea that these multiple shifts might favour highly skilled 'flexible' female labour is espoused by Fong and Paull (1992) when they suggest that 'many women – because of experience and education – have acquired strong positions in potentially expanding sectors, such as consumer goods and service industries, particularly financial services, commerce and trade, and information technology. They have also developed entrepreneurial skills that could prove advantageous in the private sector'.[5] Developments to date, however, have not borne out this hope. New technology has tended to oust female workers. The process of privatization has also been slow and hence has not provided a rich source of alternative employment. In addition, West European experience would suggest that employment in this sector can worsen women's labour market position. The service sector has contracted rather than expanded (Wagner, 1992, p. 80). It is important that more research be done to get a sense of whether longer-term developments will be more favourable for women's employment opportunities.

At present, however, job prospects for women are constrained by a double set of discrepancies:

- between available female skills and the requirements of particular sectors, such as banking and finance under market conditions (see Engelbrech, 1991; Knothe, 1993, p. 12; Nickel, 1993), hence a great need for retraining skilled women workers;
- between women's aspirations (based on their past self-image arising from their working identity) and the diminished possibilities of realizing that self-image due to current labour market problems and social policies (Engelbrech, 1991).

New technology

There is evidence to suggest that the introduction of new technology, even prior to the currently rapid fundamental economic reform, was linked to the displacement of women. Despite the fact that new production aids such as information technology, flexible automation, or robotization mean a qualitative improvement in working conditions, which might suggest the creation of a more woman-friendly working environment, women's share of those sectors in the former GDR showed a continuous decline during the 1980s, even taking into account the creation of female jobs in microelectronic and chip production (Winkler, 1990, pp. 49–50). This tendency for women to be pushed out of formerly female-dominated occupations by the introduction of new technology is confirmed by figures showing substantial decreases in the percentage of East German girls beginning vocational training in data processing, electronics and other technical occupations between 1980 and 1989 (see Schenk, 1992, pp. 36–38).

Ladó has registered a parallel tendency in Hungary (Ladó and Tóth, 1989). Sutherland notes that this trend operates in both Eastern and Western Europe. For example, in computers, software tends to be viewed as women's domain while hardware is male-ascribed, and salaries get adjusted accordingly. She cites a report of the Commission of the European Union showing a similar pattern of gender-based segregation operating in the field of information technology (Sutherland, 1990). This would seem to suggest what might be deemed a reversal of gender stereotypes. As new technology makes jobs cleaner and more highly skilled, men opt to move into them, leaving women to perform the simple and repetitive tasks or the lower-status jobs which do not offer career-enhancement opportunities (on Russia, see Khotkina, 1994).

Privatization

Privatization has been slower to develop than was at first expected (OECD, 1992). In the Czech Republic, privatization of small businesses, especially small retail outlets, has progressed to a considerable degree. There is a lack of concrete data as yet, but it is suggested that these largely family-based firms employ women for long hours for little remuneration (on Poland, see Pine, 1994, pp. 31–33). The expectation in East Germany too is that the majority of female employment in private retail outlets will be based on unprotected and part-time contracts (Wagner, 1992, p. 81).

Current labour market strategies in East Central Europe are predicated on the assumption that women, worn out by their double burden of full-time work and domestic labour, may favour part-time or more flexible working hours more easily compatible with family responsibilities. Western and developing country experience with recession and restructuring suggests, however, that the move to more 'irregular" or 'atypical' patterns of work, responsible for much of the recent growth in female employment, is linked with exploited and unprotected labour conditions, job insecurity and a weak position in the labour market (i.e. few career prospects and frequent spells of unemployment) (see, for example, Fong and Paull, 1992; Paukert, 1984, p. 54).

Much hope has been vested in self-employment (on Hungary, see Szalai, 1995). However, patchy and largely undocumented evidence so far suggests that while women *are* active in setting up new businesses, existing data may overestimate female participation in the new private sector. An example of misleading data is that former *apparatchiks* in several countries are thought to name their wives as owners to mask their own move from the *nomenklatura* or management of state-owned enterprises to their buy-out, or the establishment of private companies.

In addition, many new entrepreneurs set up their businesses as a second or third job in addition to what they perceive as relatively more secure employment in the state sector. This could operate as a constraint against women taking up such opportunities, because of their additional domestic responsibilities (Hübner, Maier and Rudolph, 1991), and is, therefore, thought unlikely to diminish the gender imbalance in unemployment statistics (OECD, 1992, p. 256).

In any case, self-employment, however much it is seen as the ultimate expression of enterprise and initiative in the new market conditions, can only ever offer a solution for a minority of the unemployed (Khotkina, 1994, pp. 105–108; ILO, 1994b, p. 16). An OECD report concludes that only a substantial boost in service sector employment could appreciably improve women's job prospects (OECD, 1992, p. 256).

Development of the service sector: shifts in sectoral importance

The transition to the market and the parallel process of restructuring described earlier lead to shifts in the relative importance of economic sectors. While the obsolete technology of heavy industrial plants in East Central Europe is compounded by the general worldwide shift away from industrial economies based on heavy manufacturing and mining, the transformation is based on the assumption of an expected concomitant growth in light industry and the service sector. This has yet to materialize. On the contrary, 1989–91 saw a marked decline in employment (OECD, 1992, p. 243). Within these two years, the wholesale and retail trades in East Germany had halved the number of their employees, and there was a substantial drop in employment in hotels, restaurants and catering (Maier, 1993, p. 275).

Decline in manufacturing industry affects not only male workers in mining, steel, automobiles and mechanical engineering, but also female workers in the administrative and clerical branches of those sectors. Women's structurally caused unemployment is further exacerbated by the collapse of female-dominated industries such as textiles, electronics, precision tools, optics and food-processing.

Before 1989, women dominated the service sector. In Hungary, Poland and Romania, more than half of all female workers were employed in services (Watson, 1993, p. 78; on Russia, see Khotkina, 1994; Mezentseva, 1994). Despite gender-neutral schooling under state socialism, girls still tended to choose vocational training in occupations traditionally seen as 'women's work'. In the former GDR, for example, over 60 per cent of female school-leavers opted for training in a mere 16 out of a total of 259 occupations. Girls made up 95 per cent of trainee textile workers and 99 per cent of trainee garment workers in

1989. And close to 100 per cent of trainee secretaries and salespersons were, of course, girls. Very similar patterns operated in Hungary, where in vocational schools in 1990–91, only 0.7 per cent of apprentices in metallurgy and 1.1 per cent in engineering were girls, but 98 per cent of apprentices in the textile and garment industries were girls (Ladó, Adamik and Tóth, 1991, pp. 22, 66; Schenk, 1992, pp. 36–38; Einhorn, 1993, pp. 120–21). These trends, together with the gender segregation of retraining courses, suggest that even when the service sector begins to expand, it will provide very limited job opportunities for women. Indeed, the introduction of new technology and the case of banking and insurance, discussed earlier in the chapter, might suggest a displacement of women workers.

The case of banking and insurance

The example of financial services is an illuminating one. For a centrally planned economy, banking and insurance were of minimal importance, and their workforce was heavily female-dominated in all of the state socialist countries. By contrast, they compose a sector of crucial importance to a market-based economy. Does this suggest employment opportunities for women, or will it result in a displacement of female by male workers as status and career opportunities within this sector become enhanced? An initial case-study of the *Sparkasse* (savings banks) in the former GDR shows that their pre-1989 workforce was 90 per cent female, compared with 60 per cent in West Germany. While there was a predominance of women at middle management level (branch managers and deputy managers) in the GDR, there were few women managers in West Germany. Yet initial findings from this case-study suggest two trends that work against female employees from the former GDR. The first is the import of a Western structural model, which leads to female managers being displaced by men. The second is the mismatch between the training and skills of employees in the new federal Länder and the needs of this sector under market conditions. This second factor tends to favour West German at the expense of East German female employees. Thus East German female employees are suffering a double form of competition, in the sense that they are starting out at a disadvantage because of their unfamiliarity with and lack of training for the specific structures and requirements of this sector in a market economy. In addition, many firms operate gender-biased recruitment policies. Nor are women in the new Länder acquiring the relevant skills. Recent apprenticeship figures show a decline in the proportion of female apprentices in previously heavily feminized occupations, such as bookkeepers and finance clerks, where women had held more than 90 per cent of jobs (Maier, 1993, p. 275; Nickel, 1993).

Conclusion

This chapter has argued that in the short run women's employment opportunities in the newly marketizing economies have been severely curtailed. They form the majority of the unemployed and are facing discriminatory hiring practices and other disadvantages when seeking re-employment. Nor are there sufficient well-targeted retraining programmes available to enable them to adapt their high-level but often inappropriate skills to the requirements of the new market conditions. Nor, in the medium term, does optimism about the potentially favourable outcomes of modernization and the introduction of new technology appear to be well-founded in terms of its spin-offs for female employment opportunities. State intervention is necessary to ensure that women workers are not the losers in the transformation process.

Broadly speaking, there have, in the past, been two types of policy response to the special problems faced by women in their dual role as workers and mothers. Protective legislation tends to govern working hours and conditions and bars women from jobs considered unsuitable for them, especially during pregnancy. Originally designed to protect women and children in 19th-century Britain from back-breaking physical labour in the mines, the model of protective legislation as practised in the state socialist societies of East Central Europe tended, even prior to the current process of economic reform, to restrict the number of occupations open to women. Generous maternity leave provisions, designed to cater for women's dual role, often militated against their being promoted to managerial posts.

More recent historical experience thus suggests that protective legislation may in effect hinder women's equal access to employment and career promotion opportunities, thus reinforcing gender discrimination in the labour market (Helsinki Watch, 1992, p. 4). However, the alternative of gender-neutral legislation cannot solve the problem of women's gender-specific needs. Therefore, equal opportunity legislation prohibiting discrimination on grounds of sex by itself is insufficient for the purpose of achieving gender equity in the labour market.

What is needed is a combination of anti-discriminatory legislation and some positive discrimination or affirmative action measures, especially with regard to promoting women to posts of responsibility and management in line with their qualifications and experience. In sum, the formal or legal outlawing of discrimination does not guarantee women workers the ability to activate their notionally equal rights of access to the market. Genuinely equal employment opportunities for women in East Central Europe necessitate a package of 'proactive measures'. These combine equal opportunities legislation with social provision that underwrites the capacity to exercise the right to work, especially in terms of publicly provided child-care, retraining programmes and affirmative action promotion schemes (Fong and Paull, 1992).

Notes

1. In the Federal Republic of Germany (FRG), 95 per cent of new labour contracts since 1970 have been for part-time positions filled by women. In 1983, 91.9 per cent and in 1990 89.7 per cent of all part-time workers were women. By contrast, in 1986 only 3 per cent of Hungarian, 6 per cent of Polish and 7.6 per cent of Czech and Slovak women workers were part-timers. Sources: for the FRG, Baden, 1993, table 4; Rosenberg, 1993, p. 113; for Hungary, Ladó, 1992; for Poland and Czechoslovakia, Kroupová, 1990.

2. In Czechoslovakia in 1989, only 53 per cent of women workers were employed in service activities, compared with 70 per cent in neighbouring Austria (Paukert, 1991, p. 623). Similarly, in 1989 the East German productive sector accounted for more than 60 per cent of all gainfully employed women, compared with only 50.5 per cent in West Germany, while 49.5 per cent of West German but only 31.8 per cent of East German women workers were employed in service sector industries (Maier, 1993, p. 271).

3. For the former GDR, see Rosenberg (1991, p. 13), who cites 1978 figures of 8.5 per cent of tenured professors, 49 per cent of doctors, 52 per cent of dentists, 64 per cent of pharmacists, and for 1986, 52 per cent of judges who were women. Einhorn (1989, pp. 289–90), gives 57 per cent of dentists and 52 per cent of doctors who were women in 1983. These figures compare favourably with Western figures for 1987, showing 4 per cent of lawyers and 16 per cent of doctors who were women in the UK; 15 per cent of judges, 14 per cent of lawyers, 23 per cent of doctors, and 20 per cent of dentists who were women in West Germany; but only 8 per cent of lawyers, 6 per cent of dentists, and 17 per cent of doctors who were women in the US. Siemienska (1987), gives a figure of 54.5 per cent of Polish judges who were women in 1986; and according to an ILO report (1992, p. 9), 67.6 per cent of Polish doctors were women in 1980.

4. Dr Angela Merkel, the East German Federal Minister for Women, reflected this view when she said, in retrospect, that the GDR had lulled women into an 'illusory life situation'. She justified the hardships of the transition, which fall mainly on women, by asserting that the level of state welfare provided by the GDR 'could not be guaranteed in any society governed by competition' (my translation; Dr Merkel was quoted in *Der Spiegel* No. 24, 1992, p. 101).

5. Fong and Paull's article, 'Women's employment in Central and Eastern Europe: the gender factor', in *Transition: Newsletter about Reforming Economies*, Vol. 3, No. 6, June 1992, was based on the authors' World Bank Report No. 8213, 1992.

References

Baden, S. (1993) 'The impact of recession on women's employment in OECD countries', paper prepared for the Interdepartmental Project on Equality for Women in Employment, Geneva, ILO.

Beer, U. and U. Müller (1993) 'Coping with a new reality: Barriers and possibilities', in *Cambridge Journal of Economics*, 17, pp. 281–94.

DIW (1992) – Deutsches Institut für Wirtschaftsforschung (German Institute for Economic Research) 'Umbruch am ostdeutschen Arbeitsmarkt benachteiligt auch weiterhin erwerbstäige Frauen – dennoch anhaltend hohe Berufsorientierung', in *Wochenbericht* 18/92, April.

Einhorn, B. (1989) 'Socialist emancipation: The women's movement in the GDR', in S. Kruks, R. Rapp and M. Young (eds), *Promissory notes: Women in the transition to socialism*, New York, Monthly Review Press, pp. 282–305.

– (1993) *Cinderella goes to market: Citizenship, gender and women's movements in East Central Europe*, London, Verso.

– and S. Mitter (1992) 'A comparative analysis of women's industrial participation during the transition from centrally-planned to market economies in East Central Europe', in UN, 1992.

Englebrech, G. (1991) 'Vom Arbeitskräftemangle zum gegenwärtigen Arbeitskäfteüberschuss: Frauen und Erwerbsarbeit in den neuen Bundesländern', in *Mitteilungen aus der Arbeitsmarkts-und Berufsforschung*, Vol. 24.

– (1993) 'Zwischen Wunsch und Wirklichkeit: Einstellungen ostdeutscher Frauen zur Erwerbstätigkeit zwei Jahre nach der Wende – Ergebnisse einer Befragung', in *IAB Werkstattbericht*, No. 8, June.

Fong, M. and G. Paull (1992) *The changing role of women in employment in Eastern Europe*, World Bank, Europe and Central Asia Region, Population and Human Resources Division, Report No. 8213, February.

Heinen, J. (1990) 'The impact of social policy on the behaviour of women workers in Poland and East Germany', in *Critical Social Policy*, Vol. 10, No. 2, issue 29, Autumn, pp. 79–91.

Helsinki Watch (1992) 'Hidden victims: Women in post-communist Poland, in *News from Helsinki Watch*, Vol. IV, Issue 5, March.

Hübner, S., F. Maier and H. Rudolph (1991) 'Women's employment in Central and Eastern Europe: Status and propects', in G. Standing and G. Fischer (eds), *Structural change in Central and Eastern Europe: Labour market and social policy implications*, Paris, OECD.

IAB (1993) – Institut für Arbeitsmarkt und Berufsforschung der Bundesanstalt für Arbeit (Federal German Labour Ministry, Institute for Labour Market and Career Research), 'Aktuelle Daten vom Arbeitsmarkt' (regularly updated unemployment statistics), in *IAB Werkstattbericht*, Nürnberg, June and October.

ILO (1992) *Equality of opportunity and treatment between men and women in health and medical services*, Report II, Geneva, ILO.

– (1994a) 'Productive employment: Women workers in a changing global environment', draft contribution to *1994 world survey on the role of women in development*, Geneva, ILO.

– (1994b) *World labour report*, Geneva.

Khotkina, Z. (1994) 'Women in the labour market: Yesterday, today and tomorrow', in A. Posadskaya (ed.), *Women in Russia: A new era in Russian feminism*, London and New York, Verso, pp. 85–108.

Knothe, M.A. (1993) 'The right to work as a way to women's independence in Poland', paper given to the Colloquium on Women's Daily Life and Equal Opportunity Policies: Central and Eastern European Societies in the Transition, held at the European University Institute, Florence, January.

Kroupová, A. (1990) 'Women, employment and earning in Central and East European Countries', paper prepared for Tripartite Symposium on Equality of Opportunity and Treatment for Men and Women in Employment in Industrialized Countries, Geneva, September.

Ladó, M. (1992) 'Women in the transition to a market economy, the case of Hungary', in UN, 1992.

– and F. Tóth (1989) 'Zwei verschiendene Welten: Die neuen Technologien und Frauenarbeit' (Two different worlds: New technology and women's work), in G. Aichholz and G. Schienstock (eds), *Arbeitsbeziehungen im technischer Wandel (Technical change and working conditions)*, Berlin, Edition Sigma, pp. 201–14.

Ladó, M., M. Adamik and F. Tóth (1991) 'Training for women under conditions of crisis and structural adjustment', paper prepared for ILO, Budapest.

McIntyre, R.J. (1993) 'The phantom of the transition: Privatization of agriculture in the former Soviet Union and Eastern Europe', paper presented to the American Economic Association/ACES Conference, Anaheim, California, January.

Maier, F. (1993) 'Frauenerwerbstätigkeit in der DDR und der BRD – Gemeinsamkeiten und Unterschiede', in Fachhochschule für Wirtschaft – Forschung 22, *Politische Ökonomie des Teilens*, Berlin.

Mezentseva, Y. (1994) 'What does the future hold? (Some thoughts on the prospects for women's employment)', in A. Posadskaya (ed.), *Women in Russia: A new era in Russian feminism*, London and New York, Verso, pp. 74–84.

Moghadam, V. (ed.) (1993) *Democratic reform and the position of women in transitional economies*, Oxford, Clarendon Press.

Nickel, H.M. (1993) 'Frauen in den neuen Bundesländer Pluralisierung und Individualisierung von weiblichen Lebensstilen oder soziale Polarisierung und Spaltung von Lebenschancen?', in B. Schäfer (ed.), *Lebensverhältnisse und soziale Konflikte im neue Europa*, Frankfurt am Main, pp. 124–31.

OECD (1992) 'Reforming labour markets in Central and Eastern Europe and the rise of unemployment', Chapter 6 in *Employment outlook*, Paris, OECD.

Paukert, L. (1984) 'The employment and unemployment of women in OECD countries', OECD paper, Paris.

– (1991) 'The economic status of women in the transition to a market system: The case of Czechoslovakia', in *International Labour Review*, Vol. 130 (5-6), Geneva, ILO, pp. 613–33.

– (1993) 'Women's employment in East Central European countries during the period of transition to a market economy system', working paper, Geneva, ILO.

– (1994a) 'Public sector adjustment through employment: Retrenchment policies in the Czech and Slovak Republics', working paper, Geneva, ILO.

– (1994b) 'Gender and change in Central and Eastern Europe', regional report prepared for the ILO International Forum on Equality for Women in the World of Work: Challenge for the Future, ILO, Geneva, 1–3 June.

– (1995) Economic transition and women's employment in four Central European countries, 1989-1994, Labour market papers, No.7, Geneva, ILO.

Pfau-Effinger, B. and B. Geissler (1992) 'Institutionelle und sozio-kulturelle Kontextbedingungen der Entscheidung verheirateter Frauen für Teilzeitarbeit', in *Mitteilungen aus der Arbeitsmarkt und Berufsforschung*, Vol. 25.

Pine, F. (1994) 'Privatisation in post-socialist Poland: Peasant women, work, and the restructuring of the public sphere', in *Cambridge Anthropology*, 17 (3), pp. 19–42.

Posadskaya, A. (1993) 'Women's daily life strategies and development of new identities', paper given to the Colloquium on Women's Daily Life and Equal Opportunity Policies: Central and Eastern European Societies in the Transition, held at the European University Institute, Florence, January.

– (1994) 'A feminist critique of policy, legislation and social consciousness in post-socialist Russia', in A. Posadskaya (ed.), *Women in Russia: A new era in Russian feminism*, London, Verso, pp. 164–82.

Rosenberg, D. (1991) 'Shock therapy: GDR women in transition from a socialist welfare state to a social market economy', in *Signs*, Vol. 17, No. 1, Autumn.

– (1993) 'The new home economics: Women in the united Germany', in *Debatte: Review of contemporary German affairs*, Vol. 1, No. 1, pp. 111–34.

Schenk, S. (1992) 'Qualifikationsstruktur und Qualifikationsbedarf erwerbstätiger Frauen in den neuen Bundesländern', in G. Englebrech, S. Schenk and P. Wagner (eds), *Bedingungen der Frauenerwerbsarbeit im deutsch-deutschen Einigungsprozess*, Beiträge zur Arbeitsmarkt-und Berufsforschung, No. 167, Nürnberg.

Siemienska, R. (1987) 'Women in leadership positions in public administration in Poland', paper prepared for Friedrich Ebert Stiftung/UNESCO Conference, Bonn, July.

Silovic, D.S. (1993) 'The status of women in Eastern and Central Europe', paper for the Project on Transition to Democracy in World Perspective, Center for Social Studies, City University of New York Graduate Center, June.

Standing, G. (1994) *Labour market dynamics in Russian industry in 1993: Results from the Third Round of the RLFS*, Budapest, ILO-CEET.

Sutherland, M. (1990) 'Women's studies and the social position of women in Eastern and Western Europe', ENWS (European Network of Women's Studies) seminar report, The Hague, November.

Szalai, J. (1995) 'Women and democratization: Some notes on recent changes in Hungary', paper presented to the Inter-regional seminar on gender and culture of the Central European University, Workshop on 'Re-Thinking Gender, Citizenship and Rights', Prague, May.

UN (1992) 'The impact of economic and political reform on the status of women in Eastern Europe', proceedings of a United Nations Regional Seminar, 8–12 April 1991 in Vienna, ST-CSDHA-19-UN, New York.

Wagner, P. (1992) 'Die Organisation weiblicher Erwerbsarbeit im Umbruch – Überlegungen zur Entwicklung geringfügiger Beschäftigung in den neuen Bundesländern', in G. Englebrech, S. Schenk and P. Wagner (eds), *Bedingungen der Frauenerwerbsarbeit im deutsch-deutschen Einigungsprozess*, Beitrab No. 167, Institut für Arbeitsmarkt- und Berufsforschung der Bundesanstalt für Arbeit, Nürnberg.

Watson, P. (1993) 'The rise of masculinism in Eastern Europe', in *New Left Review*, No. 198, March–April, pp. 71–82.

Winkler, G. (ed.) (1990) *Frauenreport 90*, Berlin, Verlag Die Wirtschaft.

4
African women workers, globalization, AIDS and poverty

GUY MHONE

This chapter tries to show that the effects of globalization in Africa appear to reinforce women's vulnerability, even though these effects are only beginning to emerge in the region. It is argued that the export processing zones (EPZs) of multinational corporations, gradually appearing in some parts of the region, actually exploit the vulnerability and disadvantaged status of the women. In the absence of regulations to protect the interests of the workers, their conditions of work in these new enterprises may not meet internationally recommended standards. More importantly, these enterprises largely employ women in low-level occupations that only temporarily fulfil the women's short-term practical needs.[1] Their strategic needs are not met. For women in the rural and informal sectors, there is a tendency for the new activities of the EPZs to displace or substitute for some of the activities customarily undertaken by them. Furthermore, for foreign investment to generate enough employment opportunities in African labour markets, there have to be sufficient openings to absorb at least some of the net additions to the labour force. The amount of foreign investment coming into African countries so far is minuscule, given the prospective investors' perception of the region's economic environment as poor.

After this, an attempt is made to indicate that the situation of women workers in Africa is being aggravated by the onset of AIDS, persisting civil strife, recurring drought and intensifying environmental degradation. The scourge of AIDS increases women's reproductive and caring roles while also undermining the viability of households. Civil strife has resulted in the displacement of large numbers of people, mainly women and children, internally and externally (as refugees), and the disabling of individuals, in addition to the decimation of populations, all of which have negatively affected women directly. Recurrent drought and environmental degradation continue to undermine women's domestic and other essential roles for their households, particularly in rural areas. In light of the above, the plight of African women is a desperate and urgent one that requires more innovative measures to resolve it than are currently being undertaken in the various countries. This is underscored by the Regional Platform for Action adopted by the African Regional Preparatory Conference (1994) for the Fourth World Conference on Women. New initiatives are needed that are comprehensive enough to address both the strategic and practical needs of women in a mutually supportive and reinforcing manner. Such initiatives should also be directly related to the economic transformation of African economies, and involve governments and all the other social partners and actors, including unions, employers, civil society, nongovernmental organizations, international organizations and donor agencies.

Overview of women workers in Africa

If 'work' is defined to include, as it should, both market and non-market activities directed at the production of exchange and use values respectively, women in Africa, as elsewhere in the world, are disadvantaged relative to men primarily as a result of the multiple roles and the implicit burdens they have to undertake. Women, by invariably combining market and non-market tasks, are compromised in their ability to exploit economic opportunities and fully realize their potential. The patriarchal legacies of both traditional and modern forms of social organization in Africa, the dualistic and often conflicting legal systems (modern and traditional), customary practices and the unequal gender-based household and social division of labour in African societies have contributed to the unfavourable situation of women.

The disadvantaged status of women workers in Africa can be characterized as that of social exclusion in several important spheres of life in both the modern and traditional sectors. Furthermore, it can be characterized as a structurally constrained inability to realize or optimize their asset and exchange entitlements in all their economic undertakings. The social exclusion and denial of optimal entitlements are manifested in grave economic inefficiencies pertaining to the manner in which human resources are allocated and utilized at the macro- and microeconomic levels. In the African context, these inefficiencies are amplified by the dualistic and enclave economic legacies reflected in the underdevelopment of the rural economy and the inability of the modern sector to generate adequate growth in productive employment opportunities. The combination of the structural features of underdevelopment and those of patriarchy are seen to result in allocative, technical and distributive inefficiencies in the utilization of both male and female labour in African economies. Economic reform measures,

which are currently the focus of attention in almost all African countries, are not only inadequate to resolve both the structural and gender
distortions in the economies, but may also be magnifying the intensity
and extensiveness of the multiple roles women have to undertake
(Commonwealth Secretariat, 1989).

Statistical dimensions

Available figures (Mhone, 1995) on labour force participation rates
of females and males refer to the proportion of the adult population
that is able and willing to work, or to engage in market-related activities
within a specified period, according to various criteria generally recommended by the United Nations System of National Accounts, and
accommodated by the various governments according to their institutional capacities and procedures. In Africa, female labour force participation rates are for every country lower than those of males.
Conventional labour force participation rates generally exclude household work and economic activities directed at the production of use
values, the primary activities of most women in Africa. It is clear, therefore, that by excluding non-market activities generally undertaken by
women, conventional labour force statistics grossly under-represent the
economic role and participation of women.

It is for this reason that the 13th International Conference of Labour
Statisticians (1993) adopted a resolution that:

> In order to have a full appreciation of the relative vulnerability of women as work-
> ers it is necessary to define 'work' more broadly than normally done in available
> statistics and analysis based on them. The scope of 'employment' and 'work' as
> actually measured in statistical surveys and censuses is usually restricted to cover
> market-oriented activities, thereby making invisible various non-market activities
> which are both socially understood to constitute work and regarded as such by the
> relevant statistical recommendations of the ILO.[2]

Essentially, these activities entail child-bearing and rearing, household
management, subsistence production, and partial involvement in market
activities, not perhaps to an extent deemed adequate for inclusion in
labour force statistics. This shortcoming in labour force statistics is now
fully recognized. Nevertheless, not many attempts have been made to
improve data collection in this area.

According to official statistics, in 1994, the sectoral distribution of
the labour force was such that in sub-Saharan Africa 75 per cent of
females, compared with 61 per cent of males, were in agriculture; 5 per
cent of females and 15 per cent of males were in industry; and 20 per
cent of females as opposed to 23 per cent of males were in the services
(UN, 1995). It may be inferred that women, in comparison to men, are
under-represented in market or modern economic activities, and that

they are over-represented in subsistence and non-market economic activities. The above, and the well-known fact that the women engage in multiple roles as workers, have profound implications for the status of women as workers in Africa, and for the manner in which they are affected by economic reform measures, technological change and globalization.

Post-independence African governments have been unable to resolve or reverse the gender bias implicit in the above sectoral distribution, whose parameters were established during the colonial period. Women have continued to bear the main burden of reproducing the labour force: subsidizing the formal sector by lowering the cost of male labour through production of subsistence goods and services, managing domestic work, and acting as a safety net for the sick, retired or retrenched from the formal sector. They also act as a labour reserve in times of need, either to resolve labour shortages in sectors in which generally men are reluctant to work, or to act as a source of cheap labour because of their weaker bargaining position as a residual labour force. In the event, women have been primarily concentrated in subsistence agriculture and rural wage labour, the informal sector and low-wage service sectors in the formal sector. The labour markets in Africa are thus largely segmented by sex in terms of occupation, jobs and differential pay, with women at the lower end.

Legal status

Customary and modern legal practices with respect to women in Africa are very diverse. Nevertheless these practices share some common features related to the subordination of women. The most common feature is the existence of a plural legal structure whereby customary or traditional, religious, and modern received, statutory and common law all coexist. They do not overlap, but contradict each other. A few countries have attempted to rationalize these practices, but many have yet to do so. While generally one might expect traditional norms to be dominant in rural areas and modern ones in urban areas, the actual situation is slightly more complex in that as a consequence of education, labour migration, government policies and choices made by both men and women, all practices continue to coexist to one degree or another even if with some bias toward rural areas with regard to customary law, and urban areas with regard to modern law (Women and law in Southern Africa, 1990a).

The plurality of the legal systems and the specific nature of almost all traditional African laws not only reinforce the subordination of women, but also make their economic and social situation highly insecure and uncertain at any given moment. Thus the need for the rationalization of African legal practices in each country cannot be overemphasized if the strategic interests of women are to be achieved. Even if a number of African governments have ratified the United Nations Convention on the Elimination of All Forms of Discrimination against Women, they have not fully lived up to it, especially in terms of ensuring its application in rural areas (Women and law in Southern Africa, 1990a).

The main aspects of international labour standards that are abrogated relate to the following. First, there is a general absence of regulations that protect the health and safety of women workers in rural areas, particularly as related to maternity care, sharing of child-care responsibilities, recognition of time for rest, limits on burdens, types of tasks that women may undertake, and protection from hazardous working conditions. Second, minimum working ages are not observed, especially for girls, who are compelled to begin their induction into the social responsibilities expected of them at a very early stage, often entailing a compromise in school attendance and marriage at puberty. Third, the fact that the roles women undertake subsidize the community and society in various ways is not taken into account as a basis for devising social security or welfare schemes that should compensate them for this task. Under such circumstances, it is not surprising that the major form of social insurance that women in rural areas can rely upon is the bearing of more children. All of the foregoing factors work to the disadvantage of women workers, especially in rural areas, given their greater invisibility and the general tenacity with which biases against them are held.

Education and training

An important aspect of the disadvantaged status of African women relates to their poor access to education. Education plays the important role of imparting skills needed for employment in terms of human capital formation and of socializing the young into their expected roles in society. The former aspect also determines their productivity and income. While there has been an upward trend in female enrolments, they remain lower than those of males, partly because of the lower priority placed on the education of girls in many poor households. Within this context, the school systems in Africa also assist in the reproduction of gender differences in human capital formation in the manner in which girls are channelled into the so-called 'female' vocational specializations. Thus girls are generally under-represented in subjects such as mathematics, sciences and technical/vocational courses, which are required in the changing work environment and ensure upward mobility in formal sector labour markets.

Economic reform measures

Chapter 2 of this volume has provided a detailed analysis of the impact of economic reforms on women workers in the different economic sectors. The continuing economic crisis in Africa has been manifested in: declining per capita gross domestic product, stagnant or declining formal sector employment, pervasive shortages of foreign exchange and goods and services, persistent budget deficits and stagnant or declining social services. Only a few countries, including the resource-endowed ones of Botswana and Gabon, have been able to sustain high rates of growth during the past two decades. The economic reform measures promoted by the Bretton Woods institutions are aimed at reversing the foregoing trends by first restoring an enabling environment conducive to the efficient operation of both the domestic and international markets, and by necessitating the switching of domestic demand and supply so as to resuscitate the latter through the increased production of tradables. Stabilization measures are geared to restoring the enabling environment, and structural adjustment measures to resuscitating production and exports.

There is, however, a general consensus that the experiment with reform has not been a success for Africa, in spite of the few showpieces such as Ghana and Uganda. While evidence on the pre- and post-economic reform status of women as workers is mixed, there is greater unanimity on the fact that the reform measures have not been adequate to resolve the structural legacies of gender bias and underdevelopment. More importantly, there is a general consensus emerging even among the proponents of the economic reform measures that not only are African countries faring poorly but that more fundamental long-term strategies are needed to promote economic transformation and growth.

Women have been adversely affected by the reform measures. In the absence of a general revival in both the rural and the formal sectors, the informal sector has not been able to carry the burden of creating viable and productive employment opportunities for women, let alone for the men. The sector continues to be plagued by the usual constraints of inadequate access to credit facilities, distribution channels and innovative techniques to acquire competitive advantage in the absence of adequate or appropriate training. Women continue to be the most disadvantaged in all these areas. Thus, economic reform measures have not been able to improve the status of this informal sector or of the women who constitute the bulk of the workers in it.

A comprehensive and coherent long-term development strategy is yet to be formulated that can adequately address the structural underpinnings of poverty in Africa generally, and also those that afflict women specifically. The United Nations launched in 1996 a special Initiative for Africa whose implementation should be closely monitored to ensure that women benefit from it.

The impact of globalization and technological change

If globalization is taken to refer to the gradual integration of national economies within an international system of production organized in large and rising measure by the actions of multinational corporations (ILO/IILS, 1994), then African countries have been experiencing this trend since the inception of colonialism. Globalization, however, is generally meant to refer to a more recent trend accelerated by new technological revolutions, entailing the geographical dispersion and interdependence of production, distribution, marketing and finance as controlled and managed by large multinational corporations. It refers also to the flow of investment, human capital and technology whereby the global marketplace is seen as one arena. Technological revolutions in information processing and transportation have overcome geographical barriers so that time and space have become relatively insignificant constraints to production and marketing. During the first two decades of independence, African countries were relatively insulated from the more revolutionary aspects of these trends because of the many policy barriers to foreign investment that were implied by statism, and inward-looking development policy regimes that discouraged foreign investment and technological transfer.

With the increasing adoption of economic reforms since the 1980s, the economic space in Africa has gradually been opened up to the effects of the more recent aspects of globalization, although not to the same degree as has occurred in the developing countries of Asia. Almost all the African countries that have adopted economic reforms see the reintegration of their economies into the international economic system as heralding the benefits of globalization. Like other developing countries, African countries believe that:

> On the whole the activities of multinational enterprises had increased or tended to increase employment opportunities and improve standards in their country. In addition, the generation of direct and indirect employment, the introduction of new technology and management practices, the provision of training, the upgrading of skill requirements, increases in productivity and competitiveness among local firms were mentioned as important benefits ... (ILO, 1992a, p. 21).

African countries have therefore found it necessary to design measures and extra incentives to attract foreign investment in order to extract the maximum benefits from emerging global trends. However, concern has been raised[3] regarding the possible negative consequences of globalization on the conditions of work of employees in multinational corporations. More radical critiques of globalization have warned against the possible further peripheralization of developing countries as a consequence of their uncritical embracing of globalization.

It needs to be noted at the outset in assessing globalization's effects on African workers that data on globalization in Africa are sparse. Nevertheless, the trends that are emerging are not too different from those that have occurred elsewhere in the developing world. The impact of globalization in Africa may be examined from at least two angles: its effects on formal and informal production processes, and the effects on women's employment and working conditions in the region. In the formal sector, the key technological developments at the centre – that is, in the developed world – relate to the revolutions in production and work organization implied by the following: automation, job fragmentation, just-in-time production, lean production, total quality control, flexible manufacturing, computer-integrated manufacturing, and biotechnology (ILO/IILS, 1994, p. 13). The above developments in various combinations have important implications for the levels and structures of employment and conditions of work, especially for women, since the growth of direct foreign investment in developing countries, as an aspect of the new globalization, has been directly related to the employment of women in the formal sector. Further, not only have these effects been limited to women in the formal sector, but they have also had indirect effects on the activities of women in the informal, rural and urban sectors. The latter sectors have also been influenced by attempts by policy-makers, donor agencies and non-governmental organizations to introduce new technologies that are spin-offs from the global technological shelf, for purposes of enhancing productivity or relieving workers in these sectors of the burdens of conventional modes of work or production.

The overall status of women as workers has not changed to a significant degree with the emergence of globalization. The reason is simply that insufficient investments have come into Africa as a result of the new economic reforms to transform these economies to any significant degree. Nevertheless, the new trends that are emerging appear to correspond to similar trends in other low-income developing countries. In the formal sector, the new global enterprises induce an increased demand for young female entrants into the labour force.

Furthermore, in the absence of government measures to protect the rights of workers, or of struggles by workers themselves to advance their rights, there is a tendency for working conditions in the new enterprises to be compromised. While employment tends to increase, jobs may be unstable and may not reduce existing levels of unemployment and underemployment, unless the inflows of foreign investment are substantial enough to more than offset retrenchments arising from 'runaway' plant closures. In the informal sectors, the impact of globalization on women has also been marginal, relative to the number of women engaged in conventional activities. However, of major interest is the displacement effect of the activities of multinational corporations in out-competing women in their conventional activities. On the positive side is the increasing tendency for women to exploit regional and international markets as intermediaries in buying and selling internationally traded goods produced by multinational corporations abroad and by informal small-scale producers at home. On the whole, however, globalization has yet to have its major impact on the economies or the women of Africa.

A major conclusion is that African governments need to take a conscious stand to promote and protect the interests of all workers, particularly women workers, who are likely to be employed by the new multinational enterprises relocated to the region, and to assess the social costs and benefits of new multinational enterprises that are likely to displace the livelihoods of informal and rural households, particularly those led by women. In this regard, the haste with which many African governments are attempting to attract foreign investors, at the cost of inadvertently undermining the welfare of their workers, needs to be tempered by rational approaches to integrate these activities into national economies on the basis of internationally and nationally recognized standards of employment and working conditions. Indeed, if such approaches were undertaken as collective agreements by regional and continental bodies in Africa, the tendency to resort to 'beggar-thy-neighbour' policies in the pursuit of foreign investment would be minimized and the interests of women workers, producers and traders would be upheld and protected.

Comprehensive studies are lacking on the exact trends in emerging EPZs in Africa. In the formal sector, a number of concerns relate to boring or alienating job tasks and content, unnecessarily long hours of work, hectic pace, inadequate maternity leave and child-care facilities, and oppressive management techniques. The nature of the international division of labour that accompanies global investments in developing countries is such that the lowest tasks are relegated to nationals of developing countries, the majority of whom will be females, while the higher and more complex tasks are monopolized by representatives of the multinational corporations or local males, if not controlled from the centre. This is a pattern that Hein was able to confirm in Mauritius, but which she partly attributed to imperatives of ownership (Hein, 1988, p. 35). Given that the activities commonly deployed to low-income developing countries consist largely of textiles and electronics industries, the resulting job tasks for lower-level workers will tend to be highly routine and repetitive, hence the degree of job satisfaction is not likely to be high. Further, in the interests of quality control and meeting production and marketing deadlines, top-down approaches to shop-floor management are likely to be most prevalent, contrary to the more participatory and team approaches innovatively used with higher levels of labour elsewhere by the same types of global enterprise. In addition, sexual harassment and exploitation of women, given their youth and their employment in unfamiliar social environments, are likely to be common.

Conditions related to hours of work, maternity benefits and child-care facilities are generally such that they are modified to the benefit of the multinational corporations in the EPZs, or that the regulations obtaining in the rest of the domestic formal sector tend not to apply. In Mauritius, for instance, overtime is compulsory in the EPZs when so required by management, while it is voluntary in the local formal sector (Hein, 1988, p. 49). Further, in Mauritius, maternity benefits are provided for, and the enterprises contribute to the running of child-care facilities. At the other extreme, the draft bill on EPZs in Zimbabwe was intended to exempt firms in the new zones from adherence to the fairly liberal Labour Relations Act, which applies to the rest of the economy, other than the public sector. This has been challenged by the Zimbabwe Congress of Trade Unions, prompting the withdrawal of the bill for re-examination. The Ghanaian bill on promoting similar invest-ments from abroad does not even address labour relations or working conditions. A common inadequacy in most of the acts establishing EPZs in Africa appears to be the laxity with which safety requirements are mandated or monitored, an issue that is of particular importance for women. There is a tendency for Factory Acts, which contain most of the regulations pertaining to safety, not to apply to enterprises operating in EPZs, an eventuality that severely compromises the safety and secu-rity of workers in these zones.

An ILO Tripartite Study Team from Zimbabwe was generally impressed by the conditions of work in the EPZs in Mauritius (ILO, 1994). Among the measures the team found commendable were the general applicability of the Labour Act to domestic and foreign firms alike; the stipulation of minimum wages and the fact that wages in the EPZs compared well with, or were even better than, those in the rest of the domestic sector; the mandatory contributions to the national pension fund and the training of workers; and contributions to scholarships and social programmes such as nursery schools (ILO, 1994). The team noted, however, that the improvements in working conditions were not implemented voluntarily, but as a consequence of struggles and negotiations with the workers. This experience underscores the importance of workers' lobbying, tripartite dialogue and government commitment to improving working conditions in these zones.

As noted above, the perceived comparative advantage of many African countries in terms of global competition is in the availability of cheap labour. So far, it appears that the type of labour called for consists of young women who are recent migrants into the modern sector, but who have some rudiments of education. This type of labour is demanded in the textile and electronics activities commonly attracted by foreign investment incentives such as those offered in EPZs. For such labour, the training and skills imparted to new recruits at the workplace represent upgrading. Nevertheless, these skills are likely to be of very limited value except in similar types of work. Given the rather low level of education currently prevailing in some parts of Africa, the main activities that foreign enterprises are likely to find cost-effective to redeploy there are those that require lower-educated labour. This of necessity limits the type of skills that can be transferred to the workers and the host economies. For the near future, African countries, particularly those south of the Sahara, are not likely to benefit from the middle- and upper-level skills that are being generated by the new global trends until levels of general education and economic development are raised to the necessary critical mass to attract higher levels of global activities.

With respect to the informal sector, women have begun to embark on initiatives to exploit the new liberalized economic environment by engaging in cross-border trade, peddling goods produced by multinationals in far-off places. Thus women have begun to act as intermediaries across nations in the exchange of wares among both formal and informal producers and retailers. Overall, however, the informal sector has not benefited much from globalization trends in the region. The majority of women continue to engage in their usual survival activities in the informal sector. Many attempts to introduce technologies, such as biotechnology, that would benefit women in subsistence and communal areas, have been experimental and limited to special projects, and have not had widespread beneficial impacts on the women and their households. The reasons include the fact that: the new technologies are costly and generally targeted at males; they may not reduce the burdens women already bear, and may even increase them; most female-headed households do not have the resources such as land, labour and cash to take full advantage of the new technologies or seed varieties; and often, after new varieties of seed have been found to be advantageous, production of the relevant crops is gradually dominated by men who begin to define and appropriate them as male crops.

Of equal concern has been the impact of the activities of multinational enterprises on rural activities, using large-scale modern technologies. Multinational enterprises have at times been able to subsume activities of communal producers, such as those related to fishing and crops, with devastating consequences for the livelihoods of the latter. The conflicts over fishing rights between large- and small-scale enterprises, common in many countries in Africa where there are large bodies of water or rivers, are illustrative. The livelihoods of many women have been negatively affected by the displacement effect of the incursion of multinational enterprises into the fishing activities of communal households. Although women do not generally engage in the actual fishing as such, they are intimately connected with male fishing activities since they generally dominate the processing and marketing of the fish. Large multinational enterprises not only displace the male fishermen, but also establish their own processing, marketing and distribution channels, which effectively bypass traditional networks normally controlled by communal households.

The impact of AIDS, drought and civil conflict

The status of African women has also been aggravated by the AIDS epidemic, frequent droughts, and persistent civil strife in many parts of the continent. The spread of AIDS in Africa is having both direct and indirect impacts on women workers. First, the women themselves are being affected at an increasing rate, a situation made worse by the early age at which sexual activity tends to begin. There are now six HIV-infected women for every four infected men in the region (UNDP, 1995, p. 28). This directly affects women's productivity. Women's caring functions are increasingly burdened by children and adult family members who are afflicted with AIDS. Married women are increasingly losing their husbands to the AIDS epidemic and have to assume the full burden of maintaining their households. Finally, women afflicted with AIDS, or whose husbands have died of AIDS, experience social stigma that severely compromises their ability to engage in productive work. Widows stand to lose their common property as well as their access to communal resources such as land. For all these reasons, women are increasingly being pushed into greater poverty and resorting to more demanding survival strategies.

African countries have not been able to develop viable strategies to fortify themselves against recurrent drought. In the Sahel region and the northern parts of coastal West African countries there is concern that desertification is spreading. Furthermore, in central and southern Africa droughts appear to be recurring more frequently. It is incontrovertible that African countries have, through economic policies of omission and commission, undermined their own ability to cope with drought and to promote viable agricultural strategies that would ensure food security for the majority of their people. The outcome is that women, who are predominantly in the rural sector, find themselves increasingly beleaguered as they attempt to counter the negative effects of drought on productivity by devising innovative survival and coping strategies.

To the effects of AIDS and drought must be added the impact of internal civil strife in a number of African countries. Currently, protracted civil conflicts are occurring in Algeria, Angola, Burundi, Liberia, Morocco, Rwanda, Sierra Leone, Somalia, Sudan and Zaire, to name only the major ones. These conflicts have displaced millions of families internally and across borders, so that more than twice the number of countries directly involved in the conflicts are now also affected to one degree or another. The scourge of masses of people, particularly women and children, being subjected to refugee status is now a common occurrence in many African countries. Not only have the livelihoods of these displaced families been undermined by persistent strife, but when the men are killed or incapacitated the burden of maintaining households is increased for women. In some countries, such as Angola and Mozambique, land mines have incapacitated thousands of people, particularly women and children, apart from making huge tracts of rural land unsafe for human habitation (UN, 1993).

Dimensions of poverty and social exclusion among women workers in Africa

The combined effects of the above developments, when added to other factors like high fertility levels and the unequal sexual division of labour, trap African women in conditions of strenuous work and poverty. Their poverty differs from that of men in degree and in kind. In

Africa, the poverty of women is widespread and endemic whether viewed absolutely or relatively. There are a number of reasons for this. First is the situational factor that African women live in one of the poorest continents in the world, where the majority of women have the lowest standards of living. Second, women are disproportionately concentrated in the rural sector, which has remained residual and impoverished, with women being the most disadvantaged. Third, a large proportion of African women is involved in low-return market activities in the informal sector, where working conditions continue to be quite appalling and degrading. Fourth, the minority of women who are engaged in formal sector employment are concentrated in low-paying and insecure occupations and jobs. Fifth, women are burdened by their multiple roles related to reproduction and production, and are subjected to discrimination and subjugation both within and outside the household.

Women's condition has been worsened by the persistent economic crisis that has plagued Africa since the 1970s and by the consequent increase in female-headed households. There is now a trend generally referred to as the 'feminization' of poverty. This may be viewed from the perspective of 'social exclusion' or that of 'entitlement'. With regard to the former, African women have been incorporated, in terms of residualness and exploitation, into the socio-economic systems that have emerged, while simultaneously subsidizing this system through their multiple roles (Wolfe, 1994; Gore, 1994). Women have been excluded from the pursuit of viable livelihoods, adequate access to private and public goods and services, participation in popular forms of organization to assert their own demands, adequate representation in decision-making, and adequate access to information that could allow them to have better control over their lives. This social exclusion can be traced to gender biases.

In the context of social exclusion, women generally do not have adequate access to assets such as land, credit, inputs and training. Within the household, they are disadvantaged in access to resources and in consumption. Further, they are systematically discriminated against in access to public goods such as education, health facilities, and agricultural extension services. The adverse entitlements of women have been exacerbated by the economic crisis and other factors discussed earlier, and also by increasing population growth.

Disaggregated data on the poverty of women in Africa are not readily available, but the nature and degree of this poverty can be deduced from socio-economic indicators (see UNICEF, 1994a, 1994b; UNDP, 1993; UNDP/World Bank, 1992). In 1985, out of the 28 countries for which data were available (UNDP/World Bank, 1992), over 50 per cent of the rural population in half of these countries was below the poverty datum-line (PDL), while more than 30 per cent of the rural population in 80 per cent of the countries was below the PDL. When it is recalled that the majority of women are in rural areas, and that they are among the poorest groups, the extent of poverty among women in rural areas can easily be deduced. The incidence of poverty in urban areas was much less, but even then, for about 68 per cent of the countries, more than 20 per cent of the urban population lived below the PDL in 1985.

UNICEF (1994b) gives a number of indicators (relating to education, calorie supply, access to safe water, sanitation and health facilities) that indirectly inform on the nature of poverty among African women in Africa. According to *Human development report 1995*, 170 million people, almost a third of the region's population, do not have adequate food to eat (UNDP, 1995, p. 28). More generally, this report classifies most African countries in the lowest category of the Development Index. The 1995 issue, which provides disaggregation of the index by sex, shows that women were in the lowest range of this overall category.

The precise nature of the poverty afflicting African women will be fully known only when comprehensive data on relevant indices are collected on a sex-disaggregated basis. The broad outlines are quite clear. There are, however, other aspects to women's poverty that are less visible, and perhaps more difficult to measure. These relate, for example, to the psychological effects of the multiple burdens women have to bear; the accompanying stress of having to balance these roles under dire economic and social circumstances, as the individuals with primary responsibilities for household welfare; and the fact that, at the end of their life cycles, the benefits are nowhere commensurate to the efforts expended as a consequence of their multiple burdens. Women in Africa continue to be disadvantaged in both visible and invisible ways that push them into forms of poverty that are indeed worse than those endured by men.

Proposals for action

To address these diverse women's issues, a number of approaches are required, which should be seen as complementary rather than alternative strategies. In the past, there has been a tendency to view as distinctly different the various approaches related to equity, welfare, poverty alleviation, social dimensions, basic needs, women-in-development and women-and-development. These various approaches address different aspects of the same problem. Further, while none of them may be adequate to deal with the overall issue at stake, they could be seen as necessary components of a broader comprehensive strategy to address the overall issue. In this respect it is necessary first to recognize that there is a hierarchy of issues or problems pertaining to women as workers; and, second, to note that this hierarchy suggests a need to distinguish between the strategic and the practical needs of women.

Wallace and March have defined the strategic needs of women as

... needs which arise from the analysis of women's subordination to men ... Strategic gender needs may include all or some of the following: the abolition of the sexual division of labour; the alleviation of the burden of domestic labour and child-care; the removal of institutionalised forms of discrimination such as rights to own land or property, or access to credit; the establishment of political equality; freedom of choice over childbearing; and the adoption of adequate measures against male violence and control over women. (Wallace and March, 1991, p. 160)

In contrast, they indicate that

Practical gender needs are those drawn from the concrete conditions women experience in their position within the gender division of labour, and come out of their practical gender interests for human survival. Practical gender needs therefore are usually a response to an immediate perceived necessity which is identified by women within a specific context. As Molyneux has written, 'they do not generally entail a strategic goal such as women's emancipation or gender equality ... nor do they challenge the prevailing forms of subordination even though they arise directly out of them.' (Wallace and March, 1991, p. 160)

The long-term resolution of the problems women face can only be achieved if their strategic needs are met. The satisfaction of these needs is a necessary precondition for any long-term gender-responsive and gender-sensitive strategy. Meeting the practical needs of women is important, but not sufficient to resolve the fundamental issues at stake, since the efficacy of such a strategy is likely to be self-defeating if the strategic needs are not resolved. In the context of underdevelopment, another fundamental issue may be added as a component of the strategic needs of women, and this relates to the need for economic empowerment, since equality in poverty is not enough to resolve some of the underlying issues related to the poverty afflicting women. Thus the strategic needs of women have to be pursued within the context of a development strategy in the region that ensures growth with equity.

An integrated approach is called for that encompasses measures aimed at promoting the strategic, developmental, and practical needs of women as necessary and mutually reinforcing aspects of the issue. This approach does not separate equality issues from a more general discussion of economic transformation in the context of the interaction of macroeconomic, microeconomic and labour market policies of growth and development, and the resolution of the conflicting dual legal legacies. In this context, policies for equality of opportunity and treatment are likely to enhance efficiency in a manner that optimizes dynamic growth with equity. Such an approach is therefore not only a matter of common sense but one of economic rationality. Apart from governments, employers' and workers' organizations, other actors at the national, subregional, regional and international levels have crucial roles to play. They should also include non-governmental organizations, national women's machineries, regional bodies, the International Labour Organization and other international agencies. Furthermore, there is a need for co-operation, dialogue and the development of alliances between the different actors to ensure consistency and co-ordination of their action for greater impact.

Governments, in collaboration with the above social partners, civil and community bodies, should facilitate the transformation of the various onerous non-market roles of women that are directed at producing use values or at consumption-related services into activities that can be provided by the market, community or government. Relevant here is formalization of the provision of such services as: eating places, child-care facilities, old persons' homes, rehabilitation centres, retirement centres and funeral services. The aim here is to give support to finding the appropriate medium (private, communal, co-operative or public) that can provide the needed services on a sustainable and equitable basis in order to emancipate women from some of their multiple domestic roles, and thus help to enhance their human development capacities, as well as their ability to exploit the benefits of specialization for the market. Such measures would also ensure that society as a whole contributes to providing these services, which are currently performed mainly by women.

There is need for development strategies to broaden productive employment opportunities for women. Current economic reform measures are necessary but not sufficient for the promotion of growth with equity, since they are inadequate to resolve the structural nature of the region's underdevelopment and subordination of women. The market, if left to itself, will continue to reinforce the dualistic and enclave legacies and patterns of development in Africa, and the disadvantaged status of women workers is not likely to be resolved. Governments need to formulate proactive development strategies aimed at rural transformation and industrial growth so as to formalize the various informal market activities currently being undertaken by the majority of the labour force in Africa, and by women in particular. The aim would be to ensure that women have adequate access to asset and exchange entitlements, and are thus able to react to, and exploit, market opportunities.

With respect to the export processing zones, governments need to anticipate the implications of attracting foreign investors by safeguarding the rights and working conditions of the local female and other workers, especially as regards shift work, night work, security of employment, maternity leave, child-care facilities, hours of work, minimum wages and security of employment. Investors in EPZs should be legally required to respect internationally recognized workers' rights, particularly those that have been ratified by the country concerned. Governments should formulate collective agreements at regional and continental levels to safeguard the rights of women and other workers and improve their conditions of work in accordance with international standards. All governments should agree to abide by such agreements. Regional and subregional bodies in the region, such as the Organization of African Unity (OAU), the Economic Community of West African States (ECOWAS), the Southern African Development Coordination Council (SADCC), the Southern African Labour Commission (SALC), the Common Market for Eastern and Southern Africa (COMESA), the Africa Development Bank, and the Organization of African Trade Union Unity (OATUU), should also play a leading role in the formulation of such agreements. Indeed, such agreements need to be advocated by the various international bodies that have direct relations with foreign investors, and by the major donor agencies.

Special welfare-oriented social safety nets should be introduced, targeted at the most needy women, and especially female heads of households. Poverty-alleviation measures in the form of developmental programmes are required to enhance women's asset and exchange entitlements.

Education, training and skill diversification of girls and women should be emphasized. Policies need to be formulated and seriously implemented to reverse the increasing drop-out and low retention rates of women in primary and secondary schools. African governments should aim at promoting universal primary education at least. In addition, governments, in partnership with women's organizations, should develop programmes to make girl pupils aware of the need to move away from traditional subjects and careers and into more competitive, flexible and productive ones that are needed in the present liberalized and changing economic environment. The promotion of entrepreneurship and self-employment activities should also be stressed.

Mobilization of women workers into groups is essential for strengthening their capacity and bargaining power, as well as for effective lobbying of the relevant bodies to address their strategic and practical needs. Such groups include grass-roots associations and other groups in the formal and informal sectors. They can initiate negotiations for asset redistribution and use; establish and run substitute services for the non-market roles of women, in the form of co-operatively run services; and set up savings mobilization and credit allocation schemes, training projects, co-operative marketing and distribution services, and employment services.

Employers' organizations have an important role to play. They can, for example, implement equal opportunity and treatment policies and establish adequate mechanisms for monitoring and evaluating their implementation, and for airing and resolving gender-related complaints at the workplace. They can hold constant dialogue with employees and organizations representing women's interests to promote women workers' rights.

There must be a systematic attempt to tackle the dearth of data and analytical conceptual work on African women workers. In this context, governments should provide resources for the periodic collection of data, such as on the valuation and analysis of women's non-market activities. The dynamic nature of the world of work and the various changes brought about by socio-economic developments, and their gender differential impact, make necessary the regular collection of data, and updating the analytical and conceptual base and the measurement instruments relating to gender equality issues, to provide a relevant basis for planning appropriate policies and effective action.

Notes

1. Practical needs of women are basic short-term needs such as income and food. Strategic needs are long-term needs involving their empowerment through changing their subordinate and unequal situation in society. Examples are women's equal participation in decision-making and their full and equal access to productive resources.

2. See the Resolution adopted by the 13th International Conference of Labour Statisticians on the Economically Active Population, Employment, Unemployment and Underemployment, ILO, Geneva 1993. In this Resolution, reference is made to the concept of 'economic activity' as defined by the System of National Accounts 1993, prepared by an Inter-Secretariat Working Group and published by the Commission of the European Community–EUROSTAT, International Monetary Fund, Organization for Economic Cooperation and Development and the United Nations in 1993 (United Nations ST/ESA/STA/SER.F/2/Rev.4).

3. For example, the International Forum, June 1994 and the ILO Tripartite Seminar on Women, Work and Poverty in Africa, Harare, October 1994.

References

Commonwealth Secretariat (1989) *Engendering adjustment for the 1990s*, London.

Gore, C. (1994) *Social exclusion and Africa south of the Sahara: A review of the literature*, Geneva, IILS, DP.621.

Hein, C. (1988) *Multinational enterprises and employment in the Mauritian export processing zone*, Geneva, ILO, Multinational Enterprises Programme, WP.52, ILO.

ILO (1992a) *'Follow-up on the high-level meeting on employment and structural adjustment'*, Committee on Employment, Governing Body, Geneva.

— (1992b) *Workshop on advancement of women in rural workers' organizations in Africa – Report*, Geneva.

— (1994) *Report of the tripartite study tour to Mauritius and Kenya to look into the development of export processing zones with special focus on the (non-) application of labour laws*, Harare.

—/IILS (International Institute for Labour Studies)(1994) 'Women workers in a changing global environment', framework paper for International Forum, Geneva, June.

Mhone, G. (1995) *African women workers, economic reform, AIDS and civil strife, Geneva*, IDP Women/WP-23.

UN (1993) *News*, Department of Humanitarian Affairs, New York.

— (1995) *The world's women 1995, trends and statistics*, New York.

UNDP (1993) *Human development report, 1993*, Oxford University Press.

— (1995) *Human development report, 1995*, Oxford University Press.

—/World Bank (1992) *African development indicators, 1992*, Washington, DC.

UNICEF (1994a) *The state of the world's children, 1994*, New York.

— (1994b) *The progress of nations: The nations of the world ranked according to their achievements in health, nutrition, education, family planning, and progress for women*, New York.

Wallace, T. and C. March (1991) *Changing perceptions: Writings on gender and development*, London, OXFAM.

Wolfe, M. (1994) *Some paradoxes of social exclusion*, Geneva, IILS Discussion Paper 63.

Women and law in Southern Africa (1990a) *The legal situation of women in Southern Africa*, Harare, University of Zimbabwe Publications.

— (1990b) 'Uncovering reality: Excavating Women's rights in African family laws', Working paper No. 7, Harare.

5
Innovations in work organization and technology

SWASTI MITTER

In the past decade, the nature, volume and conditions of women's employment have been influenced by, among other factors, changes in the organization of work at enterprise level, and the introduction of new technologies. In fact, innovations in work organization have been prompted precisely by the need to have the continuous workflow that the expensive technologies require, in order to be cost-effective. The trend, at the corporate level, has generally been to adopt a lean and quality-conscious management in order to remain competitive (Humphrey, 1992).

A perceptible rise in consumer preference for variety and quality, especially in the world market, has also prompted firms in the modern sector to experiment with new forms of work organization and choice of technologies. Ensuing corporate strategies have, in the process, altered skill requirements and employment contracts of both male and female employees. The impact of these changes on the quality and quantity of employment in the modern urban sector has been explored, but the differential impact of these changes on women and men has not yet been the subject of a detailed enquiry.

In the context of the modern industry and services sectors, changes in the organization and methods of production observed in the 1980s have been viewed by many as a paradigm shift. It is debatable whether the much-quoted contrasts in production models, shown in Table 5.1, really represent a fundamental switch. Some of the work organization in the new model, such as the use of a flexible number of workers, and subcontracting, are age-old practices reoriented to meet the emerging challenges of marketing and business strategies. Likewise, flexibility and variety in products and design as a marketing strategy may prove less significant in the 1990s if the world recession persists; a demand for mass-produced goods and services may again lend the 'economies of scale' much greater weight as a strategy than the 'economies of scope' that cater primarily to the niche markets of affluent societies. Nevertheless, the contrasting models prove useful in identifying the impact of current changes in technology and work organization on women employees.

Table 5.1   Paradigm shift in production model: from Fordism to post-Fordism?

	Taylorism and Fordism	The new model: Post-Fordism
The basic production technology	Process-dedicated semi-automatic machines and simple manual tools	Industrial robots. Computer numerical control (CNC) machines. Computerized testing equipment. Computer-aided design/computer-aided manufacturing (CAD/CAM) systems. Flexible manufacturing systems (FMS)
The model of work organization	Production line or functional manufacture	Group technologies or modified production line
The paradigmatic type of work task	A) repetitive and fragmented work tasks with short cycles in assembly and machine minding; B) more skill-demanding auxiliary work tasks in repair, maintenance and quality control	A) highly deskilled (and gradually disappearing) work tasks in the technological gaps of the production processes; B) semi-skilled work tasks in automated settings (enlarged repetitive work); C) skilled auxiliary work tasks in repair and maintenance
The focus of rationalization	*Manual labour* by time and motion studies and piece-work systems	*Capital rationalization* by increasing the turnover of inventories (just-in-time, subcontracting) and utilization of production machinery (flexible automation, flexible working times and flexible use of labour)

Changes in work organization

Increased internationalization of production and distribution of industrial products and information-intensive services have imposed the dictates of quality-conscious and lean management on modern sector firms, both in developed and in developing countries. Central to lean management has been the just-in-time (JIT) method, based on a

Japanese management philosophy that stresses the benefits of reducing inventories and waste of materials and of final goods and services.

The success of JIT relies on being able to deliver an assured quality and quantity of goods without delay. JIT's main thrust is a 'quick response strategy' to a swiftly changing market through organizational flexibility. JIT thus advocates organizational ability to deliver high-quality products, respond rapidly to changes in demand, and be more cost competitive.

Companies that embrace JIT philosophy basically follow a two-pronged policy:

(a) establishing an effective network of subcontractors that ensures a fail-safe delivery of quality goods, services or materials at all times;

(b) eliminating inefficiency and waste, in defective work and waiting time, through streamlining work organization and diversifying employees' skills.

The network between the subcontractors and the main company is generally described as the 'external' side of JIT. The emphasis on organizational efficiency, quality control and reskilling of workers, in contrast, is known as the essence of 'internal' JIT. Both sides of JIT have affected the structure and nature of employment, with a markedly differential impact on women and men.

External JIT

Until recently, the external side of JIT received greater attention from researchers and policy-makers who were involved with gender issues. This was because subcontracting networks entailed an increase in the relative share of employment in the small-scale units that generally provided jobs for women.

Subcontracting in manufacturing Since employers in large-scale units are required by law to offer certain benefits to employees, it often proves cheaper to hire women in small-scale units that are exempt from legal obligations related to redundancy payments, child-care facilities or maternity benefits. In the last decade, however, it is not only the cheapness of production that has prompted subcontracting; large retailers and distributors often rely on specialized small-scale units for supplies of high-quality goods catering for the emerging niche markets in richer countries. An increased reliance on small-scale and medium-scale production units has definitely benefited women in terms of quantity of employment in sectors as diverse as garments and electronics (Gaeta *et al.*, 1992). Yet, this overall expansion of small-scale units in the 1980s has in some cases also meant a marked reduction in overall employment at large-scale factories, with a concomitant increase in feminized employment in small-scale subcontracting units (Gothoskar, 1995). In India, for example, there has been a steady trend for smaller production units to become ancillaries of large companies (Banerjee, 1995). The trend has been particularly visible in light consumer-goods manufacturing, a sector that provides much employment for women. Large and small units previously shared 'common markets' on the basis of the sector's horizontal division; they now share a 'common production process', as different stages of production become fragmented and specialized. This is described as the vertical integration of the production process. In Calcutta, for example, small units have for a long time produced ready-to-sell electric fans; more and more of these units have now switched to working on orders for smaller parts or for specific production processes. Similarly, in the consumer electronics and automobile industries, the production of spare parts and components accounts for an average of 60 per cent of employment; most of these items come from subcontracting units (Banerjee, 1991). Increased reliance on subcontracting units can be observed in other developing countries, as in the case of the automobile industry in Brazil or the garments industry of the Philippines (Posthuma, 1990; Ofreneo, 1987).

The beneficial impact of external JIT has often been discussed in terms of a shift in the paradigm of industrial structure, described as flexible specialization or a model of productive decentralization. The experiences of industrial districts in 'Third Italy' (the central and northeastern regions of Italy) were the focal point in assessing the desirability or inevitability of such a shift. In this region, small-scale factories, generally employing no more than 10 people, have played important roles in economic regeneration around industrial districts. These small factories essentially produce parts or the whole of textiles and other industrial goods for big manufacturing retailing companies (Pyke and Sengenberger, 1992). These small, so-called 'network' firms also produce for each other, displaying horizontal as well as vertical interdependencies (Bellussi, 1992). In such subcontracting units, employers are less encumbered by the employment and labour legislation that usually adds to the recruitment costs of bigger companies. The implicit organizational efficiency of this subcontracting network, understandably, has captured the imagination of policy-makers – in Europe and beyond – particularly for its significance for the decentralization of economic power and opportunities for self-employment (Pyke, Becattini and Sengenberger, 1990; Amsden, 1990).

Women in Italy, and in some developing countries, have benefited quantitatively from the expansion of subcontracting but it is debatable whether they have experienced much improvement in the quality of their work. Admittedly, small-scale units, in ideal situations, generate a better employer/employee relationship. It is much easier to feel involved and to be instructed in a working environment that is bureaucratically less impersonal and hence less daunting. Such units could also provide informal work training, at a pace and in a form that is more accessible to women, who generally have lower formal qualifications than do male employees. Nevertheless, conditions of work are generally worse in small-scale units compared with large-scale ones; wages are lower, benefits are negligible and there is little monitoring of health hazards (Mitter (ed.), 1992b). Even in the much-vaunted Third Italy, the decentralization of work led in some cases to erosion of the rights and privileges of women employees. In small firms, in the absence of institutional procedures, women find it difficult to get redress against sexual harassment (Franzinetti, 1993).

There is always scope for self-employment for women in the small-scale sector. In most societies, it is possible to locate some successful businesswomen, but rarely a woman industrialist. In Italy, the model of productive decentralization has indeed allowed women to carve out niche markets for entrepreneurship – especially in the area of fashion and design (Gaeta et al., 1992). This experience, albeit limited, has some educative effects on women in developing countries. However, a successful transition from waged employment to entrepreneurship in the modern sector involves expensive, complex skills, including in some cases computer literacy. Without a well-formulated programme for training and business education, women in the developing world are unlikely to benefit from the prospect of self-employment that the flexible specialization model, in principle, holds out for them.

Externalization of services Externalization of parts or the whole of the production process is not limited to manufacturing. It is spreading in the services sector – most notably in office work. Innovations in computers and office equipment, and changes in telecommunications technology, international organizations and regulation of telecommunications services have resulted in a virtual fusion between the office machinery, computers and telecommunications sectors. These new developments have affected the volume of employment and the structure of work organization. Increased use of new technology for information processing in a wide range of industrial and service activities has given rise to an accelerating requirement for the preparation and entry of data into computers; women, rightly or wrongly noted for their dexterity and typing skills, have received a large proportion of these new jobs related to data entry (Mitter and Pearson, 1992).

The increased flexibility offered by new hybrid technologies has also enabled major users of information processing work to decentralize the preparation and entry part of their operation. Large companies are able to utilize the flexibility offered by innovations in telecommunications, computers and office technology to separate the physical location of labour- and space-intensive operations – such as invoicing, payrolling, stock control, sales records, market analysis and routine accounting procedures – away from the headquarters of the company to a location where the costs of labour and office accommodation are considerably lower. The decentralization of office work has in fact taken a variety of forms, which are often grouped together under terms that tend to be used interchangeably: 'teleworking', 'telecommuting', 'distance working', 'remote working'. These terms refer to a range of organizational strategies that have evolved to take advantage of the flexibility and cost savings inherent in geographically separating various tasks connected with data preparation and processing.

The range of technology-related work which can be decentralized using new information technology is extensive. However, a major demarcation can be made between the programming and software development work of professionals and the basic data entry carried out by clerical workers (Mitter, 1995). The division between programming/software development and data-entry work reflects a difference in the gender composition of the labour force, with women being concentrated in data entry, while professional work is mainly, though not entirely, carried out by men (Mitter and Pearson, 1992). The increased number of data-entry jobs for women has allowed clerical workers to have access to some degree of computer literacy, which could be a stepping stone to more skill-intensive and financially rewarding occupations. Yet, to make this progression a reality, well-formulated training programmes specifically targeted at women will be essential. For decentralized data-entry workers, national initiatives are crucial, as it is difficult for companies to organize a well-coordinated training programme for geographically dispersed workers. The task becomes even more difficult when the decentralized workers are seen and defined legally as self-employed, especially when they work for more than one company.

The spread of telework or electronic homework has been rather limited in the developing countries. The homes of clerical staff in the developing world are not often suitable for installing the equipment essential for distance working. However, the prevalence of such work can already be identified in Malaysia, the Philippines and the

Republic of Korea (Kelkar and Nathan, 1992). Decentralization of white-collar work has allowed a small but growing number of women to set up as successful entrepreneurs in the information business. In the sample surveys, especially in developed countries, core companies valued women entrepreneurs' social competence, communication and 'people skills' as of special significance in the business. However, for those women who were successful, the hours of work reported were often extremely long and unpredictable, five to 16 hours a day, sometimes seven days a week (Mackinnon, 1991). Male consultants faced similar challenges, but women's generally heavier commitment to home-making made the routine especially demanding. In addition, self-employed consultants – women and men – had to forgo the security provided by employers, such as superannuation rights, job tenure, sick-leave or holiday pay.

Offshore decentralized work   There has been a marked differentiation in the quantity and quality of relocated information-intensive jobs by region as well as by gender. Despite a dramatic growth in the international subcontracting of software programming to a number of poorer countries (Mitter and Pearson, 1992), those countries' overall share in the production of software has been small. Women's role in this sector has been minuscule. In contrast, women in developing countries have gained a major share of semi-skilled data-entry jobs – especially when they have been relocated from high-wage countries. This work is parallel to much of the teleworking carried out in industrialized countries by women working as homeworkers, or as part-time workers in satellite/branch offices, and to a lesser extent in independent distant working enterprises.

The predominant form of enterprise in developing countries undertaking data entry is that of distant work enterprise, or satellite/branch office. Many offshore data-entry facilities are fully or majority-owned subsidiaries of American or Australian companies, which are set up to carry out data entry for their parent corporation. American Airlines initiated its data-processing facilities in Barbados in 1984 in this manner. However, such enterprises, including American Airlines' own expanded subsidiary, Caribbean Data Services, also subcontract data-entry work for other clients.

'Offshore data entry or data processing' is the term applied to the relocation of new technology clerical work to low-wage developing countries. The major location of such activities has been in the Caribbean, principally in Barbados and Jamaica and more recently in the Dominican Republic, with a handful of facilities in the smaller

Caribbean islands, such as St Lucia, St Christopher-Nevis and St Vincent. Other facilities are known to operate in China, India, Ireland, the Philippines and Singapore.

Most of the foreign-owned subsidiaries in the Caribbean region and elsewhere are located in the free trade zones, which provide incentives to foreign investors parallel to those offered to offshore manufacturing. Incentives available to foreign-owned data-entry firms in Jamaica's Montego Bay free zone include low-cost space, tax benefits and full repatriation of profits and dividends to the home countries. Employment to date is difficult to estimate and no comprehensive source of data exists (Mitter and Pearson, 1992).

There are similarities between the working conditions of offshore data workers and those of electronic distance workers (teleworkers) in industrialized countries (Pearson and Mitter, 1993). This is particularly true of the insecurity of their contractual and earnings situation. In Jamaica it is frequently the case that workers are hired only after a lengthy period of selection and training, during which they are paid a training allowance whilst actually processing data for commercial contracts. Once a proper offer of employment is made, remuneration is dependent as much on reaching (variable and non-negotiable) productivity targets as on a fixed weekly or monthly wage. The basic wage is rarely more than half of the stated average earnings, with productivity-related piece rates accounting for the remainder. It is also quite common for workers to be laid off without pay, or to receive only the minimum payment, when there is insufficient work to occupy the whole workforce.

In spite of the precariousness of employment contracts and low basic wage rates, total remuneration for offshore data-entry clerks often compares well with earnings in other local employment. Even so, in comparison with prevailing rates in the developed countries, the cost advantage for employers is very clear. One study estimated that wage costs in the early 1980s (calculated on the basis of hourly wage rates) were between six and 12 times higher in the United States than in third world offshore locations (Pearson and Mitter, 1993). A more recent source estimates that the wages of Filipino keyboard operators in 1989 were one-fifth those of equivalent employees in US-based companies, indicating that – at least in some locations – the gap may be narrowing as demand for efficient data-entry operators increases (Pearson and Mitter, 1993). However, there are no systematic data allowing a reliable comparison of wage rates, and no comparative data on total labour costs including non-wage employee costs.

The situation regarding data-entry employees' rights to organize in labour unions is also unclear. Employment in free trade zones often precludes the right to organize, as is the case in the manufacturing sectors of the Republic of Korea and Malaysia (though not, it should be said, of Jamaica, Mexico or the Philippines). However, it was clear that in Jamaica there is no unionization among data-entry workers; in both Jamaica and Barbados keyboard operators were encouraged to think of themselves as white-collar employees, apparently to pre-empt the development of militancy characteristic of organized industrial workers. Management styles are often based on notions of responsibility for the employees' welfare, highlighting caring rather than conflictual relationships between workers and management (Pearson and Mitter, 1993). In the Philippines, managers stressed the benefits granted to their employees, including bonuses, medical care and profit-sharing plans, while confirming these employees' non-union status.

Employees in onshore offices The working conditions of employees in decentralized data-processing onshore offices of developing countries differ from those in the offshore data-entry sector. Employees in these offices retain their status as core public sector employees, but often consider that their jobs have become deskilled and standardized according to Taylorist management principles. In Brazil, workers employed at a decentralized (branch) office of a large public administration agency complained that lack of contact with the head office meant they had no say on questions of skills, training decisions and job content, in spite of the flexibility required from them in carrying out their tasks. Supervisors and electronic surveillance took increased control over task performance and the physical fragmentation of the workplace into individual workstations effected a deliberate minimization of communication between workers. Data-entry clerks were forbidden to talk during working hours, were allowed only limited rest periods, and were further discouraged from sentiments of group solidarity by the payment-by-results system, which encouraged not only continually increased productivity but an individual rather than a collective work ethic. The fact that the majority of data-entry workers are women was often used by management to justify restrictions on communications, since women are (stereotypically) considered to waste time by gossiping (Pearson and Mitter, 1993).

Before the decentralization drive took place in Brazil, unionization and militancy had been increasing among information-processing workers. After decentralization, employees found it harder to sustain union activity because of lack of communication with the head office and difficulties in organizing under the new conditions.

A survey carried out in Japan on the effect of working with computer terminals in banking and other sectors tends to confirm the pessimism felt by the workers in the Brazilian study. The Japanese office workers felt that their working conditions had deteriorated as a result of computerization. They complained of a high level of electronic surveillance, restrictions on their physical mobility, high levels of exhaustion, and dissatisfaction with the monotonous and repetitive nature of the work (Pearson and Mitter, 1993).

Health and safety concerns A number of health and safety issues affect all information-processing workers who use computers. Because of the intensive nature of these workers' tasks, and the long hours for which they are immobilized in front of their computer terminals, often under close human and electronic surveillance, these issues are of particular relevance to the low-skilled sector of the new white-collar workforce, where the majority of all employees, particularly women, are concentrated. In industrialized countries, where the dissemination of new technology is more thoroughly monitored by government agencies and labour organizations, the existence of potential health risks arising from the intensive use of computers is well documented. But such control is extremely rare in the developing world, especially with respect to health hazards related to VDUs (visual display units or terminals) (Pearson, 1995).

Health hazards said to be associated with computer-based information-processing work are of five types (Soares, 1992):

- musculoskeletal disorders
- deterioration of visual capacity and related problems
- stress and fatigue
- skin complaints
- reproductive hazards.

These conditions are attributed variously to:

- poor ergonomic design of workstations
- radiation emission from VDUs
- static electricity and chemical emissions
- overuse of eyes and muscles without breaks or rest.

In summary, offshore and onshore data-processing jobs have improved women's employment opportunities. But as yet few studies have been made to assess the quality of their work in terms of:

- security of contracts
- training for long-term employment
- upgrading of computer literacy
- health hazards arising out of intensive use of VDUs (Mitter and Pearson, 1992; Pearson and Mitter, 1993).

External JIT augmented internal and international subcontracting by large companies. It is timely to evaluate the impact of such a phenomenon on the quality and quantity of jobs received by women in rich and poor countries.

Internal JIT

Modern management techniques have changed the structure of work and the nature of employment also within the core sections of large manufacturing and service-sector organizations. Streamlining of work and personnel, a precondition for quality-conscious production and described as internal JIT, has not necessarily meant a reduction in the number of employees, but they have definitely altered the kinds of skills and expertise needed by major companies.

Internal JIT complements external JIT both in the services sector and in manufacturing. Crucial to internal JIT is the philosophy of total quality control, which demands that organizations be geared to all aspects of quality, including zero defects, after-sales servicing and guaranteed standards of products, aspects that are of key concern to customers and thereby to company competitiveness. The main targets of the philosophy are:

- cost reduction
- time reduction
- defect reduction
- improved customer services.

These goals, along with the flexibility needed for a quick response strategy, have made it increasingly imperative for companies to shift from 'Fordist' assembly-line work to a team-oriented philosophy. Total quality control (TQC) is often referred to as total quality management (TQM), precisely to emphasize the significance of an integrated quality approach in an emerging management policy.

TQM, or internal JIT, offers contradictory possibilities to women employees. At the organizational level, the approach entails a transition from the traditional division of labour between different sections and categories of employment, to a more integrated approach linking functions, skills and experience within a company. The key to success is viewed in terms of 'interfunctionality' between different sections of the company, so that efficient communication among employees can be established in order to improve the quality and timing of product and service deliveries. This paradigm shift in management practices demands of employees:

• complex and multiple business and technical skills
• craftsmanship
• professionalism
• high educational levels
• flexibility/ability to change.

As women are generally in the lower occupational categories and have limited access to relevant education and training, it is understandable that the introduction of TQM is likely to lead to displacement of women workers at core enterprises. The impact of TQM on women employees has hardly become a research topic. However, this should be given serious attention at a time when mainstream research emphasizes the demanding responsibilities that workers are or will be expected to assume in order to keep their positions in quality-conscious commercial companies. Studies of firms in Brazil (Ruas, 1993; Fleury and Fischer (eds), 1992), for example, show that the workers are now expected to take responsibility for:

• quality control with production work
• participation in the definition of norms and procedures related to quality inspection
• filling out of statistical process control (SPC) charts or control charts
• participation in groups which solve problems or seek improvements
• preparation and adjustment of equipment
• rotation of jobs
• routine maintenance.

Even in the expanding and dynamic telecommunications companies of the European Union countries, women, while providing the bulk of the workforce, are poorly represented in employment categories that demand and impart the above skills (Mitter, 1995).

Figure 5.1 Summary of employee profiles of the survey companies by gender in the telecommunications sector of the European Community

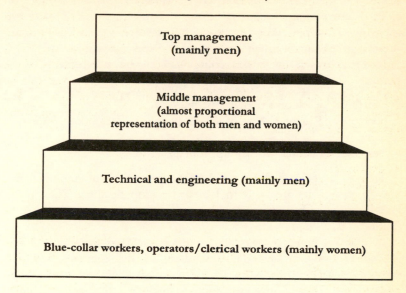

Source: Swasti Mitter, Gillian Shapiro & Paul Levy at the Centre for Business Research, University of Brighton, UK.

Without a specific gender focus in training programmes within and outside companies, it is highly unlikely that women will have access to the necessary expertise. In the absence of countermeasures, internal JIT or TQM are therefore prone to affect the quantity of women's opportunities in an adverse way.

TQM, at least in principle, holds promises as well. The move away from the 'Fordist' approach to the division of labour implies new flexibilities in existing bureaucracies. TQM replaces traditional vertical hierarchical relationships with a matrix form of horizontal project teams. The companies engage in innovative democratic practices, such as quality improvement programmes, team-building programmes, customer-care programmes or investment and training in ready-made (black box) technologies. The democratic approach requires employee involvement. TQM companies consider that the alienation of employees, a feature of 'Fordist' organizations, can be lessened by opportunities and training for self-development through resource centres, discussion groups, action learning sets[1] and so on. The aspect of TQM that gives special emphasis to people's involvement is becoming significant in the context of new accreditation for quality control. Accreditation by the European

Foundation of Quality Management (EFQM) is one such example. The EFQM's specific standards for Quality Awards are followed by companies in Europe, and in some developing countries. The EFQM draws on many of the principles of the main TQM approaches but strongly stresses 'people involvement' as a condition for ensuring quality.

In this approach, the quality-conscious company is expected to:

- preserve and develop core skills through the recruitment, training and career development of its people
- promote the involvement of all its people in continuous improvement
- empower its people to take appropriate action.

Thus, in an industry where a substantial proportion of employees are women, companies are likely to benefit by adopting those TQM practices that aim to elicit greater involvement from their women employees (Mitter *et al.*, 1993).

In practice, however, women are often excluded from quality improvement sets or groups. The members of the sets are generally selected by existing managers who are, by tradition, used to a 'top-down' approach and unaccustomed to including blue-collar women workers in decision making. In the absence of a conscious change in the culture of the organization, women, in practice, do find it difficult to join groups that assess the management of quality (Mitter *et al.*, 1993).

In some cases, a partial application of TQM simply accentuates the intensification of work and thereby health and occupational hazards for women employees. Increased expectations on the part of employers lead to increased physical stress. Applications of JIT/TQM have been known to contribute also to emotional stress. TQM expects employees to think of continuous improvement or Kaizen[2] in quality circle groups. The innovative, challenging ideas that women or men give in the quality circles make them feel important or involved; yet it leads to suspicion or fear that management gains experience from blue-collar women workers without any compensation or assurance against redundancy, tension and added responsibilities (Roldan, 1993a). Research in Argentina again shows that when temporary technology groups (TTGs) are formed,[3] they give rise to stomach ulcers and nervous ailments. Quality circles or groups do not always lead to women employees' progression and access to multiple skills. Thus, in Argentina, even in an electronics company where women make up the whole of the blue-collar workforce, quality control takes place in a different department and is the preserve of male engineers and technicians (Roldan, 1993b). Women operators, instead of acquiring polyvalent skills, simply learn a new way of rotating circuit board assembly so that they can assemble all the different models needed by customers without added involvement in expensive training or technology. The experience of blue-collar workers in the telecommunications industry in the European Union has been similar.

New technologies and women's employment

The observed changes in work organization as well as in work practices generally are a preparation for a smooth and cost-effective transition to advanced technologies. New technologies generally refer both to biotechnologies and computer technologies.

Biotechnology

Biotechnology is usually associated with the techniques of genetic engineering (i.e. recombinant DNA and cell fusion). These are what may be called 'new' techniques. Biotechnology, however, also involves some 'old' techniques such as fermentation, the use of enzymes in biological reactions and tissue culture. To date, the application of new techniques of biotechnology has been small in the developing countries. However, the technology is relatively cheap and is already spreading.

Food processing, the pharmaceutical and many other chemical industries, which represent some of the major sources of employment for women in developing countries, are already undergoing visible changes. The impact of biotechnology is likely to be even more deeply felt than that of computer technology in the late twentieth and early twenty-first centuries, and it will bring revolutionary change to both developed and developing countries. Improved and new methods of agricultural and industrial production in the industrialized countries, for example, will displace more traditional products from the developing countries (Mitter, 1995).

In the sugar industry the application of biotechnology is displacing workers. Fructose made from maize grown in the industrialized countries is emerging as an economically viable and widely used substitute for cane sugar. This has spelled disaster for cane sugar exporting countries, as they can no longer control the price of exports or compete in quality. They are losing an export crop, and the industrial workforce involved in sugar production and related processing industries is being displaced (Mitter, 1987). The application of tissue culture technology may cause further displacement of women from the manufacturing workforce in developing countries. This technology has distinct advantages over the traditional technique of extracting chemicals from plants. Tissue culture yields products that are more easily purified and ensures that both the quality and the quantity are predictable and planned. Given these advantages, it seems likely that there will be an increasing shift towards tissue culture production, even in some developing countries. This shift, however, will imply the replacement of direct labour, as the number of workers needed for tissue culture production tends to be much lower than that for traditional industries that produce chemicals from plants. Moreover, the tissue culture factories themselves are unlikely to generate significant employment, since these factories are highly automated through the use of computer-guided production techniques.

It is too early to assess the full implications of the introduction of biotechnology on the structure of employment, yet the emerging evidence indicates that new jobs, in the age of biotechnology, are going to be those that demand a high level of technical skill and managerial competence. Consequently, women's prospects for retaining their share of employment in industries such as food processing or chemicals will depend on the following factors:

(a) the ability of developing countries to create an institutional and educational infrastructure that will promote the necessary skills;

(b) the success of the developing countries in resisting recent moves towards imposing intellectual property law on the fruits of research undertaken in the developed countries;

(c) the willingness and support of national governments and intergovernmental organizations in extending opportunities to acquire relevant skills to women and men alike (Mitter, 1995).

Computer technologies

Implementation of biotechnology is still at an early stage in the developing countries. Computer-aided technologies, in contrast, have already made their impact on women's employment. Such technologies, combined with telecommunications and satellite technologies, have changed the skill requirements and the quantity of industry and service jobs available to women employees.

In the field of manufacturing, the applications of computer technology have been most widely made in computer-numerical control of machine tools (CNC), computer-aided design (CAD), automatic materials handling and more recently flexible manufacturing systems (FMS) (Bessant, 1991). A move away from 'islands of automation' to an integrated system is also being experienced through computer-integrated manufacturing systems (CIM) (Ebel, 1990).

The application of information technology has revolutionized automation in production, since this technology is much easier to apply to the whole series of processes involved. Earlier control systems used pneumatic or hydraulic means for sending messages to the machines and were limited as tools for automation. Computer-aided technology, however, results not only in automation. It allows important flexibilities into production, such as the modular production of components in different locations. The production of cars and television sets are examples of such modularization of products. In some cases, information control systems help to miniaturize production equipment, as in printing machinery. The technology thus opens up fresh possibilities for decentralizing production within and across countries. The use of computer-aided technology that includes telecommunications has significant managerial implications; it permits the centralized management of production units that are geographically dispersed. The technology thus alters the organization and location, as well as the nature and volume of industrial work (Mitter and Rowbotham,1995).

The impact of computer technologies on women's work has been in many ways complex and in some ways contradictory. Digital automation and robotic technologies, by replacing the importance of feminized labour-intensive work, reduce the scope of employment opportunities for women (Mitter and Rowbotham, 1995). Much of the documented decline of women's employment in the textiles industry of Argentina and Brazil in the last decade has been attributed to the introduction of computer-aided technology (Acero, 1991). The introduction of computer-aided technologies has likewise been a contributory factor in the dramatic decline of women's employment in the large-scale manufacturing sector of India in the 1980s (Gothoskar, 1995).

Computer technology gradually erodes the developing countries' comparative advantages that, in the past, were based on the cheap labour of their women blue-collar employees. As computer-aided machines make the role of labour-intensive work less significant, multinational companies do not locate work in developing countries for the sake of cheap labour. The current flow of foreign direct investment demonstrates that it is the countries which offer the promise of cheap but skilled labour that receive sizeable foreign direct investments. ASEAN countries have been, significantly, recipients of such investment: there, women have a relatively better chance to obtain the requisite training and skills (Mitter, 1992a).

Domestic companies also look for different expertise in the wake of new technologies. Manufacturing companies, even in a labour-surplus country, now adopt a certain number of labour-replacing methods of manufacturing to achieve speed, flexibility and quality control. As a result, even in the middle of diverse patterns and directions of manufacturing employment in all parts of the world, one can identify certain trends in the corporate sector, in that:

• the cost of capital is rising
• the input of labour is falling
• the demand for multiskilled operators is increasing
• new skills requiring hardware and software development are becoming important
• expertise in material resources planning and total quality management is proving crucial
• marketing skills are becoming significant
• skills in the management of organization as well as of technologies are becoming essential.

The changing nature of skill requirements often means displacement of women workers even in an expanding industry. In Malaysia, for example, the introduction of JIT in the semiconductor sector increased the demand for expertise in material control systems such as materials requirement planning (MRP) and materials resource planning (MRP II).[4] Most firms in Penang have reduced machine set-up time, ideal time and manufacturing lead time. Increased overall productivity, however, has meant a reduction in the share of female employment in the electronics industry of Malaysia. Whereas up to 80 per cent of the workers were women in the first phase of the industry, a 1986 survey showed that female representation had fallen to 67 per cent. The percentage is even lower in the 1990s. Computer technologies have affected the quality of women's employment as well. By lowering the number of highly repetitive manual operations, computer-aided technologies, for example, have reduced the physical strain of assembly-line work. Yet, the increasing production rates achieved by the same technological progress have also reduced employees' opportunities to regulate their work rhythm (Alasoini, 1991). Workers frequently had to pace their work within ever-narrower limits set by the ever-quicker machines to which they feed parts or whose products they have to test. In these situations, job rotations and group technologies were at times viewed by women employees as managerial strategies to ameliorate the work intensification following the introduction of CAD technologies.

With the implementation of CAD/CAM technologies, assembly workers' tasks are becoming more versatile and changing qualitatively, from manual assembly line to machine feeding, machine minding, quality control and routine maintenance. The implementation of computer technologies has thus altered the required skills at enterprise level. In the production process of semiconductors, for instance, cheap labour alone does not guarantee a foothold in the internationally competitive market. In the pioneer days of Thailand's electronics industry, for example, employers needed the nimble fingers of women workers for connecting tiny wires to a semiconductor. The same task is now being done by a machine, with as many as 10 machines under the charge of just one woman. It is not only the labour content that is decreasing; the quality of labour that is being demanded of electronics workers is rising at the same time (*Financial Times*, 1990).

Computer technology, decentralization and women's opportunities in entrepreneurship

Computer technology itself has been instrumental in shaping the growth of the small- and medium-scale sectors both in the rich and in the poor countries.

Changes in technology have facilitated the possibilities of decentralization through:

* miniaturization of machines, as in printing and publishing
* modularization of products, as in television
* fragmentation of the production process, as in garments and pharmaceuticals.

The process of decentralization has been enhanced also by:

* government policies which encourage the small-scale sector as a cost-effective way of creating employment
* the increased role of new forms of investment (NFI) by multinationals in the shape of joint ventures with smaller firms less encumbered by intellectual property rights.

Women's opportunities in entrepreneurship and high-tech decentralized units proved limited in management jobs. Success in this sector depended on having specific marketing and business skills (see Table 5.2). Even when women acquired production skills they frequently failed in the world of business for lack of the requisite marketing and business skills (Mitter, 1995).

Table 5.2 Requisite marketing and business skills in the era of new technology: Quick response and flexibility in design and delivery

Conditions of success	Strategic issues
Offer consistently low defect rates	Quality
Offer dependable delivery promises	Delivery
Provide reliable/durable products	Design
Provide high performance products	Design
Offer fast deliveries	Delivery
Customize products and services to user needs	Customization/flexibility
Profit in price-competitive markets	Price
Introduce new products quickly	Product innovation
Provide effective after-sales service	Service
Offer a broad product line	Variety/flexibility
ISO9000[5]	International standard for quality

In the developing world, it is in the services sector, especially in clerical and data-entry work, that women have become the main beneficiaries of new employment opportunities. Over the last decade, owing to the development and application of micro-electronic technologies, the office as a workplace has come under closer scrutiny in assessing the impact of computer technologies on women's employment. In the early 1980s, analyses of office activities focused on areas where deskilling and automation were taking identifiable forms, specifically in the application of word processing to text production. More recently, however, broader computing applications such as the development of network systems and the integration of office and manufacturing production via control and management systems have become widespread, demanding a greater level of skill and a knowledge of organization from certain types of office workers and secretaries. Limited evidence, mostly from the developed countries, indicates that the application of micro-electronic technologies does not necessarily impede the upgrading of secretarial skills; in fact, information technologies, and more precisely microcomputers in the office, provide secretarial workers – potentially – with a wide range of experience and activities, such as database management or desktop publishing, which broaden their jobs and expertise. Appropriate training that enhances the hands-on skills, which are learned on the job, benefits the companies as much as the secretaries.

In the 1990s, faced with the prospect of skills shortages in strategic areas, businesses in the western world have started to regard the new-technology secretarial skills of women as increasingly valuable resources. In progressive and forward-looking companies, training programmes and better working conditions are being offered to secure their commitment, and to exploit their tacit skills, and some efforts have been made in structuring ergonomically sound computer-aided offices for the secretaries. In the services sector generally, the use of computers has been generally women-friendly. The QWERTY keyboard of computers allowed women to use their typing skills in many information-processing jobs. In banking, insurance and telecommunications, the entry of women has been impressive both in the richer and in the poorer parts of the world (Tremblay, 1991). In India, in some of the major foreign banks, 70 per cent of the workforce are women. In the 1970s, the comparable figure was 5 per cent (Gothoskar, 1995). A similar rise in women's jobs in the telecommunications sector has also been documented in Malaysia (Ng Choon Sim and King, 1995). In Brazil, women on average hold more than 25 per cent of jobs related to software programming (Gaio, 1995).

Women's visibility in management and technical positions, however, is still nil or negligible in all these countries. As women are excluded from the decision-making process, women-specific concerns receive less attention. In the context of low-paid white-collar jobs, the emerging issues are in the areas of:

- decline in the number of unionized jobs
- rise of VDU-related health hazards (Pearson and Mitter, 1993).

In-depth investigation of these issues, particularly in the context of developing countries, is still rather scant.

Conclusion

Knowledge-intensive modes of production are going to be one of the major features of the twenty-first century. The pervasiveness of information technology and the steady spread of biotechnology, as shown in the chapter, require new technical, management and business skills. Thus, in the 'learning society' of the coming millennium, women would be able to compete with men on an equal footing only if they were given access to relevant cognitive skills.

A programme that will ensure such access has to be innovative. In a world of work where most workers, including the elite ones, have flexible employment, it becomes difficult to guarantee continuous on-the-job training. Flexibility in the workplace, a logical outcome of increased subcontracting, likewise makes it problematic to target education and training to dispersed workers in small units. Women form the majority of the flexible, casualized and dispersed workforce. Their representation in core employment and knowledge-based occupations is less common. In a plan of action for equality at work, therefore, innovative training methods and institutions ought to receive urgent priority.

It is not only the quantity but also the quality of work that should be the focus of attention. The emerging health and safety hazards, in new-tech occupations for example, are relatively unknown to women in developing countries.

Rapid changes in the organization of work make it particularly important to re-evaluate the efficiency of the existing mode of collective action. As women are most likely to find employment in decentralized work units, the trade unions need to reorient their traditional modes of operation, which have been geared mainly to the needs of male employees of large-scale organizations. Furthermore, the question of enabling women to combine their productive with their reproductive role should play a central part in policy dialogues, among the employees, employers and trade unions, in the context of knowledge-based modes of economic operations. Finally, research materials on the impact of technological change are an essential precondition for effective policy-making.

Notes

1. Action learning sets: a management development concept originated by Reg Revans in the UK. It is based on the idea that managers learn by doing and reviewing what they have done, and one provides opportunities for them to carry out this activity in a variety of different circumstances.

2. Kaizen, or continuous improvement, is the practice of institutionalizing the search for improvement. This can be done by forming groups of workers (quality circles, small group activities) and management task forces to seek better (less costly) ways of doing things. Kaizen works best when (i) JIT and TQC have simplified production systems so that their workings are transparent, and (ii) workers are organized into teams and have some knowledge of jobs other than their own.

3. A temporary technology group (TTG), more often called an 'amoeba', is a term used in the context of TQM and cellular flexible manufacturing that involves two or more employees for production of a given model or 'family' of goods.

4. Materials requirements planning (MRP) refers to a technique which takes a forecast of anticipated sales over time and produces a breakdown of the total materials requirements – raw materials, components, subassemblies – for meeting those targets. From such information a series of activities – purchase orders, subcontract orders, in-house production of component orders – can be initiated. Materials resource planning (MRP II) extends the concept of materials requirements planning by introducing the idea of a *master production schedule* which is generated by a mixture of forecasting of sales demand and actual customer orders. From this master schedule a materials requirement plan and a capacity requirements plan are

generated and used in connection with the *bill of materials* to produce orders for materials. MRP II differs from MRP in its strategic nature, taking into account the entire operational resource base of the company.

5. ISO9000/4: The International Organization for Standardization has developed a series of standards for total quality management. ISO9000 provides guidelines for their selection and use. ISO9001 covers product design, development, production, installation and servicing. ISO9002 covers production and installation and ISO9003 covers final inspection and testing. ISO9004 includes all elements of standards 9001–9003. Countries which adopt similar standards should be able to have them recognized by other countries and, in theory, this mutual recognition of standards should lead to freer trade.

References

Acero, L. (1991) *Textile workers in Brazil and Argentina*, Tokyo, United Nations University Press.

Alasoini, T. (1991) 'Technological changes and gendered division of labour in the light electrotechnical industry: Observations from a Finnish study', in I.V. Eriksson *et al.*, *Women's work and computerization: Understanding and overcoming bias in work and education*, Amsterdam, North Holland.

Amsden, A. (1990) 'Third world industrialization: "Global Fordism" or a new model', in *New Left Review* No. 182, London.

Banerjee, N. (1988, 1991) 'The unorganized sector and the planner', in A.K. Bagchi (ed.), *India: economy, polity and society*, Delhi, Oxford University Press India.

— (1995) 'Something old, something borrowed: Microelectronics in Calcutta', in Mitter and Rowbotham (eds), 1995.

Bessant, J. (1991) *Managing advanced manufacturing technology*, Manchester, Blackwell.

Bellussi, F. (1992) 'Benetton Italy: Beyond Fordism and flexible specialization. The evolution of the network firm model', in Mitter (ed.), 1992b.

Ebel, K-L. (1990) *Computer-integrated manufacturing: The social dimension*, Geneva, ILO.

Financial Times (1990) 'Survey of Thailand', 5 December.

Fleury, M.T. and R. Fischer (1992) (eds), *Cultura e poder nas organizacões* (São Paulo, Editora Atlas, 2nd edition).

Franzinetti, V. (1993) 'The informal sector in an industrialized country: Textile and garment workers in Northern Italy', paper commissioned by the Interdepartmental Project on Women in Employment, Geneva, ILO.

Gaeta, R., F. Belussi and S. Mitter (1992) 'Pronta moda: The new business ventures for women in Italy', in Mitter (ed.), 1992b.

Gaio, F.J. (1995): 'Women in software programming: the experience of Brazil', in Mitter and Rowbotham (eds), 1995.

Gothoskar, S. *et al.* (1995) 'Computerization and women's employment in India's banking sector', in Mitter and Rowbotham (eds), 1995.

Humphrey, J. (1992) 'The management of labour and the move towards leaner production systems in the Third World: The case of Brazil', paper presented at the International Institute for Labour Studies Conference on Lean Production Management, Geneva, November.

Kelkar, G. and D. Nathan (1992) 'Social impact of new technologies', background paper prepared for ESCAP All-China Youth Federation Seminar on the Effects of New Technologies on the Working Life of Young People, Zhuhai, China, 20–24 October.

Mackinnon, A.G. (1991) 'Autonomy and control: Women, work and computerization', in I.V. Eriksson (ed.), *Women, work and computerization: Understanding and overcoming bias in work and education*, Amsterdam, North Holland.

Mitter, S. (1987) *Women in industrial development in developing countries: Trends and perspectives*, Vienna, UNIDO, Unit for the Integration of Women into Industrial Development.

— (1992a) 'New skills requirements and appropriate programmes for the enhancement of participation of the female labour force in industry in selected economies of the Asian/Pacific region', paper presented at the Regional Workshop on Promoting Diversified Skill Requirements for Women in Industry, ESCAP, Chiang Mai, Thailand, 23–27 March.

— (ed.) (1992b) *Computer-aided manufacturing and women's employment*, London, Springer-Verlag.

— (1995) 'Information technology and working women's demands', in Mitter and Rowbotham (eds), 1995.

— *et al.* (1993) *A new approach to positive action programmes in the European telecommunications industry*, Centre for Business Research, University of Brighton.

Mitter, S. and R. Pearson (1992) *Global information processing: The emergence of software services and data entry in selected developing countries*, Geneva, ILO, Sectoral Activities Working Papers, Salaried Employees and Professional Workers' Branch.

Mitter, S. and S. Rowbotham (eds) (1995) *Women encounter technology: Changing patterns of employment in the third world*, London, Routledge.

Narayan, S. and R. Rajah (1990) 'Malaysian electronics: The dimming prospects of employment generation and restructuring', mimeo.

Ng Choon Sim, C. and C. King (1995) 'Information technology, technology and employment: a case-study of the telecommunication industry in Malaysia', in Mitter and Rowbotham (eds), 1995.

Ofreneo, R.P. (1987) *Industrial homework in the Philippines*, Geneva, ILO.

Pearson, R. (1995) 'Gender perspectives on health and safety in information processing: learning from international experience', in Mitter and Rowbotham (eds), 1995.

— and S. Mitter (1993) 'Employment and working conditions of low-skilled information processing workers in less developed countries', in *International Labour Review*, Vol. 132, No. 1, Geneva.

Posthuma, A. (1990) 'Japanese techniques in Brazilian automobile components: Best practice model as basis for adoption', paper presented to the Conference on Organization and Control of the Labour Process, Aston University, Birmingham, UK, 28–30 March.

Pyke, F., G. Becattini and W. Sengenberger (1990) *Industrial districts and inter-firm cooperation in Italy*, Geneva, International Institute for Labour Studies.

Pyke, F. and W. Sengenberger (eds) (1992) *Industrial districts and local economic generation*, Geneva, ILO.

Roldan, M. (1993a) 'Women organizing in the process of industrialization: JIT, technological innovations, industrial restructuring and gender relations', in A. Chhachi and R. Pittin (eds.), *Confronting state, capital and patriarchy: Women organizing in the process of industrialization*, Macmillan, London.

– (1993b) 'Industrial restructuring, deregulation and new JIT labour process in Argentina: Towards a gender perspective?', in J. Humphrey (ed.), *Quality and productivity in industry: New strategies in developing countries*, IDS Bulletin, Vol. 24, No. 2, April, Sussex.

Ruas, R. (1993) 'Notes on the implementation of quality and productivity programmes in sectors of Brazilian industry', in J. Humphrey (ed.), *Quality and productivity in industry: New strategies in developing countries*, IDS Bulletin, Vol. 24, No. 2, April, Sussex.

Soares, S.A. (1992) 'Telework and communication in data processing centres in Brazil', in U.E. Gattiker (ed.), *Technological innovation and human resources*, Vol. 3, Technology-mediated Communication, Berlin and New York, de Gruyter.

Tremblay, D-G. (1991) 'Computerization, human resources management and reflection of women's skills', in I.V. Eriksson *et al.* (eds), *Women, work and computerization: Understanding and overcoming bias in work education*, Amsterdam, North Holland.

PART II
Working conditions and social security

6
Sexual harassment at work

LINDA WIRTH

Sexual harassment is a new term to describe the age-old problem of unwelcome conduct of a sexual nature. It is a social phenomenon that can occur anywhere. The term 'sexual harassment' was coined in the 1970s in the United States, which at that time began to recognize it as a specific type of conduct prohibited by the law. However, such behaviour has also been given other names in the past in other parts of the world. More recently, in Japan the term 'seku-hara' has been adopted. A Tanzanian report cites workers as saying: 'sometimes a supervisor will say or hint that he will be a bit lax on your reports if you are "good to him"'.[1] This chapter focuses on sexual harassment in the work situation.

While both women and men can be subjected to sexual harassment, more women suffer from it than men. In a number of countries, sexual harassment is regarded as a form of sex discrimination. This began in 1977 with a United States court case, which determined that sexual harassment constituted sex discrimination, reasoning that 'but for her womanhood (the complainant's) participation in sexual activity would never have been solicited ... She became the target of her superior's sexual desires because she was a woman, and was asked to bow to his demands as the price for holding her job' (reported in ILO, 1992).

It is estimated in the United States that at least one out of every two women experiences sexual harassment at some point in her academic or working life (Fitzgerald and Ormerod, 1991). It happens to women in their first job and to women who have been in the workforce for years. Women's groups in Malaysia point out that unwanted sexual attention is a form of sexual harassment often encountered by women in most public places. In such instances, one can ignore or walk away from it. But sexual harassment at the workplace is more disturbing – it becomes an irritant, a source of embarrassment and discomfort when encountered constantly. Under such circumstances, sexual harassment becomes a form of discrimination, as it can become a barrier to an individual's freedom of movement, full employment or opportunities at work.[2]

Over the last two decades, sexual harassment has been increasingly recognized as a common problem. It is considered a violation of human rights[3] and an affront to the dignity of the person. In particular, it is regarded as a manifestation of violence against women, an issue on which women's organizations in many countries are mobilizing.[4]

Sexual harassment at work has also been regarded as a contravention of obligations imposed by the law to be a good employer. According to the Commission of the European Union, as sexual harassment is a form of employee misconduct, employers have a responsibility to deal with it as they do with any other form of employee misconduct, as well as to refrain from harassing employees themselves. Since sexual harassment is a risk to health and safety, employers have a responsibility to take steps to minimize the risk as they do with other hazards (Commission of the European Union, 1992).

There has been a steady growth in awareness of the serious consequences of sexual harassment for working women and for the achievement of equality. Awareness has also increased of the detrimental effects of sexual harassment on the efficiency of enterprises. Many countries have moved to legislate or are considering doing so.

The consequences of sexual harassment for the victim range from emotional stress resulting in feelings of humiliation, anxiety, fear, anger, anguish, powerlessness and depression, as well as physical reactions such as headaches, nausea, insomnia and high blood pressure (Fuentes *et al.*, 1988). This in turn may cause increased absenteeism and lower productivity and can eventually lead to the person quitting the job (Danish Gallup Institute, 1991). Refusal to grant sexual favours can mean failure to gain promotion. It can also be the reason behind the dismissal of many an employee whose work performance had formerly been satisfactory. For the enterprise, the cost of sick leave and employee turnover can be significant. Employers in those countries where court action may successfully result in awards for damages also run considerable financial risks if they do not put in place and enforce an explicit policy against sexual harassment.

The issue of sexual harassment is sensitive and difficult to address. When it occurs in the workplace, it is not so much a product of the working environment as a reflection of traditional social behaviour between the sexes and of social attitudes towards women. It is extremely difficult for victims to complain about it without making their situation worse or for fear of losing their jobs. This is because sexual harassment in the workplace is not generally regarded as an employment issue, but rather as a 'personal' problem between those involved. Without a policy explicitly indicating that sexual harassment will not be tolerated and that offenders will be sanctioned, would-be harassers may not even realize the harm they can cause not only to the victim, but also to the enterprise.

Sexual harassment is increasingly being recognized as a legitimate trade union concern, but the whole of the trade union movement is not yet fully at ease with the subject. This may be, as the Canadian Labour Congress acknowledges, because 'there are situations in which one union member is harassed by another union member'. Similarly, for employers sexual harassment is not an easy subject. A few years ago, employers tended to argue that sexual harassment is a question of individual behaviour. Many employers are now recognizing it as a discipline problem, which can have detrimental effects on enterprise efficiency. With increasing awareness of the problem of sexual harassment, and of women's rights and the need to promote gender equality, it is also being increasingly recognized that much can be done by employers and trade unions at the workplace on this issue. Governments and nongovernmental organizations can also play an important role.

An attempt is made below to illustrate the importance of understanding what sexual harassment is and why it occurs. Secondly, it identifies practical ways of providing protection and of preventing the problem so that employees enjoy the right to a work environment free of sexual harassment. The chapter brings together data generated by a number of national reports on sexual harassment covering both the developed and the developing worlds.

What is sexual harassment?

Sexual harassment has been defined in various ways. The definitions typically refer to unwanted conduct of a sexual nature, where either the rejection or imposition of such conduct can have negative employment consequences for the victim, as well as undesirable effects on the work environment. The Bureau of Women and Young Workers in the Philippines has, for example, identified two types of sexual harassment: sexual coercion and sexual annoyance. Sexual coercion has a direct consequence on the worker's employment status or the gain or loss of tangible job benefits. Sexual annoyance is sexually related conduct that is hostile, intimidating or offensive to the employee but has no direct links to any tangible job benefits or harm. This annoying conduct creates a bothersome work environment and the worker's terms and conditions of employment are dependent on the worker's willingness or capacity to endure that environment. This is especially experienced by women in non-traditional jobs.

In reviewing definitions of sexual harassment, the Bureau identified three forms: verbal, physical and use of objects or pictures. Furthermore, the four basic components of sexual harassment were observed to be that: it is unwanted; it is repeated; it may be deliberate or done unconsciously; and it emphasizes a person's sexuality over her role as a worker.[5]

Some definitions clearly place the phenomenon of sexual harassment in the context of power relationships and/or sex discrimination. For example, the Organization of Tanzania Trade Unions (OTTU), in its sexual harassment policy and complaint procedure, defines sexual harassment as 'one person(s) exercising power over another (others)'. This includes: unwanted or unwelcome and unreciprocated behaviour that is offensive to the recipient; unnecessary physical contact ranging from touching and patting through to rape; suggestive and unwelcome remarks or jokes, sexual propositions, unwanted comments on dress or appearance or verbal abuse of a sexual nature; leering and compromising invitations, display of pornographic pictures, suggestive movements and gestures, such as winking and touching; demands for sexual favours; physical assault and rape.[6]

The African Regional Federation of Commercial, Clerical, Professional and Technical Employees (AFRO-FIET), in a resolution on sexual harassment in November 1991, defined sexual harassment as 'any unwanted explicit or implicit, verbal or physical, sexual advances towards women workers in the workplace and in the trade union; sexual harassment is a hidden issue because it causes embarrassment and humiliation to women; and very few, if any, laws exist to protect women workers'. Furthermore, 'sexual harassment contributes to undermine the confidence of women, is a humiliating form of gender oppression of the worst kind and is a legitimate trade union issue' (AFRO-FIET, 1991).

Definitions of sexual harassment at work can be classified into two types:

(i) a demand by a person in authority, such as a supervisor, for sexual favours in order to keep or obtain certain job benefits, be it a wage increase, a promotion, training opportunity, a transfer, or the job itself. In the United States this definition has been legally termed as 'quid pro quo' sexual harassment (this for that), which involves a type of abuse of authority. Sometimes this type of sexual harassment is also referred to as 'sexual blackmail'.

(ii) unwelcome sexual advances, requests for sexual favours or other verbal, non-verbal or physical conduct of a sexual nature which interferes with an individual's work performance or creates an intimidating, hostile, abusive, offensive or poisoned work environment. In the United States this definition has been legally termed as 'hostile working environment sexual harassment' (ILO, 1992).

There is an increasing tendency to include both these dimensions in the formulation of legal definitions. However, sometimes only one form is used, as in the French legislation enacted in 1992 which included only the 'quid pro quo' type. On the other hand, a Japanese court ruling in 1992 endorsed a definition of sexual harassment which refers only to the creation of a hostile work environment, and in 1993 the Labour Ministry in Japan recognized sexual harassment as 'unpleasant speech or conduct with sexual references that creates a difficult work environment' (*The Times*, 1993).

The essential characteristic of sexual harassment as being conduct of a sexual nature which is unwanted by or unwelcome to the recipient distinguishes it from friendly behaviour which is welcome and mutual. Determining whether such conduct is unwelcome or not has led courts in a number of countries to indicate that sexual harassment is conduct that the individual knew or ought to have known was unwelcome. More recently, courts in Canada, Switzerland, the United Kingdom and the United States have opted for the 'reasonable woman's' viewpoint as to whether the behaviour was wanted or not, as it is women who mainly experience sexual harassment.

There are many kinds of verbal, non-verbal and physical acts which may be considered sexual harassment. They vary according to cultural and social practices and the social contexts in which they occur. For instance, in some cultures physical touching upon greeting or communicating may be normal social behaviour, while in other societies this would be interpreted as a sexual advance, whether wanted or not. Furthermore, in some traditions, a woman's explicit rejection of sexual advances may be regarded as a sign of her positive interest in the person making them. In some countries cultural difficulties still exist in understanding whether a woman finds a proposition of a sexual nature welcome or not. Thus, the Canadian Trade Union Congress supports the slogan 'No Means No', which is part of a national campaign to stem violence against women. In workplaces, the display of sexually suggestive posters would be tolerated by many workers and be considered by just as many others as offensive. A report on sexual harassment in Jamaica[7] notes that 'sexual by-play' makes sexual harassment a problematic issue in the Caribbean as it is an accepted part of communication styles between men and women. Therefore it is not always easy to determine what is offensive and to whom. It is also often difficult for victims of sexual harassment to express their rejection of such behaviour, because of fear or embarrassment.

Another issue in defining sexual harassment is whether the conduct has to be repeated to be considered as such. Usually, conduct of a sexual nature is regarded as harassment if it persists once it has been made clear that it is unwelcome. However, one incident may be regarded as sexual harassment if it is sufficiently serious, such as sexual assault or a demand for sexual favours in exchange for a job benefit.

The most common form of harassment reported by surveys is that involving unwelcome verbal comments, jokes, teasing and propositions of a sexual nature. This is followed by unwanted physical touching and fondling. More serious forms of sexual harassment, while generally occurring to a lesser extent, can have particularly detrimental employment consequences for a significant number of victims. In the Philippines one survey reported that testimonies produced evidence of emotional stress, fear and voluntary job loss because of sexual harassment. The victims reported devastating economic effects, such as denied job promotions, poor job evaluation and job transfer. Seventy-five per cent were harassed by supervisors or other individuals having direct influence on hiring, evaluation or promotion of the harassed women. Nineteen per cent were harassed by co-employees, mostly in the form of verbal harassment.[8]

How widespread is the problem?

In quite a number of countries, surveys have been conducted to determine the extent to which sexual harassment occurs, the groups which are typically affected, the profile of a harasser, the forms that harassment takes and its consequences. The validity of certain surveys, which up till now mainly emanate from the industrialized countries, can sometimes be questioned due to inadequacies of the samples, types of question posed or the time frames used. Comparison between countries and cultures is also difficult owing to the widely varying survey samples and methodologies employed. The surveys nevertheless provide some insight into the nature and extent of the problem.

While estimated percentages vary considerably, a significant number of employees, the majority of whom are women, claim to have been sexually harassed. A study in 1988 commissioned by the Government of the Netherlands found that an overall 58 per cent of women working in a small business, a large municipality and an industrial company had experienced sexual harassment at work (ILO, 1992). Similar results were obtained by a 1992 survey of 25 companies and international organizations in the city of Geneva in Switzerland (Bureau de l'égalité, 1993). A government survey in Japan in 1993 showed that 26 per cent of working women in Tokyo had suffered 'at least one unpleasant sexual experience at work in the past two years' (*The Times*, 1993). In the United States a survey of 23,000 federal employees in 1980 found that 42 per cent of women reported some form of sexual harassment.[9] At the lower end of the scale, women reporting sexual harassment represented 11 per cent of those surveyed in Denmark, 17 per cent in Sweden and 21 per cent in France (ILO, 1992).

A few surveys in developing countries also show that sexual harassment at work is a problem for many women workers. In Tanzania a survey of 10,319 women in 135 workplaces from 13 regions in 1988–89 found that sexual harassment was a common problem affecting women workers. Sixty per cent of the women indicated that sexual harassment occurred at their workplace and was so common that they did not report it.[10]

According to the Committee for Asian Women, in Thailand, women workers returning home from night shift in factories are at risk of being sexually abused, and some workers are sexually harassed by management and administrative staff. If the women refuse to give in, 'they will be dismissed or harassed until they resign. Many employers deliberately select good-looking women when they recruit new workers' (Committee for Asian Women, 1991).

In India, a study of indigenous women labourers in Bihar, India, describes the sexual exploitation of these women by their employers, contractors and co-workers as the greatest humiliation that these women are subjected to as a consequence of their extremely exploitative working conditions and lack of bargaining power. Rape and sexual abuse are common. Frequently the women are held in bondage and if they manage to escape it is not always possible to go back to their villages. Many end up in prostitution or just disappear altogether (Prasad, 1988).

The results of some surveys would tend to suggest that the reported percentage of those experiencing sexual harassment is only the tip of the iceberg. There are more women who indicate that they know of others who have been sexually harassed than there are women who acknowledge having been sexually harassed themselves. In a Côte d'Ivoire radio programme in early 1993, callers commonly indicated that while they had not been sexually harassed themselves, they all knew of women who had been victims. Similarly, in a survey in Japan in 1991 by the Tokyo Metropolitan Government, 51 per cent of respondents reported having heard about sexual harassment cases.[11]

Given the reluctance and difficulties involved in making complaints, assessments made on the basis of the number of complaints filed in courts or made within enterprises or public administrations are only an indication of what is likely to be a more widespread phenomenon. The fact that sexual harassment is often viewed as a personal problem and not recognized as a legitimate labour issue, and the consequent lack of complaints' mechanisms make reporting the incidence of sexual harassment a heroic effort on the part of victims. Fear of losing one's job, of reprisals or making the workplace even more unbearable are very real obstacles for a victim of sexual harassment and, therefore, limit reporting.

Who is harassed and who harasses?

The link between the incidence of sexual harassment and women's relatively weak position in the labour market cannot be ignored. Sexual harassment of women workers is bound to persist while women occupy more precarious and lower-paid jobs than men. With economic restructuring in many countries and the subsequent rise in more precarious forms of employment, particularly for women, the problem of sexual harassment at work is likely to be exacerbated.

A number of surveys have identified the greater vulnerability of certain categories of women workers, such as those on precarious contracts, young women, single women, migrant workers and domestic workers. In addition, women working in sectors or occupations where women predominate or alternatively women working in traditional male jobs are also particularly at risk because of the imbalance between the sexes at the workplace. In some cases sexual harassment appears to occur least in situations where an equal number of men and women are employed in positions but more frequently when the traditional roles of men and women are challenged by women taking up employment in a traditionally male-dominated sector or when women are employed in higher-level positions.[12]

The Federal Human Rights and Equal Opportunities Commission in Australia has found that two-thirds of all cases heard by the Commission related to small businesses of under 100 employees. Over half of them involved sexual harassment. The complainants held mainly clerical and retail positions reflecting the occupations dominated by women. The Commission has also reported dealing with a number of complaints from male-dominated work areas, particularly by women promoted to a more senior level than many of the men.[13] In addition, 75 per cent of the sexual harassment complaints which proceeded to a public hearing in Australia involved women under 20 years old. Young women are particularly vulnerable to sexual harassment in the workplace because of their age, inexperience and limited knowledge of their rights and remedies (Elliot and Shanahan Research, 1990). Over half had difficulties in finding employment prior to their harassment, and in most cases it was their first job.

The General Union of Workers in Spain found that women between 26 and 30 years old were more likely to be harassed than other age groups, given that this group of women combined what were regarded as important characteristics: youth and supposed sexual experience. Women who were separated, divorced or widowed were not only more likely to be subject to sexual harassment, but they also experienced stronger forms of harassment (Fuentes *et al.*, 1988). A survey of federal employees in the United States indicated that women have the greatest chance of being sexually harassed if they are single or divorced, between the ages of 20 and 44, have some university education, have a non-traditional job, or work in a predominantly male environment or for a male supervisor.[14]

Domestic workers are also among workers most exposed to sexual harassment. A Jamaican study in 1989 on domestic service reported sexual harassment as a problem, particularly for women from rural areas working in private homes in towns.[15] Studies in Indonesia and Sri Lanka have shown sexual harassment to be a serious problem for women from these countries working as domestic employees in the Middle East (ILO, 1993). The Malaysian Trade Union Congress has reported a high incidence of sexual harassment of Filipina domestic workers in Malaysia.

In the Philippines, a report based on small surveys and reported incidents from labour unions concluded that sexual harassment exists in different work environments and can affect anyone – an ordinary worker, a professional, an executive or an elected trade union official. However, there appeared to be a higher incidence of the problem in industries where physical appearance is important, such as in hotels, restaurants, banks, media and entertainment; and in industries where women predominate, such as in garment and electronic manufacturing. A high incidence of sexual harassment has been observed in export processing zones, where male supervisors reportedly demand sexual favours from subordinates, mostly young and single women, in return for employment stability, promotion or better working conditions.[16]

Sexual harassment may be perpetrated by a person in authority, such as a supervisor, or by a co-worker or a client. Some surveys have not found significant differences between the representation of these groups. For example, in a French study the harasser was identified by 29 per cent of the harassed women as the employer himself, by 26 per cent as a superior, by 22 per cent as a colleague and by 27 per cent as a client.[17]

A study of Zimbabwean women in industry noted that sexual harassment of women workers by male supervisors is becoming a problem. 'Because women are in insecure and often casual positions, they are vulnerable to male supervisors who threaten them with dismissal if sexual favours are not granted.' One woman organizer said that she had received numerous complaints from women, who, when seeking casual employment in industry, were bluntly told by male supervisors that jobs were only available to 'those willing to provide favours' (Made and Lagerström, 1985).

Consequences of sexual harassment

The effects of sexual harassment on the victim include emotional distress (stress, tension, feelings of humiliation and threat, depression, loss of self-esteem, absenteeism and a decrease in productivity) and physical illness. Others include loss of employment benefits, dismissals and resignations. In the Netherlands 25 per cent of the harassed women claimed that there had been negative job effects, with a deterioration in the work environment and with some women actually leaving their job or transferring elsewhere.[18] A study in Germany found that 6 per cent of the women interviewed had resigned from their job as a result of being sexually harassed. A Danish poll revealed that, in 17 per cent of reported cases of sexual harassment, there was a change of workplace and, in 8 per cent of cases, the women had been dismissed.[19]

In terms of financial loss to enterprises, a study of 160 companies in the United States in 1989 found that sexual harassment had cost the corporate employers an average of $6.7 million per year due to absenteeism, low productivity and employee turnover (Husbands, 1992).

An extremely serious consequence of sexual harassment that is beginning to be documented is the infection of victims with HIV and, therefore, AIDS and eventual death. This is particularly the case in those parts of the world where infection levels are high and where submission to sexual demands in the work context thus runs a high risk of HIV being transmitted.

Why does sexual harassment persist?

Sexual harassment has more to do with power relations than with sexual interest. For many it is a form of oppression, victimization or intimidation based on relationships of power and authority. In some instances abuse of power is linked only to hierarchical rank, but in many countries women's groups, workers' and employers' organizations and government agencies link abuse of power with the traditional status of women in society and observe that when harassed, a person's identity as a sexual being takes precedence over her identity as a worker.

On the other hand, fear of losing power or advantage can also be at the root of the harassing behaviour. Fellow workers may use harassment as an intimidation tactic to discourage women from applying for and working in traditionally male occupations. Sexual harassment can also be used to undermine the authority of women supervisors. A national trade union group (FNV) in the Netherlands points out that sexual harassment 'is not a temporary phenomenon because men feel threatened in their status and authority by women's improved access to the labour market'.[20]

The 14th Conference of the Asian and Pacific Regional Organization of the International Confederation of Free Trade Unions, in August 1988, identified sexual harassment at the workplace as a 'further discrimination suffered by women'.[21] A study in the Philippines notes that 'the existence of sexual harassment in the employment environment can be partly rooted in the society's concept of traditional sex roles. The notion which regards men as the economic providers and women as the inferior sex whose main role is tied to their reproductive capacities has produced inappropriate behaviour among male workers in the workplace'.[22]

In a survey by the Tokyo Metropolitan Government, 50 per cent of respondents thought that sexual harassment occurred because women were not seen as equal partners; 21 per cent put it down to lack of education on equality between men and women and 19 per cent to women being seen as sex objects.[23] Sexual harassment also persists due to public opinion and lack of legal measures specifically sanctioning it as well as low levels of cases reported.

In 1983 a survey in the fish conservation industry in Peru found that 'unsolicited sexual advances' generally involved men in a position of authority in the enterprise and that the silence around these incidents was due to the women's need to keep their jobs, the conviction of being unable to oppose a superior, and distrust and fear of the scorn of their colleagues.[24]

Combating sexual harassment

While sexual harassment has only fairly recently been recognized as a problem, there has been a remarkable response around the world in terms of awareness and adoption of legal and other measures within both public and private enterprises. Tackling sexual harassment, like many problems, involves changing social attitudes and perceptions, and is a long-term process covering the whole social and political spectrum and the adoption and enforcement of a range of measures.

Acknowledging the problem

A first step is the recognition of sexual harassment in general as a problem, and in particular as a labour issue. National mass media and informal means of education have an important role to play in this respect. Recognition of the phenomenon of sexual harassment, in turn, contributes to its elimination. Initial court cases in countries often tend to attract media attention and start off a chain reaction.

A report from the Côte d'Ivoire, cited above, indicates that for legal protection from sexual harassment and effective enforcement, the laws need to be accompanied by an extensive awareness-raising campaign led by public authorities, employers, trade unions and human rights organizations to prevent and discourage the practice of sexual harassment. Such an effort should not be restricted to the modern economic sectors, but should extend also to rural areas and the informal sector where the majority of workers are to be found.

A number of government agencies, women's groups and trade unions have conducted awareness-raising activities in their countries. They have produced leaflets and guidelines, and organized meetings and debates to make sexual harassment a subject for public discussion. Once the barrier of silence is broken, sexual harassment cases tend to be increasingly reported, as victims feel more encouraged to step forward.

Women's organizations have often initiated the launching of sexual harassment as a public issue in many countries. For example the European Association against all Forms of Violence against Women at Work, based in Paris, aims to raise the awareness of enterprises and trade unions about the need for a policy to combat sexual harassment. It has also proposed texts for legislative reform in France and issues a periodical publication on sexual harassment and violence against women.

Similarly, in a number of developing countries this is occurring in the context of campaigns to combat violence against women. The Tanzanian Media Women's Association assisted in setting up a Crisis Centre on Sexual Harassment, Domestic Violence and Discrimination against Women and Children in Dar es Salaam. The Centre provides medical, legal and counselling services to women and children. A Committee has also been established, with membership from different professional groups, that works for legal reform and focuses on stimulating people and groups to become aware of prejudice and discrimination. It identifies sexism as the root cause of violence against women and also promotes education about the problem using community radio, folk theatre and popular educational materials.[25] Women's groups in the Philippines have published articles and conducted seminars and other activities to bring the issue to the attention of government, community organizations and the general public.[26] Trade unions have, in some cases, actually spearheaded national awareness-raising campaigns. For example, in 1988 the Malaysian Trade Union Congress launched a national campaign to combat sexual harassment, which received wide media coverage and to which the government has responded with a commitment to study possible legal measures. In Nicaragua, the Association of Agricultural Workers identified, in its 1993–94 'plan of struggle', protection against 'sexual blackmail' as an issue that should be included in the promulgation of a new labour code.[27]

In many countries, the mass media (television, radio and newspapers) are already playing a crucial role in raising awareness of sexual harassment. It has even become a popular subject for film making. In Sri Lanka sexual harassment has surfaced as an issue in video films and teledramas broadcast on the national networks.

Governments in several countries have initiated awareness-raising campaigns. In 1989–90, the federal Human Rights and Equal Opportunities Commission in Australia launched a national media-based public awareness campaign targeted towards young women (SHOUT – Sexual Harassment is OUT). A campaign by the Belgian government involved the production of posters, stickers, pamphlets and information kits which were sent to employers and workers in the public and private sectors, trade unions and women's organizations.[28]

Legal protection

Major problems encountered in dealing with sexual harassment and sexual violence against women within the legal systems of many countries are the patriarchal concepts, unsympathetic judiciaries (the majority of whom may be men), the fact that the burden of proof rests on the complainant and the importance attached to the character of the victim. Moreover, in many countries discriminatory traditional customs are still in place, despite the fact that the statute books outlaw discrimination against women.

Quite a number of countries, however, have begun to adopt legislation which specifically addresses sexual harassment. This is particularly so in industrialized countries, although a few developing countries have recently begun to do likewise. In 1995, for example, both Costa Rica and the Philippines adopted laws specifically prohibiting sexual harassment. In the Caribbean, model legislation on violence against women has been prepared, with the assistance of the Commonwealth Secretariat, which includes the prohibition of sexual harassment.

Unless sexual harassment is explicitly recognized as a distinct legal wrong, labour laws which deal with sexual harassment indirectly through unjust dismissal cases are inadequate in addressing the problem. Similarly, criminal laws which treat sexual harassment as criminally indecent behaviour are not particularly effective in addressing the problem owing to the strict requirements for proving allegations. If sexual harassment remains a 'hidden problem', the development of preventive measures will be hindered and victims will be discouraged from undertaking what can be lengthy and costly court procedures.

Depending on the national legal system, different types of law may be used explicitly to prohibit and actively prevent sexual harassment. These include equal opportunity, labour, tort and criminal laws. Their implementation depends on the application of effective remedies and sanctions. Court cases can further interpret these laws or shape the law itself in countries with a common law legal system.

Equal opportunity laws which prohibit sex discrimination in employment have been used to provide protection against sexual harassment in a number of countries – Australia, Canada, Denmark, Ireland, Germany (Berlin), New Zealand, Sweden, the United Kingdom and the United States. In a number of these countries sexual harassment is specifically mentioned in the statute, while in others courts have interpreted sexual harassment as a form of sex discrimination. In most of these countries, a victim of sexual harassment may find it easier to file a complaint because of the special procedures and institutional authorities that have been created under the equal opportunity laws. These may take the form of an equal opportunities or human rights commission, a board, an ombudsman or a commissioner (ILO, 1992). In Puerto Rico a law adopted in 1988 specifically prohibits sexual harassment and recognizes it as a form of sex discrimination. The law makes the employer responsible for acts of sexual harassment in the workplace, whether committed by the employer or the employer's representatives or by supervisors and whether or not the particular acts were authorized or prohibited by the employer and independently of whether the employer knew or should have known of these acts. The law also provides for the award of financial compensation for damages and civil remedies whereby the employer could be ordered to promote or reinstate the employee and ensure that the sexual harassment ceases.[29]

Labour laws have been amended in a number of countries (Belgium, Canada, France, New Zealand and Spain) explicitly to prohibit sexual harassment. In Belgium the law directs the employer to protect workers against sexual harassment at work, including any actions of a verbal, non-verbal or physical nature which one knows or ought to know would offend the dignity of men and women employees. Canada's federal Labour Code states that all employees are 'entitled to employment free of sexual harassment' (ILO, 1992).

The 1992 Labour Code in the Dominican Republic provides that no employer may 'commit any act against a worker which might be considered sexual harassment, or support or refrain from intervening in the event of his representative committing such an act'.[30] In Namibia the 1992 Labour Act provides that a labour court may issue orders that unfair acts of harassment on the basis of the sex of an employee be discontinued or that the person harassing an employee perform or refrain from performing any acts specified in such orders.[31] The 1995 Anti-Sexual Harassment Act in the Philippines declares all forms of sexual harassment in employment, as well as in the education and training environment, unlawful.

Tort law can also afford protection against sexual harassment in most countries. A tort is a legal wrong, other than a breach of contract, such as a personal injury, for which a court can grant a remedy, most commonly in the form of damages and interest. Tort law encompasses both negligent acts resulting from carelessness or inattention, and intentional acts that can cause harm. Sexual harassment is by its nature an intentional act and would qualify as an intentional tort under most circumstances. Tort law has been found to prohibit sexual harassment in a number of countries (Japan, Switzerland, the United Kingdom and the United States). It can theoretically be applied to virtually all countries, except where a statutory scheme is the exclusive remedy, as in Canada (ILO, 1992).

Criminal law, while also potentially applicable to sexual harassment, presents more difficulties in bringing a case to court, as the burden of proof is more substantial and in most countries the state prosecutor must decide whether the situation justifies bringing criminal action against the alleged harasser. This is the case in France, which has recently adopted a specific penal law on sexual harassment, designed to have general application to any abuse of authority involving requests for sexual favours (ILO, 1992).

In a few countries the law requires positive action on the part of employers to prevent sexual harassment. In Sweden the equal opportunity law requires an affirmative action plan to be submitted annually by employers with more than 10 employees; the plan should include an indication of what positive steps are to be taken to prevent sexual harassment in the workplace. The Canadian federal Labour Code requires employers, after consulting with the workers or their representatives, to issue a policy statement concerning sexual harassment. Belgian labour law also requires employers to adopt a policy against sexual harassment, and to institute certain procedures for complaints. French labour law has a provision that allows the works Safety, Health and Working Conditions Committee to propose measures to prevent sexual harassment (ILO, 1992).

To establish legal protection for victims of sexual harassment, it is logical that legal definitions be formulated so that legal action can be effectively pursued. Such definitions may be included in legal texts which specifically seek to prohibit, prevent or sanction sexual harassment, or may be defined in case law as a consequence of civil, labour or penal court proceedings.

In a number of countries sexual harassment has been recognized and defined by a court decision (Australia, Canada, Ireland, Switzerland, the United Kingdom and the United States at federal and state levels). For example, the Supreme Court of Canada has broadly defined sexual harassment in the workplace as 'unwelcome conduct of a sexual nature that detrimentally affects the work environment or leads to adverse job-related consequences for the victims of the harassment ... When sexual harassment occurs in the workplace, it is an abuse of both economic and sexual power ... Sexual harassment in the workplace attacks the dignity and self-respect of the victim both as an employee and as a human being'.[32]

In most of the industrialized countries that have not enacted specific legislation on sexual harassment, it has been defined by implication as an activity which is in violation of a statute covering a subject other than sexual harassment, such as unfair dismissal, negligent or intentional acts causing harm, or criminal behaviour (ILO, 1992). This is also the case for some developing countries such as Brazil and Tanzania.

Enforcement problems can arise when laws against sexual harassment are passed without providing a legal definition. This is the case in Peru. The passage of proposed laws to address sexual harassment can also be delayed as a result of difficulties in defining sexual harassment or due to differing opinions as to which aspects should be legislated for. For example, in Argentina a number of draft laws addressing sexual harassment have been unsuccessfully tabled in Parliament during recent years.[33]

Legal definitions may be very specific and detailed as to the type of behaviour constituting sexual harassment. One problem with listing the types of conduct prohibited is that this may be limiting, and other acts which could also amount to sexual harassment may go unrecognized as such.

On the other hand, legal definitions may employ broad terms to refer to the actual behaviour and focus more on the employment consequences of unwanted conduct of a sexual nature. For example, the United States Equal Employment Opportunities Commission, the federal agency responsible for the enforcement of Title VII of the Civil Rights Act, which deals with employment discrimination, defines sexual harassment as a form of sex discrimination and indicates that 'unwelcome sexual advances, requests for sexual favours and other verbal or physical conduct of a sexual nature constitute sexual harassment when (1) submission to such conduct is made either explicitly or implicitly a term or condition of an individual's employment, (2) submission to or rejection of such conduct by an individual is used as the basis for employment decisions affecting such individual, or (3) such conduct has the purpose or effect of unreasonably interfering with an individual's work performance or creating an intimidating, hostile, or offensive working environment'.[34]

Combating sexual harassment successfully through law depends also on how legal enforcement of such measures is undertaken. In this respect the issues of liability, complaint procedures, relief and damages for the victim and penalties need to be addressed. The issue of liability is important both from the point of view of potential damages which can be claimed and for its preventive effects. The Canadian Human Rights Act refers to the 'liability of the person' which can include both the employer and the alleged harasser, while the Canadian Labour Code indicates that the employer has a responsibility to 'make every reasonable effort to ensure that no employee is subjected to sexual harassment'.

Procedures which allow the filing of sexual harassment complaints with the minimum of delay, cost and embarrassment are extremely important to facilitate the coming forward of victims. Such procedures also help more data to be collected on the nature and extent of the problem of sexual harassment and encourage its prevention.

Finally, the possibility for victims of sexual harassment to obtain monetary damages is important to compensate for any financial loss as a result of dismissal or missed promotion, as well as for injury to feelings and humiliation suffered. In the United States damages can amount to $100,000 or more, although smaller amounts are also common. In most other countries awards have been relatively small, of $10,000 or less, although theoretically they could be larger, particularly under unjust dismissal claims which often provide for six months' salary to be paid.

Courts may also order cessation of the harassment or action to repair harm caused, or both. Sanctioning of the harasser by transfer, demotion, temporary suspension or dismissal is usually the prerogative of the employer, although courts may determine whether to uphold this right or not in the case of dispute. Courts can also impose fines or prison sentences or both. The awarding of damages and/or the imposition of penalties are significant elements in combating sexual harassment at work as they can encourage victims to speak out and provide a stimulus for employers to take preventive action.

Enterprise policies and procedures

Whether explicit legal protection against sexual harassment is available or not, private enterprises and public administrations can make an enormous contribution to ridding the workplace of sexual harassment. Policies adopted unilaterally by management or through collective bargaining expressly to forbid sexual harassment at work as unacceptable behaviour, which will not be tolerated, give a clear message to staff that sexual harassment will be taken seriously. To enforce such policies effectively, assurance must be given that any complaints will be investigated speedily in a confidential and sensitive manner, and that alleged offenders found guilty of acts of sexual harassment will be disciplined.

Enterprises, both public and private, are beginning to adopt such policies and procedures, particularly in those countries where there are laws specifically prohibiting sexual harassment or where there has been court action condemning it. Some enterprise procedures include advice to employees that before making a complaint they should attempt to make it clear to the alleged harasser that the conduct is offensive and unwanted. There are informal procedures which usually try to promote a process of conciliation to avoid if possible the need for a formal complaint and investigation. If this fails then management staff are required to undertake a full investigation.

Sometimes various groups have collaborated in order to assist employers. In South Africa the ANC Women's League, the Institute of Directors of Southern Africa, the UNISA Centre for Women Studies, the Women's Bureau of South Africa and the Institute for Personnel Management worked together to research the problem of sexual harassment, and formulated guidelines and a model enterprise policy. Government bodies and municipal authorities in a number of countries have also produced guidelines to assist employers in dealing with sexual harassment. Sometimes government agencies and municipal authorities, in their role as employers, have led the way by having a sexual harassment policy and complaint procedure.

Trade union action

Trade unions in a number of countries are beginning to put the issue of sexual harassment at work on the *collective bargaining* agenda. For example, since 1989 the National Union of Workers in Chad has included sexual harassment in its collective bargaining negotiations, as has the National Union of Public Workers in Barbados, which usually includes in collective agreements a clause requiring employers to ensure protection against sexual abuse. The Public Services Association of Trinidad and Tobago deals with sexual harassment as a grievance as and when it develops.[35]

The American Federation of State, County and Municipal Employees (AFSCME) reports that most collective agreements have anti-discrimination clauses that cover sexual harassment. The Ghana TUC promotes awareness, among women workers, of sexual harassment. It hopes that this will pave the way for the problem to be covered in collective bargaining.[36] In Spain collective agreements have been negotiated at the sectoral level to impose sanctions on employees committing acts of sexual harassment and to provide disciplinary measures for offences (ILO, 1992).

Some trade union bodies have also developed model sexual harassment clauses to be included in the drawing up of collective agreements by their affiliates. The Malaysian Trade Union Congress has, for example, published in three languages (English, Malay and Tamil) a trade union guide on sexual harassment at work which contains a sample clause and grievance procedure to be included in collective agreements.

Trade unions can raise awareness of, and provide training on, the problem of sexual harassment at work. However, this is a particularly difficult challenge for many trade unions as they are often headed by men who may not be sensitive to the issue. Study material for East African women in trade unions, produced by women trade unionists from COTU in Kenya, JUWATA in Tanzania and NOTU in Uganda, includes sexual harassment as a topic. AFRO-FIET has called on its affiliates to develop and distribute educational materials to inform members of the nature of sexual harassment, to advise them on what to do if they become victims and to publicize the issue through articles in union newsletters and discussions at trade union meetings (AFRO-FIET, 1991).

The Civil Service Union in Argentina has produced a brochure on sexual harassment which defines and gives recommendations for trade union action (Secretaria Gremial, 1991). Trade unions in the industrialized countries have produced numerous guides and leaflets in addition to running awareness-raising programmes for their members and training seminars for trade union officials. The Irish Congress of Trade Unions has, for example, produced guidelines which also include a model agreement.

Advisory services

Advisory services can help victims identify ways to act and provide much-needed emotional support. A major challenge in this respect is the situation in smaller enterprises, where it may be the actual employer who is perpetrating acts of sexual harassment. In these circumstances, trade unions, governments and women's organizations can provide the advisory services to assist victims of sexual harassment to identify the course of action to be taken.

A women's group in the Philippines, the General Assembly Binding Women for Reform, Integrity, Equality, Leadership and Action (GABRIELA), provides support services to victims of sexual harassment, such as counselling, legal assistance and lobbying for speedy investigation and resolution of cases.[37] The Women Against Sexual Harassment organization (WASH) in the United Kingdom offers free and confidential advice to anyone who has been sexually harassed at work (WASH, 1990). The Employment Equality Agency in Ireland advises complainants on their legal rights and the procedure for lodging complaints (Employment Equality Agency, 1990).

International action

Intergovernmental organizations and international organizations of trade unions and employers are also addressing the problem of sexual harassment. Concern with sexual harassment at work has, for example, been expressed by the International Labour Organization through resolutions, adopted by the International Labour Conference in 1985 and 1991, several seminars and other meetings and publications (ILO, 1992; Husbands, 1992). It has emphasized the need for combative and preventive action and has also pointed to the need to address the problem both as a sex discrimination issue and as a problem of the working environment.

Action by the United Nations includes calls for specific measures to prevent sexual harassment at work by: the Nairobi Forward-Looking Strategies for the Advancement of Women and the Platform for Action, adopted in 1985 and 1995 respectively by the Third and Fourth World Conferences on Women; and the United Nations Convention on the Elimination of All Forms of Discrimination against Women, 1979.

The Commission of the European Union is probably the regional organization that has been most active in trying to address the problem of sexual harassment at work. Over the last decade a number of initiatives, such as a resolution and a recommendation with a code of practice, have been taken to address the issue.

International trade union and employers' groups have also been active in addressing sexual harassment. For example, in 1986 the Women's Bureau of the International Confederation of Free Trade Unions (ICFTU) published a trade union guide on sexual harassment at work (ICFTU, 1986). In 1992, at its 15th World Congress in Venezuela, the ICFTU adopted a resolution in which it confirms that sexual harassment is a legitimate trade union concern (ICFTU, 1992). The Union of Industrial and Employers' Confederations of Europe (UNICE) agrees that sexual harassment at work must be condemned and prevented and that employers and employees both have the responsibility to create a climate at work which is free from unwanted conduct of a sexual nature.[38]

Conclusion

In many parts of the world sexual harassment has now been recognized and measures taken to combat it. However, progress is uneven and much effort is still required to mobilize governments, employers' and workers' organizations to address this 'occupational hazard'. While laws can do much to provide a framework for action, it is public opinion and changes in social attitudes towards women that will eventually have the greatest impact on eradicating sexual harassment. Recognizing the phenomenon of sexual harassment as harmful to victims, enterprises and society is the first and most important step, as well as probably the most difficult. A major shift in consciousness is needed to ensure that sexual harassment at work is not perceived as a trivial and personal matter and that it is treated as an act of sex discrimination and an unacceptable condition of work. Raising awareness in schools, universities and other educational institutions is of strategic importance for setting the stage later on in workplaces and social structures.

Acting on the problem of sexual harassment must include providing avenues for the victim of sexual harassment to complain without fear of retaliation or ending up as the accused through the stringent tests involved in proving allegations. Appropriate workplace complaint procedures are an ideal way to provide such guarantees. Legislation and government agencies can go a long way in assisting complainants where solutions cannot be found within the enterprise. Special attention will need to be given to devising ways of reaching women most vulnerable to sexual harassment.

Notes

1. Women and Youth Directorate, Organization of Tanzania Trade Unions, 'Protection against sexual harassment at work in developing countries' Tanzanian country paper prepared for the ILO, September 1993.

2. Selangor Consumers Association, Women Graduates Association, Women's Aid Organization, Young Women's Christian Association and the Malaysian Trade Union Congress' Women's Section.

3. United Nations, 'Declaration on the Elimination of Violence Against Women', New York, A/RES/48/104, General Assembly, 20 December 1993.

4. Selangor Consumers Association, Women Graduates Association, Women's Aid Organization, Young Women's Christian Association and the Malaysian Trade Union Congress' Women's Section.

5. 'Women: Where do you go from here?' in *Philippine Labour Review* (Manila), Vol. 15, No.1, January–June 1991.

6. Women and Youth Directorate, Organization of Tanzania Trade Unions: 'Protection against sexual harassment at work in developing countries', Tanzanian country paper prepared for the ILO, September 1993.

7. 'Measures to prevent sexual harassment in Jamaica', Country paper prepared for the ILO, August 1993.

8. Country monograph on sexual harassment in the Philippines, prepared for the ILO, October 1993.

9. United States Merit Systems Protection Board, 1981, 'Sexual harassment in the federal workplace – Is it a problem?', Washington, US Government Printing Office.

10. Women and Youth Directorate, Organization of Tanzania Trade Unions: 'Protection against sexual harassment at work in developing countries', Tanzanian country paper prepared for the ILO, September 1993.

11. Tokyo Metropolitan Government: Koyo biyodo o kangaeru 5: Sexual harassment he nanda ro? (Thinking about equal employment No. 5: What is sexual harassment?); Koyo biyodo o kangaeru 6: Romu kanritoshiteno sexual harassment (Thinking about equal employment No. 6: Sexual harassment: A labour relations issue), March 1992.

12. Study commissioned by the Dutch Government and conducted by the University of Groningen. Information on sexual harassment in the Netherlands reported to the ILO by Alie Kuiper, May 1992.

13. Information reported to the ILO in 1992 by Quentin Bryce, Australian Federal Sex Discrimination Commissioner at the time.

14. United States Merit Systems Protection Board, 1981, 'Sexual harassment in the federal workplace – Is it a problem?', Washington, US Government Printing Office.

15. 'Measures to prevent sexual harassment in Jamaica', Country paper prepared for the ILO, August 1993.

16. Country monograph on sexual harassment in the Philippines, prepared for the ILO, October 1993.

17. Secrétariat d'Etat aux droits des femmes et à la consommation, 1991, *Le harcèlement sexuel; enquête auprès des français: Perception, opinions et évaluation du phénomène (Sexual harassment: Survey of the perceptions and opinions of the French and evaluation of the phenomenon)*, Paris.

18. Study commissioned by the Dutch Government and conducted by the University of Groningen. Information on sexual harassment in the Netherlands reported to the ILO by Alie Kuiper, May 1992.

19. 1991 survey of approximately 1,350 women by the Danish Gallup Institute. Information reported to the ILO by Hanne Petersen and Gitte Mogensen, February 1992.

20. Women's Secretariat, FNV.

21. Resolution of the 14th Conference of the Asian and Pacific Regional Organization of the International Confederation of Free Trade Unions, meeting in Bangkok, Thailand, 4–6 August 1988 on the Promotion of Equality in Employment and Development for Women, in *Asian and Pacific Labour*, July–August 1988.

22. Country monograph on sexual harassment in the Philippines, prepared for the ILO, October 1993.

23. Tokyo Metropolitan Government: Koyo biyodo o kangaeru 5: Sexual harassment he nanda ro? (Thinking about equal employment No. 5: What is sexual harassment?); Koyo biyodo o kangaeru 6: Romu kanritoshiteno sexual harassment (Thinking about equal employment No. 6: Sexual harassment: A labour relations issue), March 1992.

24. M. Barrig, M. Chueca and A.M. Yañez, 1984, 'Anzuelo sin carnada. Obreras en la industria de conserva de pescado', Lima.

25. The Committee against Sexual Harassment, 'Domestic Violence and Discrimination against Women and Children', Dar es Salaam, Tanzania, October 1991–May 1992.

26. Country monograph on sexual harassment in the Philippines, prepared for the ILO, October 1993.

27. Resolution of the Association of Agricultural Workers, VIII Assembly of the Movement of Agricultural and Livestock Women Workers for Employment, Property and Equality. Not a Step Backwards, 6–7 March 1993, Managua.

28. Secrétaire d'Etat à l'emancipation sociale, 1986, 'Sex collègue Ex-collègue: Un dossier sur le harcèlement sexuel sur les lieux de travail', Brussels.

29. Act No. 17, 22 April 1988, Puerto Rico.

30. Dominican Republic, Section 47(9), Act N° 16-92 of 29 May 1992 promulgating the Labour Code.

31. Labour Act, 1992 (Act 6 of 1992), dated 26 March 1992, Government Gazette of the Republic of Namibia, 8 April 1992, No. 388, pp. 2–151.

32. Janzen v. Platy Enterprises, 1989, op. cit.

33. *Clarin*, Buenos Aires, 17–23 August 1993.

34. 45 Federal Register 74,677 (10 November 1980), codified in 29 Code of Federal Regulations (CFR), Section 1604.11(a).

35. Responses to ILO Survey on Collective Bargaining and the Promotion of Equality, 1992.

36. Ibid.

37. Country monograph on sexual harassment in the Philippines, prepared for the ILO, October 1993.

38. UNICE comments on draft recommendation on the protection of the dignity of women and men at work, Brussels, 1991.

References

AFRO-FIET (1991) 'Resolution on sexual harassment', Regional women's seminar for English-speaking Africa, Lusaka, Zambia, 11–14 November.

Bureau de l'égalité (1993) *Harcèlement sexuel, la réalité cachée des femmes au travail* (Sexual harassment, the hidden reality of women at work), Geneva.

Commission of the European Union (1992) 'Recommendation on the protection of the dignity of women and men at work and code of practice on measures to combat sexual harassment', in *Official Journal of the European Communities*, Vol. 35, L.49 (Brussels), February.

Committee for Asian Women (1991) *Many paths, one goal: Organizing women workers in Asia*, Hong Kong.

Danish Gallup Institute (1991) *1991 survey of approximately 1,350 women*, Copenhagen.

Elliot and Shanahan Research (1990) 'Young women in the workplace – An awareness and attitude survey – Sexual harassment', in Pemberton Advertising, North Sydney.

Employment Equality Agency (1990) 'Annual Report', Dublin.

Fitzgerald, L. and A. Ormerod (1991) 'Breaking silence: The sexual harassment of women in academia and the workplace', in F. Denmark and M. Paludi (eds), *Handbook of the psychology of women*, New York, Greenwood Press.

Fuentes, M.C. *et al.* (1988) *Discriminaciyn y acosa sexual a la mujer en el trabajo (Discrimination and sexual harassment of women at work)*, Madrid, Fundación Caballero.

Husbands, R. (1992) 'Sexual harassment law in employment: An international perspective', in *International Labour Review*, Vol. 131, No. 6, Geneva, ILO.

ICFTU (1992) *Resolution in equality: The continuing challenge – strategies for success*, 15th World Congress, Caracas, Venezuela, 17–24 March.

ICFTU Women's Bureau (1986) *Sexual harassment at work: A trade union guide*, Brussels, December.

ILO (1992)   *Combating sexual harassment at work, Conditions of Work Digest*, Vol. 11, Geneva.

—— (1993) 'A comprehensive women's employment strategy for Indonesia', Final report of an ILO/UNDP TSS1 Mission, Bangkok.

Made, P. and B. Lagerström (1985) *Zimbabwean women in industry*, Harare, Zimbabwe Publishing House.

Prasad, S. Sahay (1988) *Tribal women labourers: Aspects of economic and physical exploitation*, New Delhi, Gian Publishing House.

Secretaria Gremial (1991) *Acoso Sexual*, Subsecretaria Gremial de la Mujer, Union del Personnel Civil de la Nación, Buenos Aires, Argentina.

The Times (1993) 20 October, London.

WASH (1990) *Sexual harassment of women in the workplace: A guide to legal action*, London, Women Against Sexual Harassment.

7
Equality of treatment between men and women in social security and in family responsibilities[1]

ANNE-MARIE BROCAS

Instruments of international labour legislation reflect progress in the way the concerns of women have been taken into account. The traditional concept of women's protection, which focused mainly on their maternity and reproductive role, has subsequently been broadened to guarantee equality of treatment between men and women in employment. This development is reflected in international labour conventions including Convention No. 100, concerning equal remuneration (1952), and 111, dealing with elimination of discrimination (employment and occupation) (1951). The process accelerated in the 1970s and found expression in resolutions adopted and in the United Nations Convention on the Elimination of All Forms of Discrimination against Women (1979). One particular outcome is the recognition that men as well as women have family responsibilities and that men and women workers with such responsibilities should be granted specific protection to guarantee them equality of treatment with those without such responsibilities. It is in this spirit that international labour Convention No. 156 and Recommendation No. 165 concerning workers with family responsibilities were adopted in 1981. Furthermore, in 1985, the International Labour Conference adopted a resolution on equality of opportunity and treatment in employment, which called for measures to remedy situations in which women receive social security benefits not equal to those of men. In addition, the ILO Governing Body's Working Party on International Labour Standards in 1987[2] and the ILO Committee of Experts on the Application of Conventions and Recommendations in 1989[3] identified equality of treatment between men and women in matters of social security as requiring new international labour instruments. To this end, there are ongoing studies. The Platform for Action adopted by the Fourth World Conference on Women (1995) also called for review of social security systems to ensure equality in them between women and men.

From the 1980s, a number of countries have made real progress in equality legislation and in obtaining a massive flow of women into gainful employment. Significant developments occurred in social security legislation aimed at ensuring that women were given equality of treatment with men in this sphere. Nevertheless, the economic difficulties that have affected most regions of the world over the past 15 years, and other socio-economic changes, have slowed down progress considerably. Moreover, there is no certainty that objectives of even the recent past are still valid in the current changing context.

Rising levels of women's employment have made it possible to improve women's right to social protection. However, there are limitations to these improvements and the first section of this chapter tries to determine why this is so. The analysis shows just how heavily the bearing and raising of children still weigh on women, and how severely women's maternal responsibilities penalize them in their employment and career opportunities. The development of arrangements to reconcile employment and family responsibilities seems more than ever the key to any progress towards equality of treatment. The next section of this chapter examines the actual scope of social security arrangements that have been introduced and their impact on the employment of women. In the past, progress in women's employment and changes in the way men and women share roles within the family have suggested that perhaps the time has come to abandon the concept of 'derived rights' in favour of autonomous social protection for non-working women, in the form of 'personal rights'. Current thinking on this matter is the subject of another section of the chapter. 'Personal rights' refer to the rights of an individual to social benefits in her or his own name. These rights may stem from the individual's own employment activity or residence in a particular country and are independent of marital or family situation. 'Derived rights' are an individual's rights to social benefits because of her or his dependence on another individual (usually a spouse) who is covered by social insurance.

Improvement in women's social protection rights, but more required

The progress in women's employment has made it possible to broaden social cover for women in most countries, by means of social security schemes based on the criterion of gainful employment. These are basic schemes in countries with a Bismarck-type social security system and occupational schemes in countries with a Beveridge-type system. Under the Bismark-type social security system, individuals make contributions to it and derive benefits dependent upon their level of contribution. Under the Beveridge-type system, contributions are made to it by the state. This type of system is geared to the needy. However, the above newly acquired women's rights are still of limited scope because of the flexible nature of many women's employment and other specific ways in which women are integrated into the world of work and their great vulnerability to fluctuations in business activity. Achievements to date may be measured by considering the scope of social protection granted to women in gainful employment, taking into account the specific characteristics of women's employment, and the comparative level of rights granted to women and men in comparable employment situations.

Prospects for extending social cover for working women vary from country to country and from region to region. In the industrialized market-economy countries, progress has been appreciable but less rapid than might be expected from the growth that has occurred in women's employment. Rising female employment has had extremely positive effects on women's social rights. However, this improvement has been limited because growth in the employment of women has been mainly in part-time and intermittent wage-earning jobs, or in self-employment. Since in these jobs women work only a limited number of hours, or have earnings which do not exceed a set level, they are often excluded from the protection provided by social security schemes, especially those of the occupational type. To improve women's social cover, social security schemes have to give priority to making these types of jobs eligible for an adequate level of social protection. A number of countries have taken steps in this direction, and also towards protecting women working with their spouse in a family enterprise.

Paragraph 21 of the international labour Recommendation on Workers with Family Responsibilities 1981 (No. 165) states that: 'the terms and conditions of employment, including social security coverage, of part-time workers and temporary workers should be, to the extent possible, equivalent to those of full-time and permanent workers respectively; in appropriate cases, their entitlement may be calculated on a *pro rata* basis'. In the same way, Article 6 of the international Convention on Part-Time Work 1994 (No. 175) lays down that 'Statutory social security schemes which are based on occupational activity shall be adapted so that part-time workers enjoy equivalent conditions to those of comparable full-time workers'. However, Article 8 of this Convention also accepts entry thresholds, except in the case of employment injury benefits and occupational diseases, provided that these thresholds are sufficiently low not to exclude an unduly large percentage of part-time workers. Furthermore, the European Court of Justice has ruled that the exclusion of part-time workers from a private pension scheme or from entitlement to sickness payments is contrary to the provisions of the Treaty of Rome, when such a measure affects a much greater number of women than men, unless the enterprise or the member state can demonstrate that such a measure is attributable to factors that were objectively justified and in no way related to any discrimination based on sex. Moreover, some countries have changed the conditions for granting social benefits so as to adjust the method of calculation and reduce or eliminate minimum periods of employment or minimum wage levels, which have the de facto effect of excluding persons working beneath these thresholds from benefiting from ordinary social protection. Nevertheless, initiatives of this type continue to be dispersed and fragmentary. Among the examples of countries with adjustments in the method of determining entitlement to, and amounts of, social benefits in part-time work are Belgium, France, Italy and Canada.

In many family firms, the work done by the spouse, most often the wife, is essential, although the business does not always generate enough profits for the spouse to be paid a real wage, even though she or he may be a co-owner. A number of national initiatives have reflected concern that this work should be duly recognized. Germany, Luxembourg and the United States are among the examples of countries where social protection has been established for persons working with a spouse who is an individual entrepreneur or farmer.

Any attempt to increase social cover for women working in special types of employment is confronted with the problem of the woman's own ability to pay the related contributions. It would, therefore, seem difficult significantly to improve women's situations without requiring greater financial redistribution from persons holding stable, well-paid jobs to persons working in precarious, poorly paid jobs. In this respect, there is a worrying trend towards making some social security schemes more contributory. This trend can be seen in practice in the expanding role being accorded to private occupational schemes whilst, at the same time, the basic level of protection is cut back.

In the countries of Eastern and Central Europe there is danger of regression, linked to the effects of economic liberalization and adjustment of employment and social security schemes. In the past, all benefits stemmed from employment and everybody without due dispensation had the right and duty to work. Rights to social benefits were derived from employment and were therefore in practice guaranteed to all. Social protection was financed globally. With the current

transition from central gove
these countries, there is now a
working women against social conti
tion in these countries is undermining
protection, under which women benefited
This includes in particular: maternity and dep
enabling them to reconcile gainful employment and
ties in a satisfactory manner (this point will be develo
low-priced basic commodities and services (food, hous
transport), which took some pressure off the family budget it
ally managed by women. Second, there is a reappearance of previ
half-forgotten risks in these countries. They include increasingly expen
sive basic commodities and services and, more generally, price inflation
of key items in family budgets, which penalizes those receiving social
benefits, especially women (family allowances, old-age pensions); and
unemployment, which is already widespread among women.

These ongoing social security reforms need to extend the social
cover of working women. The reforms are based on efforts to clarify
social protection provisions and to distinguish between what should fall
under national solidarity (financed out of taxation) and under social insurance (financed by earnings-based contributions). Thus, in most of
the countries in question, the state has been entrusted with administer-
ing family allowances and the social security institutions with managing
the financing of health care and retirement pensions (as is the case in
Russia, the Czech Republic, Slovakia, Hungary and Romania). At the
same time, thought is also being given to the introduction of private
occupational schemes. Finally, these reforms are aimed at improving
protection against new contingencies by instituting unemployment insurance benefits, bolstering social assistance schemes and developing
rules to protect the purchasing power of cash benefits.

The changes are bringing social protection schemes of these countries closer to those of Western Europe. However, as far as working
women are concerned, they raise questions relating to health care and
old-age pensions. Financing health care through social contributions inevitably raises the problem of health-care access for inactive or unemployed persons who do not pay contributions or who are not covered
through a contributor. Similarly, with regard to old-age pensions, the
ending of the era of full employment deprives women of the guarantee
of a contribution-based retirement pension. Thus, for the future, it
will be necessary to make arrangements for providing adequate non-
contributory old-age pensions, where these do not already exist.

...gether with

, raise ques-

...social groups,

...attractions of

...re is a danger

...o women. Such

...strengthen assis-

...c minimum bene-

...veloping countries,

...ecession in many of

...ence for social pro-

...lowered basic family

...significantly reduced

...schemes. Furthermore,

the ec... ...ogrammes that were in-troduced led to ... , especially in the social sector and in food aid.

Thus, whereas economic recessi... ...tabilization tended to increase poverty and the need for aid, in most developing countries the ability of public structures and social security schemes to intervene has been whittled away. Women have been hit hard by this process. There has been a reduction in their access to care (especially for maternity and child-care) and to food subsidy needed for the survival of urban households (for which women often have a large part of the subsistence responsibility). The immediate prospect of them obtaining greater social protection (in the rural, informal and small-enterprise sectors) also does not appear to be bright.

The desirable objective seems to be wide social security coverage of the population, to benefit both men and women working in the formal urban sector just as much as those working in the informal and rural sectors. However, in view of the limited resources available, and the equally limited potential base for social contributions, it is necessary to identify priority needs accurately, target carefully the social protection introduced to meet these needs and establish social protection approaches which may vary depending on the populations for which they are intended. This also means using financing procedures into which contributions are made by those requiring cover whenever they are able; and which also permit payments to be made when the target groups are either unable or not fully able to pay.

In defining the rights which they grant their members, social security schemes still refer widely to the traditional social roles of men and women. For this reason, they grant women specific benefits that reflect their particular contribution to the support and education of their children. Conversely, the rights that women obtain from the contributions levied on their income from gainful employment may have removed from them certain advantages reserved for men in their role as head of the family. There is no denying that men's and women's roles in society continue to change considerably throughout the world. Under such conditions, various solutions have been adopted in different regions of the world towards equality of treatment in social protection. These are examined below by distinguishing between the entitlements that a woman derives for herself from her gainful employment and those that are granted to her in respect of her dependants.

In some social security schemes, the idea of a woman's dependence results in the entitlements that a woman has or could have as a dependent person prevailing over those that she acquires as a result of her gainful employment. Thus, in these schemes, a working woman, especially if she is married, has no or only reduced personal rights. However, the presumption operates in the opposite direction through the granting of automatic additional advantages to women, and to women alone, in respect of the cost of bringing up their children.

Two types of 'advantage' are granted automatically to women in a number of old-age pension schemes, which are not available to men. They are earlier retirement age, and entitlement supplements or credited periods and other forms of compensation for interruptions in gainful employment linked to the bringing up of children. It is common practice to set the retirement age for women lower than that for men. The difference is usually five years. Whatever the justifications for it, they seem lacking in conviction from the point of view of the principle of equality. The relative shortness of the working careers of some women (because of interruptions for maternity and child-care) and their greater life expectancy should encourage them to work as long as possible, in particular to improve their pensions. In addition, in a difficult employment context, the right to an earlier retirement – far from giving women an advantage – is likely to penalize them by justifying the pressure exerted by employers for them to withdraw from the labour market. Many countries have already looked at the question of reducing the gap between the retirement ages of men and women, and have decided to replace their progressive increase in the age of retirement for women with the same retirement age for both sexes. However, recently instituted retirement schemes in most developing countries – with the notable exception of Ghana (1991) – still stipulate different ages of retirement for men and women.

Pension supplements or bonuses granted automatically to women to compensate for the disadvantages of bringing up their children raise more questions. They are often granted without the woman having to give any proof that she actually interrupted her employment career to bring up her children. In actual fact, they make it possible to attenuate the overall consequences of chaotic careers and low wages on women's acquired rights. The concept of equality of treatment that prevailed in the mid-1970s was to lead to these advantages being reserved for women and men who actually did interrupt their gainful employment to bring up their children (like the old-age pension insurance for non-working parents in France). Paragraph 3 of Article 6 of the Social Protocol to the Treaty of Maastricht stipulates that the principle of equality of remuneration between men and women workers 'shall not prevent any member State from maintaining or adopting measures providing for specific advantages in order ... to prevent or compensate for disadvantages in their (women's) occupational careers'.

Furthermore, in many social security schemes, a wife – unlike the husband – has to prove that she is the family breadwinner to obtain recognition of derived entitlements for persons dependent on her, especially in the case of health care. The same condition often applies in the granting of supplements in old-age or disability benefits for a dependent spouse. Yet it is no longer unusual for a woman to provide, through her gainful employment, for maintenance of the household, either because she is alone or because her husband is unemployed. Finally, it may be that her gainful employment gives her access to a social security scheme which is more favourable than that of her husband. For all these reasons, the principle of equality of treatment has led to the recommendation that benefits or supplements for dependent persons should, at least in future, be granted under the same conditions without distinction by sex. This approach has been put into effect in numerous social security schemes in both industrialized and developing countries as regards the benefits payable to the surviving spouse of a deceased old-age or disability pensioner. The choice usually made reserves the survivor's benefits to those men or women who are actually in need, in view of their personal resources on the death of the male or female insured person.

It seems desirable to undertake, with respect to insured women's personal rights, a progressive alignment of men's and women's retirement ages, which will allow women to improve their pension rights in certain systems. On the other hand, one may question the desirability of suppressing the advantages currently granted automatically to women in old-age pension schemes. With regard to the insured woman's eligibility for benefits relating to dependants, it seems desirable to allow family allowances to be granted to the parent who makes the choice.

Arrangements to reconcile gainful employment and family responsibilities: maternity protection, family and parental leave and child-care support

Women's working lives are affected by the presence of children in the family. If progress is to be made towards equality of treatment, it is essential to make due allowance for these burdens women have to bear. Pregnancy and maternity, which are characteristics of womanhood, place women in a position in which they are temporarily unable to pursue gainful employment, and call for special social protection which reflects, by its extent and complexity, the state's recognition of this social function. Maternity protection, for example, has been constantly improved.

In almost all cases, it is the woman who assumes responsibility for looking after the children. The Workers with Family Responsibilities Convention 1981 (No. 156) and Recommendation No. 165 emphasize the principle of equality of treatment in this sphere. They therefore emphasize the development of arrangements to provide women and men with better opportunities to reconcile family and occupational responsibilities, thereby promoting the notion that both parents should play a role in raising children. The arrangements include leave of absence (parental leave) and educational leave. Finally, children in the family give rise to other types of collective responsibility: family allowances, taxation arrangements and child-care systems. These arrangements, which are spreading significantly throughout the world, make an important contribution to child-care.

Health protection and cash benefit schemes represent some of the areas of progress in social protection for pregnant women and mothers. Increasingly there is a high level of health protection in a number of regions. As part of public health policies, systematic medical check-ups (usually free of charge) have been introduced for pregnant women and young children. Very many countries have set up prevention programmes based on vaccination, medical examinations for children and health education. The general application of maternity health insurance and improvements in health schemes are aimed in particular at maternity-related care. Most countries with adequate health infrastructure pay, as part of their social security or health schemes, the cost of care and hospitalization during pregnancy, delivery and the postnatal period. This is the case in most developed countries. However, major inequalities continue in the level of health cover provided to mothers and infants. In the developing countries, the situation varies. Although most Latin American, Asian and Middle-Eastern countries have organized health protection for mothers within their social policies, in sub-Saharan Africa this protection, usually implemented through the activities of social security institutions, has not been significant.

In Eastern Europe and the Commonwealth of Independent States (or the ex-USSR), large segments of the female population have found themselves marginalized and are destitute owing to the economic crisis. The health service has also deteriorated. The ability of strictly contributory social security or even private schemes to respond to these situations is questionable. Unemployed women are excluded from arrangements of this type. In order to guarantee all mothers access to maternity care, these schemes should be at least supplemented by social assistance arrangements or free care (such as dispensaries) of adequate scope. In countries with less well-developed health infrastructures, it seems essential to give priority to basic health services such as mother and baby care and health education.

Most countries have established women's right to maternity leave and guaranteed the protection of pregnant women in their employment through maintenance of employment, seniority and old-age pension rights. Social security schemes have subsequently dealt with maternity by organizing cash benefits equal to all or part of the mother's previous earnings. This help to families when a child is born is one of the aspects of social security which is tending to expand rather than contract. Indeed, maternity protection in social security schemes has improved markedly over the past 20 years (ILO, 1995). In recent years, health care cost-containment policies have not really slowed down the trend observed since 1975. In nearly all countries which have introduced maternity protection changes, they have been aimed at making this protection more substantial.

In the industrialized market-economy countries, the scope of maternity leave has continued to expand to a position where it now covers virtually every single working woman, and the length of this leave has also been extended. In most of these countries, maternity leave is longer, and in many cases significantly so, than the minimum standard of 12 weeks laid down in the International Labour Maternity Protection Convention, 1919 (No. 3) and the Maternity Protection Convention (Revised), 1952 (No. 103). This standard has been raised to 14 weeks by the European Union (directive 92/85). Similarly, the amount of the benefits paid has been increased and adapted to the individual situation of the women in question. Nowadays, these benefits are usually proportional to the beneficiary's previous earnings. In the majority of industrial countries, this proportion is equal to or greater than the two-thirds specified in Convention No. 103. The countries of Eastern Europe had long ago instituted lengthy and very well-paid maternity leave. It seems that the changes with economic restructuring in these countries will – in the short term at least – affect the benefits granted to mothers.

In the newly industrializing countries, significant progress has been made in maternity protection. Entitlements granted have grown to reach or even, in some cases, exceed ILO standards. Thus, women workers in the formal sector in Latin America, the Caribbean and Asia are now relatively well protected in this respect. However, in all developing countries, a very large part of the population, made up of women who in fact work, remain unprotected due to the small part of the working population in the formal sector for whom social security is reserved. It would seem important to extend maternity leave to as large a proportion as possible of the population of women workers, no matter the type or nature of their job.

Moreover, according to international labour standards, maternity allowances must be paid within the framework of a compulsory insurance scheme or financed by public funds, and in no case by the employers themselves. Yet, in a number of developing countries, this principle is not observed. In Africa, for example, this is the case in many countries. Consequently, it is feared that employers use this to discriminate against women's recruitment by choosing not to recruit women of child-bearing age if they themselves are required to pay the cost of maternity leave. In Burkina Faso, however, under the pressure of the trade unions, the National Social Security Fund now pays a mother's wage for the three months of maternity leave.

Family and parental leave has also to be considered in any attempt to promote true equality of treatment and opportunity between male and female workers. The Workers with Family Responsibilities Convention (No. 156) and Recommendation (No. 165), adopted in 1981 by the International Labour Conference, recognize the importance of sharing responsibilities, by stressing that both men and women are able to take over the care of the family. Some countries, especially the Nordic ones, served as path breakers in this area from the end of the 1970s.

Currently a significant number of countries, as well as granting short-term leave of absence, provide prolonged maternity leave with supplementary leave for the bringing up of young children. During such leave of absence, which may last for a few weeks or a few years, women are granted protection against dismissal or occupational reclassification. In some cases, this leave of absence may be accompanied by a guarantee that the worker's acquired rights and social security cover will be maintained.

In order to facilitate further the harmonization of family and employment responsibilities, various countries, such as Austria, Finland, France and Sweden, allow the combination of parental leave of absence and part-time work. Finally, some countries have instituted a prolongation of parental leave entitlement for the bringing up of young children. The way in which these benefits are granted varies and ranges from linkage with the ranking of the child to means testing or the requirement of prior employment.[4]

The development of parental leave has often been accompanied by diverse types of parental benefits within the social security schemes. In many industrialized countries in particular, periods devoted to the bringing up of children are taken into account in the calculation of pension rights. In calculating the duration of insurance contributions, basic schemes based on earnings-related contributions take into account periods of interruption in gainful employment for which an allowance is paid under maternity leave.

The European Union recently carried out a study in several member states to evaluate measures to remove obstacles preventing parents from working. The results show clearly that, after payment of social security contributions and taxes and collection of social benefits, it is expenditure on care for very young children that most reduces net disposable income in families where both parents work.

Several countries have introduced a series of measures to promote child-minding arrangements. For example, France has introduced two specifically targeted allowances: family assistance for employing a qualified maternal assistant (AFEAMA), and an allowance for minding children at home (AGED). The aim is to provide compensation for the amount of social security contributions incurred in employing a person to look after the children. These measures, which have an explicit twin objective of creating new jobs and of absorbing people from the labour black market, are doubly beneficial to women since they offer employment of mothers and of women child-minders. Some countries have sometimes offered tax relief, in the form of a tax deduction or credit, for expenses incurred in the employment of domestic staff or recourse to child-minding services or establishments.

Furthermore, the establishment and development of group services may go a long way towards helping women combine a job with motherhood. In some countries, many pre-school and school-age children are looked after by individual persons, usually women such as 'family day minders' in the United States and 'minder mothers' in Venezuela, who are paid to look after children at home. This system, organized by the public authorities to guarantee a certain quality of care (such as in training and hygiene) is a minimum form of group child-minding service. Other more sophisticated group structures include public and parental crèches, approved nurses, child-care stopovers, holiday centres, playschools, kindergartens or pre-school centres.

Traditionally in the countries of Eastern and Central Europe, a vast network of free family services existed. Today, the financial difficulties faced by many of these public enterprises have adversely affected this practice. In addition, the new private enterprises may not necessarily consider it a priority to provide their employees with this type of service. The future of these arrangements, which have proved their effectiveness for women's employment, now seems to be in serious danger.

Child-care programmes have been developed in many countries of Latin America, Asia and the Middle East. They have sometimes occurred in response to a legal obligation for undertakings which employ a certain number of women to provide child-care. This obligation marks a significant advance in this area but may pose a danger for women's employment, especially when it applies only to enterprises employing more than a specific number of women. Employers may well seek to avoid this obligation simply by not hiring women at or above the prescribed threshold.

The simultaneous expansion of support services and structures, opportunities for leave of absence and the family's financial resources are an essential step towards achieving greater equality of treatment. However, the measures should avoid the trap of indirectly promoting the reconciliation of family life and occupational activity by strengthening the traditional division of functions between men and women.

Derived or personal rights in the present circumstances?

The benefits women may receive on the basis of their gainful employment are still far below the levels achieved by men, despite their increased economic participation. Responsibility for children in most cases still falls on the woman. This means that they are more often required to interrupt their employment or re-arrange their working hours or type of work, or simply give up gainful employment completely (policies in times of high unemployment may tend to encourage them to adopt this course).

In social security systems based on gainful employment, women's economic dependence on husbands also brings about dependence in social security cover. Non-working women cannot benefit from personal rights, entitlement to which is gained through the contributions of an insured man with whom they live. They can obtain entitlement in their own right only in universal schemes in which the entire resident population, gainfully employed or not, is entitled to receive the same amount of benefits, independent of their level of earned income. These schemes, which guarantee basic protection for the whole population, are usually supplemented by contributory schemes based on gainful employment, which guarantee benefits linked to previous income and higher than the subsistence level.

Debate has traditionally centred on the alternatives: personal rights or derived rights. The idea generally accepted in the 1980s was that derived rights' systems, based on the concept of a traditional family model, increasingly do not reflect reality, owing to the changes that have occurred in family structures and the growth of single-parent families. They should give way to personal rights for women. However, without financial transfers, this proposal would be hard to accept. It could be envisaged only if most women were gainfully employed. Analysis of recent social security legislation reforms shows that the effect of economic and social changes in different regions of the world has been to alter the terms of the above debate and to complicate the problem. As far as derived rights are concerned, although developing countries have continued to establish and improve survivors' benefits, industrialized countries have, for their part, attempted in particular to adapt their legislation to the new needs brought about by new economic and family trends.

These changes are, however, still restricted to a small number of countries, and the lack of synchronization between changes in the social environment and morality and changes in legislation have, thus, left gaps in social cover. The difficulty is to find answers, not as in the past for a single family model, but for a multitude of different family models. It seems desirable that, at least as a transitional measure, and for some types of scheme, derived rights should be extended to take into account a variety of family configurations in which women are economically dependent on the person insured although not joined in wedlock.

The problem of divorced or separated housewives is not restricted solely to that of survivors' benefits. These women are highly prone to financial precariousness, both in the immediate future (through difficulties of re-entering gainful employment, reduced resources linked to an occupational status usually lower than that of their ex-husband), and, over the longer term, on retirement (through low pension entitlements as a result of their limited level of work), independently of the death of their husband. Fundamental changes to the systems may, therefore, be necessary with the object of attaining, through the implementation of equality of opportunity and treatment principles for men and women, a situation that better addresses their needs. The concept of social protection requires to be changed from being based on risk to need.

Inherited as it has been from an era when women were dependent on their husbands, the majority of today's social security legislation does not grant widowers benefits equivalent to those provided to widows. Sometimes it makes no provision for the deceased wife's survivor pension rights. Often it attaches to this right a number of very restrictive conditions (total unfitness for work). Consequently, women's work does not have the same status as that of men. Nowadays, changing views mean that the couple are more and more considered as being jointly responsible for the family's well-being. Moreover, the rise in the number of working women combined with the persistence of high levels of unemployment may sometimes lead to an inversion of the sense of economic dependence between the couple. Situations in which the woman's wage is the household's sole income are no longer exceptional. It therefore seems necessary that the insurance effort should result in the same effects for men as for women. A number of countries have recently amended survivors' benefit provisions in this direction, so as to bring into line entitlement conditions for both widows and widowers (age, disability and existence of children).

In countries where the gainful employment of working women is widespread, one needs to examine whether widowers automatically have the right to a survivor's pension when the death of one or other spouse leads to a partial loss of income. The issue should also be raised whether such a right be automatic no matter what the man's situation or whether it is necessary to reconsider the eligibility conditions for granting survivors' pensions with a view to ensuring greater adjustment to the real needs brought about by the spouse's death. Improving survivors' benefits further highlights the difference between the treatment extended to widows (and widowers) and that received by other persons, such as single parents.

In relation to personal rights, the institution of non-contributory rights for housewives comes from the recognition of the value of their household responsibilities. A number of provisions allowing women who interrupt gainful employment to care for their children to maintain their personal social security rights have earlier been described. In some cases, these provisions may not extend beyond making due allowance for short interruptions in gainful employment (validation of maternity leave), whereas in others they may guarantee rights to women who stay permanently at home (such as a housewife's disability pension in Israel, and mothers' old-age insurance in France).

An interesting trend in some countries is to extend this type of protection to persons who provide care for another family member. This gives some degree of recognition to the role of home help that women are increasingly required to carry out for their aged parents or parents-in-law, or their own disabled children, and which does not bring in a wage.

The establishment of individual contributory rights for women has so far followed two courses: voluntary insurance and the sharing of rights between spouses. On account of its high cost, voluntary insurance has had only little success.

Analysis of recent developments in personal rights indicates some progress, albeit modest, in both non-contributory and contributory rights. Pension-splitting or other rights sharing, which in the 1980s was considered a possible response to the problem of personal rights, has made scarcely any tangible progress. Moreover, its underlying philosophy is hardly compatible with concepts developed in recent reforms, which tend to consider each individual as an independent economic entity. Even though it might seem desirable to institute recognized rights such as these for each member of the community, including women not in gainful employment or who have had to interrupt their employment, it is hardly likely that economic and financial conditions will make it possible to envisage their extension over coming years.

In all countries where reforms have been undertaken, their redistributory effects and their actual economic impact on different categories of women need to be examined. Until the establishment of equality in employment and remuneration, equality of social rights will probably accentuate the actual inequality between men and women. A transition will have to be arranged, all the more so since different generations of women co-exist who have not had the same opportunities of access to employment.

The changes described in this chapter point to the need to re-examine the current significance of the principle of equality of treatment between men and women in social security. Up until the early 1980s, there was a trend towards equality of employment between men and women. The principle of equality of treatment thus simply required social security policies to react neutrally to these changes. However, under the effects of economic crisis and the changes that have occurred in most regions of the world, women's employment rates have continued to rise without placing women in an employment situation comparable to that of men.

On the other hand, changes in the respective roles of men and women within the family have not contributed to the emergence of a new and uniform family model but to a great diversity of forms. The length of marriages and the forms they take nowadays vary considerably. There is no certainty that the model that places men and women in identical situations within the family will, in the final analysis, be the reference model of the future. Confronted with these developments, it no longer seems possible to consider the problem of equality of treatment between men and women in social protection solely from the point of view of the sex-neutrality of social security schemes.

More than ever in the current context, priority needs to go to labour law and social schemes that take real account of a woman's own needs as regards having and raising children. Consequently, it is necessary, throughout the world, to guarantee the protection of women during pregnancy and childbirth, starting with health cover, and by granting them, where they are gainfully employed, and no matter what type of job they are doing, paid maternity leave under conditions at least equal to those laid down in international labour standards. Over and above this, arrangements need to be developed to reconcile working and family responsibilities. Diversity in the situations of women and families continues to grow. The needs and aspirations that social schemes are required to meet are, therefore, many and varied.

Furthermore, the effectiveness of existing arrangements in achieving the objectives assigned to them needs to be assessed, taking into account the priorities set by the community that instituted them. Tax-rate adjustments and means testing in social security systems should avoid threshold effects that over-penalize households with two moderate-income workers. Child-care arrangements also deserve to be expanded. When these arrangements are made on a community basis, they offer care to the children of the least well-off, thus compensating for family shortcomings. Social security schemes must take into account the real situation of women not only when they are working, but also when they are not in gainful employment.

Nowadays, most women work in often poor conditions and without adequate social security cover. The flexibility and low cost of women workers are widely exploited to facilitate economic adjustments and the competitiveness of enterprises. In the interests of simple equity and balanced long-term growth, this employment should be recognized and it should entitle women to social security rights that match their needs.

The growing diversity in the situations of women and their families creates difficulties for social security schemes. This trend justifies the launching of studies which can accurately evaluate the needs of various categories of women for adequate consideration in social security arrangements.

Notes

1. This chapter was originally prepared in French by the author using, in part, the regional overviews undertaken by the ILO's Social Security Department for the Interdepartmental project on equality for women in employment and also, in part, other additional data generated by the author. A shortened English translation served as the background paper for the ILO Tripartite Meeting of Experts on Social Security and Social Protection: Equality of Treatment between Men and Women, Geneva 21–25 November 1994, which has since been revised and further abridged for this volume.

2. See ILO, *Report of the Working Party on International Labour Standards,* special issue, Vol. LXX, Series A, Appendix II, Geneva, 1987.

3. See ILO, *Social security protection in old-age. General Survey of the Committee of Experts on the Application of Conventions and Recommendations*, Geneva, 1989.

4. In addition, it should be indicated here that, depending on the countries in question, the benefits may or may not be taxable.

References

Euzéby, C. (1993) *Social protection, inequalities between the sexes*, Manuscript, Geneva, ILO.

Folbre, N. (1993) *Women and social security in Latin American, the Caribbean and Sub-Saharan Africa*, IDP Women/WP-5, Geneva, ILO.

ILO (1995) *Conditions of work digest on maternity protection*, Geneva.

PART III
Enhancing legal effectiveness

8
Analysis of the legal framework for gender equality in employment: Lesotho, a case-study

DAVID TAJGMAN AND EVANCE KALULA

A legal environment supporting equality of women workers in employment goes beyond strict labour law matters governing aspects of employment relationship. This is particularly so in developing countries where formal employment is a minor proportion of labouring activities of women in society. In such cases, laws affecting real and personal property rights, contract and inheritance, medical care and assistance, family life and marriage can have just as much – if not more – influence on women's ability through their work to avoid poverty, and to produce and accumulate wealth. Accordingly, any review of the legal status of women as workers must take fully into account the legal status of women as property owners, contracting parties, wives and mothers. Improvement of the position of women workers through law must therefore seek reform of a broad range of laws. This issue is examined in this chapter through a case-study of Lesotho, undertaken in November 1993.

Law as an instrument of policy

Law gives effect to policy, provided law is given effect. This simple proposition pronounces the relationship between a policy promoting gender equality in employment and provisions that must be made in the law of a country if this policy is to become a reality. In Lesotho today legal contradictions affect gender equality, possibly because there is no uniform policy on the matter. The review below addresses this issue by way of three major themes:

- **Legal impediments to equality** Certain crucial aspects of law affecting gender equality in Lesotho undermine women's equality in work and in self-employment. Equality of opportunity cannot be achieved until these impediments to equality are removed. The points that must be addressed and suggestions for their remedy are raised in this review.

- **Implementation of existing law** A number of very important sources of law in Lesotho, namely the Constitution and the Labour Code Order, establish equality *de jure* and, in some circumstances, provide special protection. Evidence available suggests, however, that these provisions are not yet given full effect. If the policy that these provisions imply is to be made a reality, steps must be taken to enhance the rule of these laws in Lesotho.

- **Ineffective laws can lead to inefficient allocation of resources** Effective laws and legal institutions can act to secure the accumulation and use of productive resources. An 'effective law' is one that is respected, can be given effect and enforced. Productive resources are more likely to be efficiently used when expectations of their use and return can be secured by effective laws. Hence, labour laws which require payment of wages on time and in legal tender – assuming they are enforceable through effective legal institutions – could help people formulate expectations that they will be paid when they work and thus ease their decision to perform work for pay. Similarly, laws that secure property rights permit the formation of expectations which encourage people to accumulate and use property for productive purposes. In Lesotho, laws that make insecure the accumulation and use by women of property, that do not effectively guarantee women's job security in the light of their natural biological functions, or do not effectively ensure workers' full access to opportunities for which they are qualified, tend to undermine the efficient allocation of these real and human resources; they hinder economic development and, for this reason, steps should be taken to remedy the situation.

The Constitution

The Constitution is of fundamental importance. It is the basic law, the basis of all laws. In specific terms and in so far as the employment situation is concerned, the Constitution contains both enabling and disenabling provisions for gender equality.

The Constitution guarantees fundamental human rights and freedoms, including freedom from discrimination. However, the section that prohibits discrimination on the basis of sex, among other criteria, makes extensive qualifications. The effect of this is that some laws and practices that would otherwise infringe freedom from discrimination are valid. As a result, women are denied protection against discrimination in a number of key areas of the law and practice that flow from those laws, for instance, under customary law, and in relation to marriage, divorce, property acquisition and inheritance. The discriminatory elements in these laws adversely affect women's participation in the job market.

Principles of state policy that are relevant to employment are set out in the Constitution. Among them are: equality and justice; opportunity to work; just and favourable conditions of work; and protection of workers' rights and interests. However, these principles of state policy are not justiciable.

Some other provisions of the Constitution also have obvious implications – both positive and negative – for the situation of women in employment. A systematic review of the Constitution needs to be undertaken not only to remove discriminatory provisions but also to make it gender-neutral.

General legal position of Basotho women: minority status, land rights, inheritance, contractual capacity and pension rights

Lesotho has a dual legal system: customary law and Roman-Dutch common Law, two parallel systems of law operating side by side. In some respects, particularly in the areas of marriage, divorce, inheritance and property, customary law applies to the traditional population, while the common law regulates the affairs of those Basotho who have adopted the modern life style. As in many countries which were British colonies, the common law, Roman-Dutch law in the case of Lesotho, supersedes customary law when the two are in conflict.

Much of the adverse discrimination that women face is a result of their legal position. Under both the customary law and common law, women in Lesotho are generally regarded as minors, without full legal capacity. The consequences can be summarized as follows: the women possess no legal capacity to enter into contracts unless they are assisted by husbands or guardians. This position is clearly reflected when a woman needs to acquire property and to have access to credit;[1] women do not have capacity to acquire and own property unless assisted. This is true in terms of ownership of fixed property and movables; women have no *locus standi in judicio*; they cannot be sued and sue in their own names; women do not have capacity to enter into employment contracts without their guardian's or husband's assistance.[2]

The 1976 Insurance Act contains provisions enabling women over 18 to take out life insurance policies as single persons or married persons without their husband's or guardian's consent. This is a positive development that women could take advantage of.

Women have a very disadvantaged status regarding land and other property rights. Under customary law a woman does not acquire any rights over land. The widow's right over land previously held by her husband is a limited right of use (usufruct). She cannot dispose of the property because she holds it on behalf of the heir, usually the eldest son of the deceased's first wife, if it is in a polygamous family, or any male appointed as a customary heir.

The Land Act No. 14 of 1979 regulates acquisition of land generally. In 1987 a Land Policy Review Commission was appointed with broad terms of reference. The Commission was to review land tenure arrangements and administration under the existing law with regard to ownership of land by women.

Section 8 (2) of the Land Act provided, *inter alia*, that at the instance of the death of an allottee, the interest in the land should pass to the first male issue of the deceased allottee or, in his absence, to a person nominated by the surviving member of the family as heir of the deceased allottee's land. Subsection (3) provided further that the surviving female spouse or a minor child of the deceased allottee were 'entitled to remain in occupation of the land during her lifetime'. The provision did not give the widow full title or rights over such land. The first male issue therefore acquired full title while the widow remained in occupation only. These sections were amended by Order No. 6 of 1992 to give the widow full title rights over any land acquired by the deceased. However, such land reverts to the family of the original allottee in the event of remarriage by the widow.

Section 14 of the Deeds Registry Act, 1967 provides specifically that a woman who is married in community of property may not register land. She cannot acquire land in her own name. All such rights are registered in the husband's name, who is the sole administrator of the joint estate. A Land Reform Commission was in the process of being set up in November 1993. This Commission should deal with the issue of women's rights over land as a matter of priority.

The husband as the sole administrator of the joint estate may alienate or mortgage part of the estate without the wife's knowledge or consent. There are legal remedies: for instance, an urgent application may be made to the High Court to restrain the husband from alienating community property if the wife is lucky enough to do it before alienation is effected; or she may apply to the court for it to declare a husband a prodigal or wastrel. These remedies are usually impracticable for most women on account of legal illiteracy and prohibitive legal costs.

A woman who is subject to her husband's marital power requires his assistance to contract. For example to buy a house, obtain a site, get a loan, start a business, purchase furniture or a car on a hire purchase agreement.

In relation to inheritance, under customary law women generally do not inherit in Lesotho. Upon the death of the husband, the eldest son of the first wife is the heir. Where there is no male issue the widow acquires the right of use and occupation (usufruct). She can administer the property but she has no right to dispose of it. The family has the right to appoint the customary male heir.

Under common law, a woman inherits at least half of the estate as a wife, or as a daughter she is entitled to a child's share of her late father's estate (interstate succession). The provision of a will, theoretically speaking, would avoid this discriminatory problem. Again, the question of choice of law arises. A problem is created by Section 3(b) of the Administration of Estates Proclamation, which states that Roman-Dutch law does not apply to estates of Basotho except those who are clearly proved to have abandoned the customary way of life and adopted an western way of life. However, the majority of Basotho make oral wills and dying declarations which have no legal force and effect. It is not common to make written wills.

In contractual terms, under both customary law and common law a woman is generally regarded as a minor without full legal capacity. The position under customary law is that of perpetual minority under guardianship of father, brothers, husband and other members of extended family during and upon the husband's death. Under common law unless a woman marries under an ante-nuptial contract, she marries in community of property under her husband's marital power and is therefore a minor in law. Most women perceive an ante-nuptial contract as a curse on the stability of the prospective marriage and do not take advantage of this type of marriage contract. Besides, many women are unaware of the possibility of contracting a marriage under an ante-nuptial contract.

Concerning *locus standi in judicio*, the piecemeal amendments made to improve the situation of women are limited. A married woman does not have *locus standi in judicio*. Under both customary and common law systems a woman generally cannot sue or be sued in her own name. She has to be duly assisted by her husband.

The incapacities flowing from women's minority status in law are major obstacles to equality for women in most spheres of life in Lesotho, including employment. Minority status restricts women's capacity to realize their full potential and therefore contribute to national development. Reform in this area is therefore a matter of top priority.

In the past, the law was discriminatory against women, with respect to pension rights and job tenure. The situation has now been redressed by the Pensions (Amendment) Order No. 12, 1992 in the case of pension rights. The new Order amended the 1964 Proclamation and gives all women civil servants entitlement to pension rights whether they are married or not. However, pensionability is still optional, with gratuity payment at the end of 10 years for some women.

Some women civil servants are, however, still discriminated against in paid maternity leave. Women on permanent employment terms get paid maternity leave, while the rest do not. This position has not been changed by the 1992 amendment to the Public Service, which affects pensions only.

The Labour Code Order, 1992

The Labour Code Order, 1992 (hereinafter, the Code) very clearly establishes a principle of non-discrimination and equality. This is done in section 5 in a way entirely consistent with international labour standards. There it pronounces:

(1)   The application by any person of any distinction, exclusion or preference made on the basis of race, colour, sex, marital status, religion, political opinion, national extraction or social origin, which has the effect of nullifying or impairing equality of opportunity or treatment in employment or occupation, is incompatible with the provisions of the Code.

(2)   Sexual harassment, as defined (the offering of employment or threatening of dismissal or threatening of the imposition of any other penalty against another person in the course of employment as a means of obtaining sexual favours or the harassing of workers sexually), shall be prohibited.

(3)   Men and women shall receive equal remuneration for work of equal value.

(4)   Any distinction, exclusion or preference in respect of a particular job based on the narrowly defined inherent requirements thereof shall not be deemed an act of unlawful discrimination.

(5)   For the purposes of this section, the term 'employment' and 'occupation' includes access to vocational and other occupationally

related training, access to employment and to particular occupations, retention of employment and any terms or conditions of employment.

As the Code is applicable 'to any employment in the private sector and to any employment by or under the Government, or by or under any public authority, save (persons employed in a non-civilian capacity in certain named disciplined forces)', it should have a broad impact on equality in employment. If there is sex discrimination in Lesotho, recourse can be taken to the legal protection in section 5 of the Labour Code. There is, however, much evidence to suggest the existence of discrimination in employment and occupation in the country. The irony is that there is not much evidence of widespread concern about the issue; the situation appears to be accepted as part of Basotho life and culture. And there do not appear to be widespread initiatives to address gender discrimination through legal recourse, even where it has been recognized. Formal complaints of discrimination to the Department of Labour based on legal rights are not numerous. There has not been one case of employment-related sex discrimination or sexual harassment taken to court – despite many accounts of such occurrences.

Are the legal mechanisms to combat discrimination in the country sufficient? The ILO's Discrimination (Employment and Occupation) Convention (No. 111), speaks in very broad terms about the subject, establishing an obligation to ban distinctions on the basis of a number of criteria, including sex, as they may occur in employment and occupation. The Labour Code in Lesotho can be used to challenge such phenomena as:

• the 'glass ceiling', which prevents women from achieving higher levels of responsibility in employment;
• explicit cases of refusal to employ on the basis of sex;
• cases of indirect discrimination, where statistical analysis suggests that there is no reason other than discrimination on the basis of sex for anomalies in employment patterns;
• failure to provide emoluments or employment-related benefits where the reason is the sex of the employee;
• refusal to admit women or men to training programmes on the basis of their sex;
• threats of discharge or disadvantage, or conditioning employment, promotion or benefit on the basis of sexual favours.

The limits of protection found in the Labour Code will not, however, be known until cases are brought, settled, won or lost. This is why legal literacy and attitudinal change towards the enforcement of gender equality rights is so important in the country.

In Lesotho, the Labour Courts' decisions are final (Code: s. 38); thus, the sensitivity of the Court to gender issues will be of critical importance in defining the limits of sexual harassment and other forms of unlawful discrimination. An important step toward ensuring a level of the court's gender sensitivity will be the appointment of women to the position of deputy president and as ordinary members of the Court. The appointed president in 1993 was male.

In addition to the Code's section 5 guarantee of equality, sections 133 to 137 of the Code address employees' maternity protection. Provisions make unfair a dismissal which takes effect during a statutory maternity leave and prohibit termination or notice of dismissal during a period of absence for confinement-related illness. While dismissal and leave protection are consistent with international standards, the non-existence of systematic medical and cash benefits in the Code for working women is not.

Evidence of practice with respect to maternity protection suggests certain difficulties in conforming to the requirements of national law. Despite the success of private sector employers in winning a provision in the Code making clear that there is no obligation to give paid maternity leave, anecdotal evidence is equally clear that there is a tendency for employers wholly to disregard the spirit of protection through a number of exploitative practices. For example, some employers are said either to dismiss a newly pregnant employee or refuse to take the new mother back after absence on maternity leave. There are also verbal reports that some discriminate in favour of women who are beyond child-bearing age. Pregnant women who attempt to forestall the consequences of these practices by hiding their pregnancy and continuing work can damage their health. These employment practices, beyond being contrary to the spirit, if not the letter, of the law, result in losses for the nation's stock and utilization of human resources. Employers who engage in these practices assume that women with children tend to leave their jobs. In fact, the opposite is possibly true under the labour market conditions in Lesotho: the burden of an additional mouth to feed and the scarcity of substitute employment are more likely keep a mother scrambling to maintain employment in remunerative work. This is especially true since men have difficulty in finding the employment needed to fulfil their traditional role as the family bread-winner.

The enforcement of maternity protection is perhaps most disturbing. According to government officials, the employer in the 'typical case' of a maternity-related discharge refuses to reinstate the worker, arguing that the dismissal is motivated by 'low productivity' and not pregnancy or maternity leave. Payment of terminal benefits and acceptance of the discharge is the resolution of such a 'typical case'. This outcome may be the result of a perceived weakness of administrative process, or from the belief by enforcement decision-makers that a maternity dismissal does not warrant a steadfast demand for reinstatement. The situation may change with the activation of the Labour Court. However, the Labour Court would be within its authority under the Code to hold that reinstatement in the case of an unfair dismissal is 'impracticable in light of the circumstances'. If the Court makes a habit of finding reinstatement impracticable in cases of maternity-related dismissals, the diseconomies suggested above would continue, and the principle of maternity protection would be evaded.

The concept of a medical and cash benefit is introduced by the international labour standard, the Maternity Protection Convention (Revised) 1952 (No. 103). While no cash benefit is obliged from private sector employers, full benefits are given in the public sector. Anecdotal evidence suggests that collectively bargained cash benefits are by far the exception rather than the rule.

Another system of serious exploitation also seems to have developed whereby the employer obliges the women seeking maternity leave to find a replacement to perform her work. Instead of the employer directly employing the replacement, the replacement worker is paid a sum by the women on maternity leave who, in turn, is paid her usual wages by the employer. Motivated by the need to maintain herself and her child during the period of maternity leave, the new mother skims a portion off the wages she passes along to the replacement. This system allows the employers to absolve themselves of responsibility either towards the pregnant employee or the replacement. The burden is placed squarely on the back of the worker, that is, precisely where national and international standards hold it should not be placed.

On the issue of medical benefits, pre-natal and post-natal care is provided on a fee-for-service basis by private and public health care providers in the country. The services available are the same for women employed in the private or public, formal or informal sector, with the rare exception of insurance coverage by a few isolated employers.

There has recently been some consideration of national shared-risk maternity-care insurance to provide a cash and medical care benefit. In the case of Lesotho, given the large proportion of women workers and the apparent attitude of significant numbers of employers, the imposition of a mandatory insurance premium to cover the costs of maternity protection would seem the best option for restricting and spreading the costs imposed by the discriminatory practices discussed above.

Section 137 of the Code requires an employer to grant a paid nursing period of one hour per day for six months following an employee's return to work, upon the request of the employee. In practice, this right is little exercised since most workers leave their babies at homes a significant distance from the workplace – making it impossible to go home, nurse the child and return within the mandatory one-hour period.

The Code makes no provision for family responsibilities. For example, there is no prohibition of discrimination on the basis of family responsibilities, either of the male or female member of the family. Paternity protection also falls under this rubric. Such provisions, if enforced, can help spread the burden of family responsibilities in the context of employment obligations. As gender sensitization grows in the country, this issue may be taken up.

Consistent with the most recent international labour standard, the Night Work Convention, 1991 (No. 171), provisions on night work in Lesotho are universally applicable to all persons working at night. However, there appear to be a number of gender-related issues in relation to night work in Lesotho. The most significant is the problem of 'winter rapes', which occur typically during communal walks home during hours of darkness after being dropped at transportation centres. The ILO's Recommendation on Night Work, No. 178, specifically suggests that measures should be taken to 'improve (night workers') safety when travelling at night' through a number of possible measures described in the related Recommendation. There should be some study of this problem in the country with a view towards its remedy.

Consistent with its international obligation under the Underground Work (Women) Convention, 1935 (No. 45), no woman in Lesotho shall be employed on underground work in any mine except under circumstances as the Minister may regulate (Code: s. 132). Many countries have reconsidered the need to protect women from the hazards of underground work through its complete ban.

The Code makes comprehensive provision for universally applicable working, safety and health conditions;[3] many of these address traditionally gender-sensitive matters. They include the provision of sanitary and changing facilities, facilities for sitting while working, protection from ionizing radiation, safety in underground works, and general obligations of workers and employers to provide and work in a generally healthy and safe working environment.

The Occupational Health and Safety Unit of the Department of Labour has detailed information of gender-related hazards in Lesotho's workplaces. They include: factories lacking ventilation and heating, resulting in environments that are too hot during the summer and too cold during the winter; a hesitancy sometimes to provide working areas with seats or to provide ergonomically correct seats; and long (although not statutorily illegal) working hours. This topic is discussed further below under the subject of enforcement.

Section 5 requires equal pay for work of equal value, consistent with the international labour standard on the subject, Convention No. 100 on Equal Remuneration. The domestic provision appears to require immediate conformity with the principle and, therefore, differs from the Convention, which has an obligation that is *promotional* in nature (i.e. the obligation is to pursue a policy of equal value, with a view towards ultimately achieving this objective).

It is also significant that the Code applies to domestic and rural workers, a large proportion of whom are usually women and traditionally vulnerable (Code: ss 2 and 3). Thus, both groups benefit from protection in their freedom of association, against discrimination, in working conditions and in other areas just like other persons employed in Lesotho. The perennial question is whether these rights and protection are used to improve the situation of these workers. Structural aspects of the workers' conditions of work have traditionally limited application in practice of these rights: the distances to be covered to inspect adequately agricultural workplaces, the multitude of domestic workers' workplaces and ease in replacing workers, are all impediments to the organization of workers and the enforcement of their rights.

Role of international obligations

Lesotho ratified 11 International Labour Conventions[4] upon admission to the International Labour Organization in 1966 and none up to the end of 1993. The Underground Work (Women) Convention, 1935 (No. 45), is the only standard which touches directly on gender issues. This standard has, however, come under international criticism as being overly protective and is due for revision. Lesotho had also ratified 15 international human rights and humanitarian instruments[5] by November 1993, some of which cover gender equality issues.

International labour standards can be of dramatic importance in guiding the formulation of national policy and law, and ensuring its application in practice. In the case of Lesotho, use has already been made of many ILO Conventions in formulation of the Code. Provisions on non-discrimination are identical to the essential obligations in the Discrimination (Employment and Occupation) Convention, 1958 (No. 111), the Equal Remuneration Convention, 1951 (No. 100), and follow closely the obligations found in the Night Work Convention, 1990 (No. 171).

The ILO's system of supervision for ensuring application of domestic law comes with the ratification of the international standards. On ratification, the government would be obliged to provide periodic reports on the application of Conventions; ratification also provides the opportunity for the social partners (employers' and workers' organizations) to comment to the ILO's supervisory bodies on the government's application of ratified Conventions. This process acts as a brake against backsliding on social progress; it also provides a focus for improvement of practical application of national law.

Ratification of certain critical international labour equality Conventions can be recommended in the case of Lesotho. Lesotho's laws have been written to conform to Conventions Nos 100 on Equal Remuneration and 111 on Discrimination (Employment and Occupation). However, as far as practical application is concerned, the country has still a long way to go; but this is the case with many ratifications by member states of the ILO. Indeed, membership in the organization implies a willingness to become internationally bound to social progress through subscription to Conventions. Through the act of ratification, this government would give an indication of its political will to give effect to national law which itself follows the obligations of the Conventions. Ratification in this case in Lesotho would be seen at the very least as a willingness to stand behind the current law of the land.

On this point, it is important to notice that the Code itself obliges domestic interpretation 'in case of ambiguity ... in such a way as more closely conforms with provisions of Conventions adopted' by the International Labour Conference. When the Labour Court becomes operational, this provision will assist Lesotho's judges in conforming national practice to the requirements of international labour conventions.

The importance of the UN Convention on the Elimination of All Forms of Discrimination against Women and other international human rights instruments in the promotion of equality generally, and gender equity in particular, cannot be overemphasized. While Lesotho has ratified a number of important international human rights instruments, it had not, by the end of 1993, ratified the UN Convention on the Elimination of All Forms of Discrimination against Women. The ratification and implementation of this Convention would be an important step in the promotion of gender equality in Lesotho. A potential ratification must, however, be seen in the context of barriers to equality in the legal system itself, particularly the minor status of women discussed in the preceding sections. Only a ratification of the Convention, coupled with corresponding changes in the legal system, would enhance gender equality.

Implementation and enforcement

It has been said that the granting of rights without their effective enforcement is equivalent to their not being granted at all. The next chapter (9) focuses in depth on this issue of enforcement. An evaluation of this in Lesotho cannot be made without more experience under the 1992 Labour Code. Equality issues in the context of existing law need to be publicized so that government, employers and workers' organizations and interested non-governmental organizations can rally behind a demand for better enforcement of legislated rights. They include main means for enforcement in the country, the labour court, labour inspection, health and safety inspection, legal literacy, code of practice. The next chapter examines them in detail.

Section 22 of the Labour Code Order 1992 establishes a labour court charged with the function of rendering substantial justice in employment disputes (Section 27). The Court could play an important role in enforcing labour rights, including those that affect women. Much will depend not only on its composition but on how the court chooses to play its role. It is essential that the Court should be equitably composed to reflect all sections of society, including women. The procedures of the Court should also be sufficiently fair and flexible to ensure that women will be able to bring gender-related complaints before it, especially those relating to sexual harassment as defined under the Code.

Labour inspections in Lesotho are conducted by Labour Officers placed in the Industrial Relations Unit of the Department of Labour. Only 34 Labour Officers of various grades are placed in 10 District Offices around the country and, therefore, the number of inspections conducted is limited.

Despite the major involvement of women in enforcement activities (25 of the 34 Labour Officers are women), the majority of women being the subject (by their overwhelming participation in the workforce) of enforcement action, there seems to be little gender sensitivity. For example, there is neither gender aggregation of enforcement statistics nor compilation of gender-related complaints or grievances. There would appear to be no particular effort to create a broader awareness amongst workers of gender-related rights, such as non-discrimination policy, sexual harassment policy or maternity protection. Such activities could include sensitization of the Labour Inspectors themselves, grassroots programmes for workers and training of trade unionists.

The Occupational Health and Safety Unit of the Department of Labour is a recent institution under the Code. With a staff of four factory inspectors for the country, some 35 inspections took place during the second half of 1993. The primary strategy for improvement of conditions in factories is through the operation of a Health and Safety Committee in places of work where more than 15 people are employed. There is little apparent gender sensitivity in the unit. No systematic assessment is conducted of the effect of harsh working conditions on the different sex groups of the populations. While this may be due to constrained resources, such analysis could lead to better allocation of resources by producing a more focused approach to enforcement activities.

The scope of the Code is broad: it applies to all employment where a person agrees to enter into the service of another.[6] However, it is apparent that these legal rights have little direct impact in small and micro enterprises. Accepting the legislation as it is,[7] key problems are the lack of enforcement and inspection, limited legal literacy, and the veiled threat of unemployment for any complainant. The Women Lawyers' Association (FIDA) continues to undertake some legal awareness programmes.

A code of practice properly devised to take into account Lesotho's particular circumstances could play a useful role in the promotion of good industrial relations generally and employment equity in particular. It could promote equality for women in employment by ensuring that non-discriminatory practices are followed, for example, in the recruitment and promotion of employees. Government and the social partners in Lesotho seem to be well-disposed towards the idea of putting a code of practice in place.

The need for a law reform commission, a statutory body charged with the function of revising and consolidating legislation as the need arises, has long been recognized in Lesotho. A law reform committee was set up under an Act of Parliament a number of years ago but it was never operational. A new initiative was taken recently.

A properly structured law reform commission, composed to reflect gender equality, could play a useful role in focusing on areas of the legal system that impede gender equality. The need for a gender-sensitive commission, not only in terms of its composition but also in terms of the issues it chooses to focus on, is therefore imperative.

Lesotho does not have any kind of social security system. The need for a comprehensive scheme was recognized as far back as 1989. There is an urgent need for such a scheme. Too many workers, particularly women, are exposed to insecurity in the absence of any contingency risk protection, unemployment, survival or old-age benefits. Apart from the government sector, a relatively small proportion of women workers have any pension rights at all. Moreover, maternity benefits (government excepted) are at best limited in most cases.

The Legal Aid Act No. 19 of 1978 provides for legal services to indigent and poor people. The bulk of the clients are women, particularly in maintenance cases. The legal office's resources are grossly inadequate. Moreover, many women not only in rural but also in urban areas are unaware of its existence. A properly structured Legal Aid Office with adequate resources could play an important role in addressing women's plight in employment, particularly in the new Labour Court.

Priority areas for action

A number of priority areas for action can be identified to create an enabling legal environment for gender equality in the country. There is a need to reform traditional and other laws, as well as the Constitution, to remove obstacles to gender equality. It is also necessary to improve application and enforcement of gender equality legislation. Attention has been drawn to the country's need to ratify and implement a number of international instruments and to adopt a comprehensive contributory national social-security system to cover contingency risks and also provide for maternity, unemployment, survivor and old-age benefits. Finally, greater effort is called for to promote the idea of shared family responsibilities.

Notes

1. As an exception, a 1971 order allows a married woman to open a bank account at Lesotho Bank in terms of Lesotho National Development and Savings Order of 1971 (which created Lesotho Bank). It expressly states that a married woman, whether under marital power or not, may be a depositor in the savings bank and may without assistance execute all necessary documents and give all necessary acquittance and be liable to all obligations attached to depositors. Credit, however, is still heavily restricted.

2. In many instances, particularly in government service, women appear to be unable to take advantage of opportunities for further training because their husbands object. Similarly some women have been forced to resign by their husbands, who do not wish them to continue in employment or on account of transfers to different parts of Lesotho.

3. With the exception of limits on lifting of weights, 50 kgs for men, 25 kgs for women; and the provision of separate sanitary facilities.

4. They include: Minimum Age (Industry), 1919 (No. 5); Right of Association (Agriculture), 1921 (No. 11); Weekly Rest (Industry), 1921 (No. 14); Equality of Treatment (Accident Compensation), 1925 (No. 19); Minimum Wage-Fixing Machinery, 1928 (No. 26); Forced Labour, 1930 (No. 29); Underground Work

(Women), 1935 (No. 45); Contracts of Employment (Indigenous Workers), 1939 (No. 64); Penal Sanctions (Indigenous Workers) 1939 (No. 65); Freedom of Association and Protection of the Right to Organise, 1948 (No. 87); and Right to Organise and Collective Bargaining, 1949 (No. 98).

5. Among them are: 1949 Geneva Conventions on Armed Conflicts; International Convention on Elimination of All Forms of Racial Discrimination; International Convention on the Suppression and Punishment of the Crime of Apartheid; Convention on the Prevention and Punishment of the Crime of Genocide; Convention on the Political Rights of Women; Convention on the Nationality of Married Women; 1926 Slavery Convention as amended; Supplementary Convention on the Abolition of Slavery, the Slave Trade and Institutions and Practices Similar Thereto; Convention Relating to the Status of Stateless Persons; 1951 UN Convention Relating to the Status of Refugees and the Additional Protocol Thereto; OAU Convention of 10 September 1969 Governing the Specific Aspects of Refugees' Problems in Africa; The UN Convention on the Rights of the Child; The International Covenant on Civil and Political Rights; The International Covenant on Economic, Social and Cultural Rights. Lesotho has also ratified The African Charter on Human and People's Rights.

6. See terms defined in section 3, including 'contract of employment', 'employee', 'employer'. See also the broad definition of 'factory'.

7. That is, not challenging the appropriateness of provisions' applicability to small and micro-enterprises on the basis of excessive cost or operational capacity.

Bibliography

Kimane, I.; M. Mtimo-Makara and E.R.M. Mapetla (1992) *Gender Planning Strategy, Enhancing the Participation and Performance of Both Female and Male Civil Servants in Lesotho*, Report for the Ministry of Public Service, Maseru, Lesotho.

Lesotho Government (1992) *Labour Code*, Maseru.

Mamashela, M. (1991) *Family Law Through Cases in Lesotho*, National University of Lesotho, Roma.

Molefi, J. (1993) *Labour Law and Industrial Relations in Lesotho: Recent Developments and Prospects*. First Regional Workshop on Labour Law and Industrial Relations in a Changing Southern Africa, Durban (Labour Law Unit, University of Cape Town).

Pholo, M.T. (1992) 'Status of Women in Lesotho – The Legal Situation', Conference on Legal Status of Women, Maseru, Lesotho, September.

9
Enforcement of equality provisions

CONSTANCE THOMAS AND RACHAEL TAYLOR

Introduction

Provisions prohibiting discrimination or guaranteeing equal rights on the basis of sex have been adopted in almost every country of the world. These provisions range from general statements contained in national constitutions to specific articles found in labour codes, employment acts or other labour-related regulatory instruments. In a growing number of countries, specific legislative acts addressing sex-based discrimination or the promotion of equality for women exist. Equality clauses are also increasingly being included in collective agreements.

These legal provisions have contributed to many of the gains made by working women during the last 25 years. Nevertheless, discrimination against women in the workplace persists and has even worsened in periods of economic recession. This harsh reality has prompted many countries to re-examine their legislative provisions and subsequently to amend them, extend their scope, repeal discriminatory provisions and attempt to increase penalties and sanctions. While the importance of formulating and adopting improved legislative texts should not be underestimated, it is their practical application that poses the greatest challenge. Practical application can be accomplished through a variety of means, including educational measures, training, legal literacy programmes, positive action and enforcement measures. All of these tools need to be used simultaneously to be mutually reinforcing.

To be fully effective, legal provisions must be enforceable. In other words, national or other authorities must be able to order or compel compliance with the rights and obligations set forth in legislation. This chapter examines, on the basis of national reports available in the ILO in relation to member states' application of relevant international labour standards, the enforcement aspect of legislative implementation. It looks at various aspects of enforcement such as access to justice, procedures, sanctions and remedies. Typical national mechanisms used to enforce anti-discrimination provisions include: administrative investigation and enforcement actions, litigation by groups or individuals who have claims of discrimination, litigation by government agencies, collective bargaining, and, to some extent, governmental incentive policies. The chapter is intended to highlight those aspects of enforcement that are key to improving the application of equality provisions. It does not provide an exhaustive review of all enforcement mechanisms nor an in-depth analysis of their effectiveness.

The effectiveness of enforcement mechanisms are reviewed in terms of, first, intended beneficiaries' ability to invoke the mechanisms in a judicial process and, second, the mechanisms' ability to produce their intended effects. Individual enforcement mechanisms are examined from the perspective of individual versus group justice theories. Individual justice theory considers whether the legal provisions can be enforced in a way that is fair to the individual complainant by redressing the discriminatory treatment individually experienced. This model is limited by its failure to take into account the more complex institutional aspects of discrimination that go beyond individual actions and relief. By contrast, the group justice perspective looks at the position of women as a whole and is more concerned with redistributive results and institutional changes, such as those achieved in affirmative action, rather than individual actions.

Despite use of these indicators, bright line distinctions between ineffective and effective mechanisms are rarely present. Clearly the judicial process is ineffective when a woman cannot invoke a law against employment discrimination because she is legally considered to be a minor and, thus, without the legal authority to bring a claim. Assessment of effectiveness and adequacy is more difficult in a situation where a woman successfully pursues a discrimination claim in court, receives her court costs and a token amount of compensatory damages, but fails to obtain the job that she was wrongfully denied. Is the claimant's favourable judgement sufficient to act as a deterrent to the continuation of the discriminatory conduct? Will women as a group benefit from this action? Is the remedy adequate in light of the time, effort and money put into the pursuit of the claim?

In-depth research into these areas at the national level can produce information useful for comparative studies at the regional or international level. The need for such study is evidenced by the paucity of existing information on the subject and by the actions undertaken by some countries over the last few years to amend procedural and penalty sections of their labour or equality legislation in the hope of strengthening their enforcement capabilities. The various efforts undertaken in this area by countries such as Australia, India, the Philippines, the United Kingdom and the United States illustrate that countries have identified the need to make the enforcement of equality provisions more effective, but are their efforts hitting the mark? McCrudden has recently summarized the limitations in the effectiveness of European equality laws as follows:

- the inadequacy of institutional assistance to, and representation of, individual litigants;
- the need to pay extensive costs to commence and complete litigation successfully;
- the lack of trained and motivated lawyers;
- the inadequacy of remedies provided, both to compensate the individual fully in financial terms, and to ensure that the individual victim secures the benefit discriminatorily denied her;
- the inadequate knowledge of European Union law principles by representatives and judges;
- the difficulty of proof of discrimination;
- the difficulty, specifically, of lack of adequate information being made available to an actual or potential plaintiff;
- the delays in the operation of the judicial process leading effectively to denial of individual justice;
- the lack of involvement by unions in addressing equality issues;
- the absence of mechanisms for tackling institutional (indirect) discrimination directly;
- inadequate settlements;
- remedies and sanctions which are addressed only to the individual plaintiff and not generalized to the class affected;
- the absence of adequate aggregate information on employer's pay or workforce composition by sex;
- lack of public bodies with a specific equality mandate to adopt a strategic approach to enforcement rather than an ad hoc reactive approach;
- understaffed, ill-equipped, badly resourced, or poorly led special enforcement bodies;
- inadequate opportunities to challenge discriminatory collective agreements.[1]

What do international labour standards say about enforcement?

The principal international labour instrument concerning the elimination of sex discrimination and the promotion of equality is the Discrimination (Employment and Occupation) Convention, 1958 (No. 111).[2] One hundred and twenty countries had ratified the Convention by November 1995, thereby committing themselves to its implementation at the national level. The Convention requires governments to adopt a national policy which prohibits discrimination and promotes equal opportunity and treatment in employment and occupation. It requires the enactment of legislation and the promotion of educational programmes necessary to secure acceptance and observance with the policy. It further requires the repeal of any statutory provisions and the modification of administrative instructions or practices that are inconsistent with the policy.

Convention No. 111 leaves it to the national authorities to determine how legislation should implement national policy and how it should be enforced. While the Convention itself is silent on enforcement measures, its accompanying Recommendation concerning discrimination (No. 111) urges that appropriate agencies be established to receive, examine and investigate complaints of non-compliance. These agencies should be able, through conciliation or other means, to 'secure the correction' of those practices that conflict with national policy. The agencies should be able to render opinions or issue decisions on the manner in which identified discriminatory practices should be corrected. Unlike those of the Convention, the Recommendation's provisions are not binding. Their purpose is to enhance countries' understanding of the Convention's requirements and to facilitate its application.

The ILO Governing Body has approved certain report forms for governments to use in fulfilling their reporting obligations on ratified Conventions in accordance with the ILO Constitution. The report form for Convention No. 111 includes questions on enforcement, such as the methods by which implementation is supervised and enforced, including information on labour inspection and decisions of courts and tribunals.

Like the Discrimination Convention, the terms of the Equal Remuneration Convention, 1951 (No. 100) allow for its application to be determined at the national level. This may be done through collective agreements, laws and wage-fixing machinery. While it mentions nothing about enforcement or the handling of alleged violations, the accompanying Recommendation No. 90 suggests that investigations be undertaken that promote the application of the equal remuneration principle. Moreover, the report form for Convention No. 100 seeks information on responsible national authorities and their methods for ensuring that relevant legislation is supervised and applied. Furthermore, it asks about court or tribunal decisions issued on the subject.

Effective enforcement mechanisms are essential to the full implementation of the anti-discrimination and equal remuneration principles contained in International Labour Conventions Nos. 111 and 100. In the future, consideration may be given to providing more explicit guidance on the enforcement of these provisions as found in the Termination of Employment Convention 1982 (No. 158).[3] The Termination of Employment Convention describes at length procedural protection and rights of appeal that should be available for wrongful termination of employment. For example, it provides that a worker who considers that his or her employment has been unjustifiably terminated shall be entitled to appeal to an impartial body that should be able to render decisions, such as a court, labour tribunal, arbitration committee or arbitrator. It further provides that the worker should not have to bear alone the burden of proving that termination was not justified. Instead, the burden of proof may be placed on the employer or some other means may be used which allows the impartial body to reach a decision on the evidence presented. The Convention also requires that certain remedies be made available to claimants such as reinstatement, adequate compensation or other appropriate relief.

Enforcement of labour laws through labour inspection is addressed by several International Labour Conventions on labour inspection. The principal Convention on Labour Inspection, 1947 (No. 81) provides that workplaces shall be inspected as often and as thoroughly as is necessary to ensure effective application of the relevant legal provisions. The provisions covered by the Convention relate to conditions of work and the protection of workers. They are very broadly defined and thus may include protection against discrimination in the workplace.

Administrative bodies to supervise and/or enforce compliance with the legislation

Labour inspection

In the majority of countries, labour inspectorates have been established to ensure the observance of legal provisions in the working environment. Firstly, they secure the enforcement of laws and regulations relating to conditions of work, labour relations, contracts of employment, and the protection of workers while engaged in their work; secondly, supply technical information and advice to employers and workers; and, thirdly, bring to the attention of the competent authority any defects or abuses not covered by existing legal provisions. Most salaried employees and apprentices are subjected under law to labour inspection. Even though labour inspectorates are often associated with the enforcement of legal provisions concerning payment of wages, hours of work, and health and safety conditions, their enforcement powers generally cover all labour laws and regulations and may cover certain aspects of labour relations. The question is, to what extent do labour inspectors use their powers to address gender discrimination in carrying out their wide range of functions?

As a general rule, labour inspectors have the power to enter premises where work is being performed, review documentation and question employers, supervisors, managers and employees. This regular investigative authority enables inspectors to obtain first-hand knowledge about, and make on-site assessments of, the terms and conditions of work. Co-operation with the labour inspectors is usually mandated by law and refusal to co-operate with them may lead to sanctions. Nevertheless, the inspectors tend to have failings in inspecting establishments for violations of discrimination. Such failings have been addressed in several jurisdictions. For example, a separate division of labour inspectors has been created in Ontario, Canada, to undertake inspections and improve enforcement of the legal provisions requiring pay equity between men and women.

The inspectors often have authority to deal with matters in the working environment that fall outside specific regulations. Even if equal pay provisions are not specified in the law, in many instances, labour inspectors during an inspection would be authorized to compare wages of men and women or compare work tasks where pay differentials give the appearance of being sex based. In Spain, as a result of using their investigatory powers, labour inspectors discovered and corrected a situation where women were doing the same work as men under different job titles and at different salary levels.

Labour inspectors also usually have general advisory powers. They frequently give advice, to both employers and employees, on matters concerned with legal rights and obligations. International Labour Conventions Nos 81 on Labour Inspection, 1947, and 129 on Labour Inspection (Agriculture), 1969, call upon the labour inspectorate to supply technical information and advice to employers and workers concerning the most effective means of complying with the legal provisions. Because this assistance ensures the effective implementation of laws and regulations, it is interdependent with and complementary to the enforcement function. In Spain, some preliminary contacts and meetings have taken place between the Institute of Women and the labour inspectorate with the aim of establishing such an information section concerning women workers. It would seem in such a situation that labour inspectors could be very influential in promoting compliance with discrimination provisions. Of course the ability to make good use of this advisory function presupposes a knowledge of discrimination issues and anti-discrimination policies that many labour inspectorates do not possess. In this regard, collaboration with national machinery on the status of women could be mutually beneficial.

In accordance with International Labour Conventions Nos 81 and 129, labour inspectors should also make recommendations on the improvement of existing laws and regulations, and notify their supervisors of any shortcomings in existing provisions. While this function appears to be accepted in principle, a review of available labour inspection reports indicates that labour inspectors are not often able to fulfil this function in practice.

The enforcement powers of labour inspectors fall roughly into two categories: the authority to bring violations (or suspected violations) to the attention of some higher administrative authority and/or to initiate proceedings to deal with such violations; and, in some areas, the power to undertake conciliation and arbitration proceedings (this latter function is a controversial subject).[4] When suspected violations arise, the labour inspectors usually must refer the matter to a court, or to the appropriate authorities, such as the labour commissioner. It may be that the use of the inspectorate for discrimination enforcement might, in some cases, reduce the need to use court procedures. Alternatively, where court procedures are followed, the inspectorate could ensure that complainants have some form of support. If properly exercised, inspectors' advisory functions and their ability to disseminate information could also be very effective in helping to prevent discrimination. Their investigative functions could allow for more direct contacts with complainants and help to obtain the perspective of a group of employees rather than just of an individual complainant. The number of enforcement actions taken by labour inspectors in matters involving sex-based discrimination seem to be few, although more information is needed to verify this assessment.

The constraints placed on the labour inspection systems must be taken into consideration in assessing the potential effectiveness of labour inspectorates in the area of discrimination. In many countries, labour inspectorates may not be utilized to their full potential due to restricted funding, lack of an efficient infrastructure, and problems of poor communications and transport. In Indonesia, for example, there are only 1,133 inspectors in the entire country who have to cover over 140,000 registered enterprises. Transportation costs are not built into their budget, which makes inspection of enterprises in remote areas, where large concentrations of women work, very difficult.[5] The inspector to enterprise ratio is even worse in other countries.

Many labour inspectorates are overburdened with the diversity of responsibilities. This results in labour inspectors not being able to spend a sufficient amount of time on enforcement activities in general, let alone the specific enforcement of equality provisions.

Another limitation concerns the level of training of the labour inspectorate. Inspectors can be effective only in areas in which they have expertise, and most do not have expertise in the area of identifying and preventing discrimination, especially indirect forms of discrimination.

Application of discrimination laws

Unfortunately, information is not available that could allow an analysis as to how often labour inspectorates use their power to bring about compliance with discrimination laws. Nevertheless, the potential for labour inspectors' participation in the enforcement of discrimination provisions is considerable because of their regular contacts with employers and workers at workplaces. In some countries, co-ordination between the labour inspectorate and the specialized agencies on the status of women has raised awareness among labour inspectors regarding discrimination issues. In Portugal, the labour inspectorate must first obtain the opinion of the Committee on Equality in Work and Employment when questions arise concerning the existence of discriminatory situations or practices.

Specialized enforcement bodies

In keeping with the provisions of international labour Recommendation No. 111, a number of countries have established specialized enforcement agencies to promote compliance with non-discrimination legislation. Some commissions are limited to employment discrimination and others cover all forms of discrimination. The scope of the agencies' coverage usually parallels the scope of the legislation that they are established to enforce. The agency with a women-only focus has the advantage of becoming very specialized in all aspects of gender discrimination. On the other hand, the agencies that cover various grounds of discrimination, such as race and sex, have the advantage of more realistic evaluation of reasons for discrimination. For example, for many ethnic women, discrimination is both race- and gender-based.

Generally, these agencies have the power to receive individual and, where permissible, group complaints alleging violation of employment discrimination laws. They also undertake investigations, assist in conciliation and make findings or recommendations. In some countries the agencies have authority to initiate complaints and investigations themselves. In other words, they need not rely solely on individual complaints to trigger their enforcement powers. Ideally, agencies should be authorized to do both – handle individual complaints as well as initiate their own actions. In some countries, such as Spain, these agencies may also render expert advice in discrimination cases in the courts.[6]

The purpose of the agencies is to assist victims of discrimination in the handling and resolving of their complaints in an informal, inexpensive, efficient and understanding manner. The procedures for the filing and pursuit of claims are much less rigid in such agencies than in court cases. In theory, they should be user-friendly and operate to facilitate application of the law. Services of the agency are usually free of charge and do not require legal representation. Discrimination law is recognized as being an extremely complex area of law often involving cases that are very difficult to prove. The handling of complaints by the agency that has specialized knowledge in the field is perhaps the greatest contribution it has to offer.

Limitation on the authority of specialized agencies can frustrate their effectiveness. Furthermore, the performance of the agencies has, in a few countries, been constrained by the excessive number of complaints, a lack of funding or lack of political will to support their enforcement actions.

Where such agencies or commissions do not exist, consideration should be given to their establishment. Staff should have specific expertise in subjects such as equal pay and sexual harassment. These agencies would be ideally suitable for providing policy advice to other government agencies and legislative bodies, particularly on legislative changes. Greater co-ordination among the specialized agencies, other enforcement agencies and the national machineries on the status of women can also be encouraged to enhance and complement each other's work. They should have the necessary power to obtain all the relevant evidence needed for decision-making in discrimination cases. Moreover, they should be accorded the necessary status for their decisions, whether recommendations or opinions, to be given due weight. Consideration may also be given to extending their powers. For example, it may be more effective for an agency to be able to undertake periodic compliance reviews of equality legislation rather than to be solely complaint-oriented.

The office of the Ombudsman

At present there are over 100 ombudsman offices or ombudsman-type institutions throughout the world. Over time, these offices have developed two primary roles: investigator of faults in administration, and provider of remedies where injustice is found. The jurisdiction of the Ombudsman varies. In some countries the office covers only the public service. For example, in Trinidad and Tobago, the Ombudsman hears complaints from employees of statutory and local authorities, including allegations of discrimination. Over time many of the offices have taken on employment discrimination complaints.[7]

The office of the Ombudsman appears to be an appropriate forum in many countries for discrimination complaints to be resolved. These offices would appear best suited to resolve individual complaints in an informal manner. They are perhaps less equipped to resolve complaints involving complex issues such as those presented in equal pay cases.

Legal aid

Legal aid centres in many countries have enabled many women to invoke the protection of discrimination laws. Such centres often serve as an initial source of information about women's rights. They also provide legal counselling and may advocate on women's behalf. Such centres may be funded publicly or privately. In the United Republic of Tanzania, the Tanzania Media Women Association (*sic*) – TAMWA[8] – has helped to establish a Women's Crisis Centre for taking appropriate action against problems of beating, sexual harassment and discrimination. The Centre has the support of women lawyers, who provide legal counselling, and also enjoys the services of social workers, journalists and other professionals.

In countries where specialized commissions or offices of Ombudsmen do not exist, the role of legal aid offices to assist in the enforcement of laws is even more important. The question is the extent to which such centres have developed the expertise needed to adequately represent claimants, particularly women, in employment discrimination cases.

Judicial action

Types of cases brought and outcomes

Although statistics are limited and the kinds of discrimination cases pursued vary between countries, it would appear that the most common types of complaints about gender discrimination in employment include actions of dismissal, promotion, equal pay, sexual harassment, job advertisements, hiring and infringements of maternity protection. In many countries the nature of the cases brought may depend as much on substantive legal provisions as on the available enforcement mechanisms. For example, in some countries, hiring decisions cannot be challenged. Where they can be challenged, the rights to remedies are often nominal, causing individual claimants to feel that such cases are not worth pursuing.

While the actual number of discrimination cases is increasing (albeit slowly), the success rate for applicants remains low, as does the overall number of cases actually being heard.

Equal pay claims before Industrial Tribunals in the United Kingdom, tabulated separately, have dropped since 1988, perhaps owing to recession, which has gripped the United Kingdom for the last few years, the appallingly low success rate experienced by claimants, and the difficult and lengthy procedures that must be followed in such cases. In Australia, the figures at the federal level show that the number of complaints is increasing.

Initiation of complaints by individuals

The mere existence of a right does not mean that an individual can exercise that right in relation to her particular case: there may be certain procedural bars or obstacles to the individual's exercise of her legal right and her bringing a legal action.

The nature of the complaint itself may prevent action. The court may not have jurisdiction to hear the complaint. In some countries a challenge cannot be made before the courts, by an individual, against a discriminatory provision in a collective agreement. The individual herself also may lack standing to bring an action. There may also be legal requirements to be fulfilled before a woman is legally considered an 'employee': for example, in the United Kingdom, the length of continuous service an individual has performed is relevant. This is a particular problem for part-time and temporary workers. An individual might also be expressly excluded from certain legislation. In Germany, the Labour Code expressly excludes public-sector workers, who enjoy only constitutional protection. Time limitations placed on the filing of complaints may also prevent the right to file an action in a court or tribunal.

Japanese law illustrates another problem related to the basic right of an individual to bring an action. The Equal Employment Opportunities Law 1985[9] provides that employers 'should endeavour' to give equal opportunities in recruiting, hiring, assigning tasks and promotion. Thus the law merely imposes a duty to strive for adherence, rather than a strict prohibition or a requirement to achieve a certain level of equality. This type of standard is essentially promotional, making a violation very difficult to prove – which must surely limit the possibility of using judicial action to enforce the provisions of this law.

Once it has been determined that a complaint may legally be brought, a host of other procedural obstacles faces a claimant who wants to pursue her case to a successful conclusion. They include the nature of the forum to hear discrimination cases, and the burden of proving the case.

An individual action to enforce rights may be brought in a number of different fora depending on the country, the legal system and the dispute resolution infrastructure. The forum can be an ordinary civil or penal court, the supreme or high court, or the constitutional court. Alternatively, in some countries, labour courts or industrial tribunals have jurisdiction over some or all labour or employment matters. A complainant may have a choice of venue, depending on the nature of the complaint, or possibly the remedy sought.

The diversity of fora makes an international comparative study of their relative effectiveness and efficiency extremely difficult. Nevertheless, significant questions have been raised about which is the best forum for discrimination cases. For example, some have questioned whether labour courts are better or less equipped than civil courts to handle complaints of gender discrimination in employment. In most instances, labour courts or industrial tribunals have a better general knowledge of labour relations and employment matters. That knowledge, however, is usually centred on the settlement of interest disputes arising out of collective agreements rather than disputes arising out of individual employment or civil rights. Perhaps the answer to the 'preferred forum' query lies not in the type of court *per se*, but rather in whichever forum has developed the most expertise, experience and jurisprudence in the area of employment discrimination and the remedies they offer.

Another factor that may influence a complainant's choice of forum is the nature of the adjudicatory process – does it seek conciliation or does it reward one adversary over another? The composition of the tribunal or court is also increasingly recognized as an important factor. Most judges in the world are men, who may not be gender sensitive.

Both overt and subtle forms of gender bias displayed by judges towards attorneys, litigants and court personnel involved in proceedings have also been documented. 'The appearance of justice is as important as justice',[10] and 'when pervasive bias by judges exists ... the system is not fulfilling its duty to assure equal justice under the law'. Regardless of the type of forum, it is important that a complainant be able to use the available forum expeditiously, inexpensively and with knowledge that the complaint will be fairly and knowledgeably determined with appropriate remedies and sanctions attaching.

With regard to burden of proof, in an employment relationship it is generally true that the employer is in a much stronger position than the employee. The employer is likely to be in a better financial position and to be in control of sources of information. During litigation, therefore, the employer is likely to have better legal representation and more relevant information under his or her control, which can be submitted as evidence. Discrimination complaints also, in many cases, involve a certain amount of investigation into an employer's 'state of mind', or other hidden factors to which only the employer has access. Such subjective evidence is often used to determine whether the alleged discriminatory practice was, in fact, based on the complainant's gender.

In court actions one party usually has to meet a certain standard of proof as to the truth of the allegations. This is the 'burden of proof', as it is called, in civil cases. Approaches vary somewhat between legal systems and countries, but in general the procedures followed in discrimination cases are the same as those followed in other civil cases. The burden of proving the allegations sometimes rests with the complainant. However, it is sometimes shifted to the employer, or shared between the two parties (although this is probably the case in a minority of countries).

Although shifting the burden of proof works to the advantage of the complainant in discrimination cases, there are many advocates for placing the entire burden on the employer, as is often done in other types of labour dispute. This would be consistent with the principle of *favor laboratoris*, which means that in labour disputes legal rules are to be interpreted in favour of the employee, especially where there is any doubt. It would also follow many countries' rules on employment dismissal.

The issue of protection against reprisals is also crucial. Persons who feel they have been discriminated against may often refrain from lodging a complaint for fear of retaliatory action such as dismissal by their employer. The concern over retaliation is not limited to prospective complainants. It extends to those employees who may have information vital to the victims' case and who may be necessary witnesses for establishing proof of discrimination.

Many countries do have provisions covering such victimization. For example, the Cyprus Equal Remuneration Law[11] states that a person cannot be dismissed for submitting a complaint, and provides a maximum fine of £1,000 for non-compliance. This sort of victimization is also an offence, subject to a fine, in Australia.[12]

All European Union Member States have legislative protection against reprisals. In Belgium, Denmark, Ireland, Luxembourg, Portugal and the United Kingdom, compensation and possible reinstatement are available, and fines may be imposed as well.

One of the most serious problems associated with individual enforcement through judicial action is the financial cost. Once a case reaches the litigation stage, a claimant is usually required (or needs) to retain legal counsel to represent her. After that point, many other costs accrue, such as lawyers' fees, filing costs and investigation costs. The employer is often in a stronger financial position than the employee to pursue the litigation. The complainant's prospect of compensation (if ordered) may in fact cover only the costs of the legal proceedings. Thus the potential costs of litigation may act as a serious deterrent to complainants, particularly to someone who has just lost her job. One solution to this problem is to make legal aid available for discrimination proceedings (it is often available for criminal and other proceedings).

In addition to the costs, adequate legal representation requires finding a lawyer who has expertise in employment discrimination or equal pay claims. In many countries this is a difficult task. The issues involved in employment discrimination cases are often very complex and may be highly sensitive. They require specialized knowledge and special procedures (in addition to group action) to be dealt with effectively. Recognition of these needs has led some jurisdictions to use specialized experts in discrimination cases. The experience of using experts appears to be mixed. On the positive side, the expert brings to the case information and knowledge which a judge or tribunal panel member usually does not possess.

Representative and group action

Class and representative actions can be effective ways of combating discrimination within the enforcement process. A class action is a procedural mechanism that allows an individual complainant to file an action of discrimination on behalf of other similarly situated persons. The findings of the court, including remedies, are extended to all persons in the identified class. The representative action is similar. It is a procedure that allows an organization to file an action on behalf of its members or on behalf of persons whose interest the organization represents. Thus, a successful class or representative action may result in positive changes for an entire group of discrimination victims.

From a group justice point of view, these actions are more effective than individual actions for several reasons. First and foremost, the class action may be the only type of action that can redress indirect discrimination. Indirect discrimination is generally defined as an apparently neutral practice or working condition which in fact has a discriminatory effect on more members of one group (in this case, women) than on the other group. It is defined by reference to a group, which makes class action one of the obvious means of combating such discrimination, or at least remedying it. The potential to correct the institutional structure or practice that created the discrimination exists in these cases. Class actions are also more likely to deter the continuation of a discriminatory practice than are individual actions. Only a few countries, however, allow class or group actions.

Use of class action procedures should not be identified only with the industrialized countries that have common-law legal systems. In Afghanistan, the Constitution lays down certain fundamental rights, and gives a right of complaint through individual and group petition to related government organs.[13] In India, a recognized welfare institution (this includes three women's groups, but it does not appear to include trade unions) may bring a complaint to court. It is also established by case-law that class action is possible in equal remuneration cases. In many countries, trade unions or other employees' organizations may bring an action of discrimination on behalf of their members.

Because of its advantages, the use of representative action on behalf of women in discrimination cases by workers' organizations, special enforcement bodies or other designated groups should be encouraged over individual actions, wherever possible.

Remedies and sanctions

Effective enforcement of equality provisions must entail an adequate and appropriate system of remedies and sanctions. Access to justice would be of little import to a claimant or group of claimants unless, at the end of successful legal action, an appropriate, adequate and effective remedy can be obtained. Such remedy and sanction from the individual claimant's point of view should be compensatory and provide relief for the harm caused. In discrimination cases, individuals may suffer both monetary and non-monetary damage. In addition to the contract and employment breach that may have occurred, a person who has been discriminated against usually suffers from mental and emotional distress. They may also have suffered past and present economic loss and anticipate future economic loss. In sexual harassment cases, they may have suffered humiliation. The complainant should be able to stop or nullify the discriminatory action.

From the group justice perspective, remedies and sanctions should be able to tackle and eliminate the cause of the discriminatory treatment or effect. If necessary, the remedy should extend beyond the individual who brought the case to others similarly affected. It should also be sufficiently punitive to act as a deterrent to the continuation of such practice. In other words it should not be cheaper for an employer to pay a minimal fine rather than to stop the discriminatory practice. Optimally, remedies should be fashioned for the specific situation at hand to remedy both the cause and effect of gender discrimination, and should prevent its recurrence. From either perspective, a remedy should not be merely symbolic. The range of sanctions and remedies in use in countries includes criminal sanctions, civil damages, exemplary damages, injunctive relief, equitable relief, costs and fees. It is probably in this area, more than any other, that efforts are being undertaken to strengthen equality laws.

Enforcing judgements

Once a judgement or opinion has been rendered by a court or tribunal, it must be followed by the employer if it is to have any effect. In cases where it is not followed, claimants need to have some means of forcing the employer to comply with the order. It is in these instances that many countries invoke criminal sanctions for non-compliance with court orders. In some countries these are called contempt proceedings. In many countries, such as France and Norway, the sanctions for failing to follow an order are harsher than the original sanctions for the discriminatory action.

Specific difficulties in the application of equal pay

The difficulties encountered in the enforcement of equal pay cases appear to be greater than in many other discrimination cases. The present enforcement mechanisms appear to require adjustment to become more effective in resolving equal pay claims. In any revision of the national enforcement mechanism, the following key points concerning the application of the principle of equal pay for work of equal value should be considered.[14] The very meaning of the term 'work of equal value' still gives rise to uncertainty and confusion in many jurisdictions. Simply put, the principle of equal remuneration for work of equal value is intended to redress the undervaluing, and subsequent lower pay, of jobs undertaken primarily by women, when those jobs are found to be as demanding as the different jobs undertaken by men. The principle thus contemplates the comparison of different jobs on the basis of their content. Accordingly, it is much broader than the notion 'equal pay for equal work' that was prevalent in most countries of the world until the early 1970s.

If the jobs of women and men are to be compared in terms of their content or 'value', there must be some means to assess and compare the actual nature and demands of the work to be performed, in other words to determine the value of jobs. The International Labour Convention No. 100 on equal remuneration specifies only that measures are to be taken 'to promote the objective appraisal of jobs on the basis of the work to be performed' where 'such action will assist in giving effect to the provisions of this Convention'. Job evaluation schemes are not, however, free from problems in implementing pay equity. Job evaluation or classification is a mechanism used to determine the hierarchy of jobs in an organization or in a group of undertakings as a basis for devising a rational pay system. Such systems were, and remain, management tools to rank the order of jobs. Accordingly, they often reflect conservative or traditional organizational structures, including a gendered division of labour. Moreover, these systems may be influenced by differing societal perceptions about the importance of factors such as education or training. Many systems for comparing jobs are unable to take account of the diverse content of the different jobs in an organization – for example, administrative workers and nurses – because they were designed to order different hierarchies of posts for each particular group of jobs, based on different evaluation criteria. Emphasis was placed on using the same criteria for both men and women in job evaluation and classification systems only in the 1980s. Precise definitions of the elements to be compared were then included in national legislation. Generally, these are based on training and experience, responsibility, physical and mental effort and the conditions in which the work is performed.

These apparently objective criteria have also proven inadequate safeguards against sex bias. In particular, they tend to upgrade certain criteria specific to male jobs at the expense of ignoring or minimizing factors considered more 'feminine', for instance, physical strength rather than the strain of repetitive work at a sustained speed, physical effort as opposed to the emotional demand of caring for very ill persons, responsibility for product control against direct responsibility for the safety, training and well-being of children. Many characteristics of women's work are invisible to both men and women. More gender-neutral factors, which give weight to the work performed by both men and women, are being developed. An example is the use of the factors of mental and emotional demands plus physical demands to determine 'effort'.[15]

Scope of comparison

Even where legislation calls for equal pay for work of equal value, observance of that principle is commonly restricted to work undertaken for the same employer or sometimes to employment in the same establishment. As occupational segregation remains a persistent characteristic of all labour markets, progress towards equal pay will be restricted unless comparisons extend outside the scope of the individual enterprise or organization. Studies appear to indicate that the more centralized the wage-fixing system – which therefore allows potential for the broadest possible field of comparison – the greater is the ease of implementing gender pay equity. Conversely, as countries have moved towards decentralization, with employers being allowed greater autonomy to fix wages, there is concern that the existing means of enforcement will prove inadequate. There are enough indications to suggest that women's disadvantaged position in the workplace, their weaker bargaining power (either as individuals or as a group) and their lack of power to influence the bargaining agenda may be further disadvantaged by the move towards individual or enterprise bargaining. Apart from the need for employers and trade unions to develop strategies that involve and protect women, there appears to be a need for the responsible government authorities to ensure that a minimum standard of equity is observed.

What constitutes pay?

All elements of the pay package need to be taken into account in the effort to enforce equal pay for work of equal value. It is often those components of pay additional to the basic or minimum wage that are operated in a discriminatory manner (though the absence of legal minimum wages in selected sectors in some countries has operated to women's disadvantage). Objective systems such as productivity bonuses may be applied selectively or subjectively. Indeed, performance or merit bonuses tend to be awarded to managers, who tend to be males. The assumption of family responsibilities by women, or rather men's disinclination to assume them to the same degree, has also had a considerable negative effect on women's pay, either directly, in terms of women's ability to remain in employment continuously or, indirectly, through traditional views about the commitment of married women or mothers to work. Seniority pay has discriminated against women whose careers are disrupted to meet family responsibilities, particularly in countries like Japan, where lifelong attachment to a particular company has been the norm. It has been noted, however, that when advancement depends more on seniority than other factors, women may better achieve higher grades than when managerial discretion plays a major role in determining progress.

Frustration with slow progress towards implementing pay equity has led some authorities to take more dynamic measures to improve enforcement. In the Canadian Province of Ontario, the Pay Equity Act 1987 was introduced to 'redress systemic gender discrimination in compensation for work performed by employees in female job classes'. A determination to establish and maintain pay equity will necessarily involve a regular evaluation of the enforcement methods and their impact; and, if necessary, action to streamline or change those methods.

Conclusion

The overall impact of administrative and judicial action is difficult to measure. Chambers and Horton[16] in a study on the impact of industrial tribunal decisions in discrimination and equal pay cases on employers in the United Kingdom, found that for the majority of employers, the tribunal had no effect on attitudes towards promoting equality. There was some evidence that an adverse decision, or at least the filing of a complaint, played a part, among other influences, in the adoption of an organizational equal opportunity policy. There was little evidence, however, that the industrial tribunal's decisions led to a review of existing equal opportunity policies. In some cases the adverse decision resulted in disciplinary action against the offending employee. Of the few recommendations made to the employers, not all were implemented.

Chambers and Horton also observed that large employers were more likely than smaller employers to take action following an adverse tribunal decision. Public-sector bodies had a higher rate of follow-up action to promote equality after tribunal decisions than did private-sector organizations. The tribunal decisions were most likely to have an effect in promotion cases. They were least likely to have a positive effect in equal pay cases.

Most mechanisms of enforcement are not meeting their potential to help redress direct and indirect discrimination in employment. Some are simply not used and are totally ignored by law enforcement personnel and employers. Others are inadequate and in need of overhauling.

Some isolated improvements and measures to strengthen enforcement mechanisms have been undertaken in some countries. With the deficiencies and problems in national enforcement mechanisms in various regions of the world, interestingly, a parallel but ad hoc pattern of remedial actions is also beginning to emerge. A comprehensive set of recommendations has to be established to assist countries in their pursuit of effective enforcement of legal provisions that prohibit discrimination and promote equal opportunity in employment. It would appear that the time is ripe for serious consideration and further emphasis to be given to developing guidance material, at the international level, on the effective enforcement of non-discrimination and equal opportunity and treatment provisions. The guidance could be aimed at both administrative and judicial national enforcement mechanisms, and include the role that could be played by each of the social partners – employers, workers as well as government – and other relevant bodies.

Notes

Much of the information for this chapter was extracted from the authors' review of government reports on ratified Conventions, submitted to the ILO under article 22 of the ILO Constitution.

1. C. McCrudden: 'The effectiveness of European equality law: National mechanisms for enforcing gender equality law in the light of European requirements', in *Oxford Journal of Legal Studies*, Vol. 13, No. 3, 1993, pp. 331, 332.

2. Convention No. 111 also prohibits discrimination on grounds of race, colour, political opinion, religion, national extraction and social origin.

3. Convention No. 158 concerning termination of employment at the initiative of the employer provides that race, colour, sex, marital status, family responsibilities, pregnancy, religion, political opinion, national extraction or social origin shall not be considered valid reasons for termination.

4. Ibid., paras 99–102.

5. ILO: *A comprehensive women's employment strategy for Indonesia*, final report of an ILO/UNDP TSSI mission, Regional Office for Asia and the Pacific, Bangkok, June 1993, p. 96.

6. Spanish country paper in A. Bronstein and C. Thomas (eds) (1994) *European labour courts: The role and use of international and European labour standards in labour court decisions, and labour court jurisprudence on sex discrimination*, Labour–Management Relations Series, No. 81, Geneva, ILO.

7. The Ombudsman Fourteenth Annual Report, The Republic of Trinidad and Tobago, 31 January 1991 to 31 December 1991.

8. ILO, 'Tanzanian Monograph on Sexual Harassment', 1993 (unpublished).

9. Japanese law respecting the improvement of the welfare of women workers including the guarantee of equal opportunity and treatment between men and women in employment, 1 July 1972 (as amended 1 June 1985).

10. 'Achieving equal justice for women and men in the courts', the draft report of the Judicial Council Advisory Committee on gender bias in the courts, Judicial Council of California, 1990, Ch. 4, p. 3.

11. Cyprus Act No. 158 of 1989 concerning the Provision of Equal Remuneration to Men and Women for Work of Equal Value, 5 May 1989.

12. The Australian Sex Discrimination Act, 21 March 1984, section 94, provides for the imposition of fines on persons who subject or threaten to subject another person to any detriment for making or proposing to make a complaint under the Act.

13. Constitution of Afghanistan, December 1987, section 28.

14. The principle of equal remuneration for work of equal value is enunciated in the ILO Convention on Equal Remuneration, 1951 (No. 100).

15. New Zealand Department of Labour and the State Services Commission, 1991, *Equity at work, an approach to gender neutral job evaluation*, Canberra.

16. G. Chambers and C. Horton (1990) *Promoting sex equality: The role of industrial tribunals*, London, Policy Studies Institute.

PART IV
The role of relevant institutions other than government

10
The trade unions and women workers: current trends

EUGENIA DATE-BAH

Mobilization of women workers in groups, such as in trade unions, is an important strategy for their empowerment. Furthermore, freedom of association is a universal human right for both men and women. The chapter provides a brief overview of current trends in women's trade unionism in the different regions of the world. It covers membership rates and representation in leadership positions. It also analyses the unions' need to cover disadvantaged groups – workers in informal and rural sectors and in flexible and other precarious forms of work.

Background

A major development within the trade unions in the current changing world is women's increased participation, linked to some extent to the rise in women's labour force participation in most parts of the world. However, with the exception of a few countries, such as some of the Nordic states and Lesotho, women's membership of unions and occupation of union leadership positions remain unequal to men's. They still lag far behind the proportion of women in the labour force. On the whole, women remain a resource that has not been fully tapped by the trade unions. A concept of trade unionism that demonstrates full commitment to gender equality and thoroughly considers women workers' issues at every stage of its work does not yet exist in most parts of the world. Factors internal and external to the unions contribute to this phenomenon.

Increasingly, women's equal representation with men in the trade unions, other societal organs and in decision-making positions is perceived as a crucial feature of real democracy.[1] So far, however, in the current debate on democracy, it has tended to be interpreted only in terms of multipartism. New concepts, such as 'egalitarian' and 'parity' democracy, have therefore emerged in recent years to portray this (Institute of Study, 1995). The trade unions cannot be described as fully democratic institutions if their membership is mainly from one segment of the working population. The ICFTU's Sixth World Women's Conference in October 1994 pointed out that just as there cannot be democratic societies without unions, so there cannot be democratic unions without women's full participation. Women and gender equality issues should therefore be an integral 'part of mainstream trade union agenda' (ICFTU, 1994, p. 9 of Appendix).

The unions' degree of commitment to women workers' questions is closely linked to the extent of women's participation and representation in the unions' membership and leadership positions. There are gains to be made not only by women but also by the trade unions through women's greater representation and more active participation within their structures. In some areas of the world, sectoral shifts and other labour-market changes have had adverse effects on union membership. For example, reductions in the labour force of the manufacturing sector – a traditional stronghold of trade unionism – have brought about considerable loss of union membership in this sector. Women's increased participation in the unions therefore becomes essential for maintaining union strength and survival. An increase in women's membership also enriches the unions through diversity.

Many unions, at local, national, regional and international levels, have adopted policies and implemented specific strategies, programmes and activities geared to promoting women's membership and participation within their structures. Examples are: adoption of a union policy showing commitment to the issue; self-analysis by the unions themselves to identify factors influencing women's participation at the different levels of the union organizations; introduction of changes in union structure; promotion of trade union education for women; and sensitization of male and female trade unionists to women workers' and gender concerns. Some unions have also taken up issues on job segregation, equal pay for work of equal value, sexual harassment and maternity leave in collective bargaining. Seats for women have been reserved on union executive committees, and some unions have established women's committees. But much remains to be done for women's equal representation and full reflection of their concerns in the unions. Trebilcock (1991), for example, concludes in a review that 'full integration of women in the decision-making processes of trade union organizations remains an unfulfilled promise'.

Overview of current trends in women's union membership in different regions

Analysis of membership trends is greatly constrained by limited availability of sex-disaggregated statistics by the unions. According to ICFTU, women formed 34 per cent of the membership of its affiliated unions in 1994 (ICFTU, 1994, p. 1). There are, however, variations between regions: 33 per cent in Africa, 41 per cent in the Caribbean, 39 per cent in Europe, 31 per cent in Latin America, 38 per cent in North America and 39 per cent in the Pacific (ICFTU, 1991). Furthermore, the countries with high women's economic participation rates, such as Sweden (Donlevy, 1995) and Lesotho (ILO, 1994), also tend to have a relatively high proportion of women's union membership. The CMTU (Confederation of Trade Unions) of Malta and the TURK-IS (Confederation of Turkish Trade Unions) have women constituting 60 and 59 per cent respectively of their total membership. In all regions, women now form a large proportion of new entrants into unions.

North America Eaton (1992) shows that women's proportion of union membership in the United States and Canada has more than doubled in recent years. In the United States, for example, two out of every three new union members are reported to be women, while in Canada the figure is three out of four. Canadian unions are portrayed as having a stronger commitment to organizing women and a greater responsiveness to women's concerns. In both the US and Canada, women tend to be concentrated in few unions because of the job segregation that exists, with women found in a narrow range of sectors, mainly those covering traditional women's jobs, such as teaching, nursing, the public sector, clerical and other services. Women still face a 'hostile environment' in unions in other sectors.

Despite similarity in the industrial profiles of Canada and the United States, differences exist between them in women's unionization trends, and in effectiveness and intensity of union efforts to mobilize and encourage women as members and leaders. Early in 1992, 29 per cent of women workers in Canada, compared to 14 per cent in the US, were unionized (Eaton, 1992). In the case of Canada, this represents a tremendous increase from 16 per cent three decades ago. The figure for the US, however, appears to be almost the same as 30 years ago. Men's unionization in the US has declined from 35 per cent to 20 per cent during the same period, while in Canada men's unionization has remained at 38 per cent. The divergence between the two countries in women's unionization is attributed to differences in policies and programmes pursued by the unions and the general attitude in the two countries towards gender equality. Canadian unions have tended, on the whole, to adopt more innovative policies towards women workers. Women's caucuses in Canadian unions are observed by Eaton to be better organized and more closely linked to relevant women's organizations outside the unions. Thus, such issues as child-care, family leave and pay equity have improved further in Canada than in the US. Unions in which women have reached a critical mass of between 40 and 50 per cent of membership, and in which women's caucuses have been formed, were observed to have implemented more courageous positive action for women.

Western Europe Women's share of union membership is on the increase (Hastings and Coleman, 1992). Declines in union density are more dramatic for men than for women. Furthermore, new entrants into the unions are mainly women. For example, in the FNV (Netherlands Trade Union Confederation) and CNV (Christian National Federation of Trade Unions in the Netherlands), women form 80 and 60 per cent, respectively, of new entrants. Cross-national and sectoral differences in union density, including that of women, are explained by Hastings and Coleman in terms of institutional and political factors, structural and economic variables as well as initiatives undertaken by the unions. These factors, however, do not sufficiently account for the observed differences in all cases. Other contributory factors include the fact that women tend to work in sectors of the economy with lower levels of unionization, and constitute a high proportion of workers in small enterprises and in casual and atypical forms of employment, which are often not unionized. In the unionized sections of the service and public sectors – the most significant sectors for women's employment in Europe and in other regions – women's level of union representation is high. For example, women constitute 92 per cent of the Chartered Society of Physiotherapy, the union of physiotherapists in the United Kingdom (SERTUC, 1994). Generally, women's concerns appear to be better covered in unions with significant numbers of women members.

Caribbean Most unions, like those in Trinidad and Tobago, are general ones. Only a few are industry- or sector-specific, such as the unions of teachers and civil servants. Women predominate in some unions, especially the National Union of Government and Federated Workers, the Bank and General Workers' Union and the Trinidad and Tobago Unified Teachers' Association, where they form 71 per cent of the membership.

Africa Women now form 33 per cent of trade union membership (Date-Bah, 1995). Several trade unions have reported growth in women's membership. However, this growth remains lower than women's participation in the labour force. In Africa, the only exception is Lesotho, where women outnumber men in most unions. The Lesotho Labour Congress, for example, reported a membership of 90 per cent women in 1993. This unique situation is related to the predominance of women over men in the country's labour force in view of the large-scale male migration for work in South Africa. Yet women's numerical strength in the Lesotho unions has not led to any high degree of gender sensitivity in union activities in terms of fighting for issues of concern to women workers (ILO, 1994). Women unionists have yet to utilize fully the power that they have, through their superior numerical strength, to change the unions. The challenge in Lesotho is not how to empower women in unions, but how to raise the awareness and sensitivity of both female and male members to focus not only on bread-and-butter matters, but also on strategic issues, especially in relation to women (Date-Bah, 1995). The proportion of women in unions in the region is linked to the history of trade unionism in specific countries and sectors, the extent of structural adjustment programme under implementation, and the adequacy and coverage of the legal instruments relevant for industrial relations; these tend to focus on formal sector workers, while the majority of workers in the region are in the informal and rural sectors. Other essential factors include differences between the public and private sectors and unequal sexual division of labour at home, which limits women's availability for union activities after work.

Latin America   There has been an increase in women's union membership (Balliache and Febres, 1993), but this numerical increase appears not to have led to an increase in women's power in the unions in terms of representation among union leaders, who participate in collective bargaining and other high-level meetings with employers, or negotiate labour disputes and strikes. One therefore needs to go beyond the mere numbers of women's union membership to assess women's current importance in trade union life and activities.

Asia   Women's percentage of total union membership ranges from less than 5 per cent, for APFTU and PNFTU Pakistan and JSP Bangladesh, to 53 per cent in CWC Sri Lanka (Phillips, 1995). In FITA/TNA Tonga, women constitute 100 per cent. On average, women in the ICFTU affiliates in Asia form 25 per cent of trade union membership. Many of the unions' women's membership figures have not kept pace with the large increase of women in the labour force. Women's union membership tends to reflect the sectors and occupations organized historically. For instance, the high female membership in CWC Sri Lanka derives almost entirely from the union's historical strength in the tea plantations. In Malaysia, women's union membership has been growing slowly, from 23.04 per cent in 1956 to 27.1 per cent in 1986.

Women's proportion in union leadership

While women are gradually becoming visible in union leadership, they remain grossly under-represented in these positions, especially at the higher levels. There has, however, been considerable progress in women's representation among shop stewards and generally at the lower leadership positions at local level.

The US and Canada differ with respect to the average proportion of women in union leadership positions. The figure is one in four for Canada, but one in eight for the US (Eaton, 1992). In both countries women's numbers in union leadership positions have been increasing gradually, in particular at the level of the local unions. The range of measures implemented to this end includes setting seats aside for women, organizing special monitoring and training programmes, and adopting other affirmative action measures. The specific leadership positions held by women tend not to be the strategic or key roles with prospects for future advancement.

In Western Europe, a positive trend has been observed in women's proportion of union leadership positions (Hastings and Coleman, 1992). However, only two out of 31 national trade union confederations covered in a survey by the European Trade Union Confederation (ETUC) had women leaders (Braithwaite and Byrne, 1994). Women continue to be under-represented at the unions' higher-level leadership and decision-making positions. Furthermore, they are under-represented in the unions' executive committees. The British TUC and the German DAG have women forming between 31 and 35 per cent of their executive committee members. In all the other unions, the proportion was lower (Donlevy, 1995). Furthermore, few women serve on the teams that engage in collective bargaining.

In Africa, women's under-representation in union leadership positions is explained in terms of the occupational segregation prevalent in the labour market, including women's limited participation in managerial and decision-making positions (Date-Bah, 1995). With respect to the Caribbean, women occupy only 25 per cent or less of union executive positions, according to one estimate (Clark, 1993). Furthermore, despite the high proportion of women in some unions, women's numbers in leadership positions remain low. For example, they constitute 6 per cent of the executives in the National Union of Government and Federated Workers' Union and 9 per cent of the executives of the Trinidad and Tobago Unified Teachers' Association. In Latin America, trade union leadership remains a 'difficult area for women to penetrate' (Balliache and Febres, 1993). Contributory factors include the unions' strong male culture and the difficulty for some women, especially those who are single parents, to combine the long hours of work demanded of union leaders with their responsibility for child-care and other domestic duties.

In Asia and the Pacific, the percentage of women in executive positions continues to be low despite progress in some areas. It is 3 per cent in Malaysia, 5 per cent in Singapore and 6 per cent in Taiwan. The highest percentages are in the Philippines (12 per cent) and Fiji (15 per cent) (Phillips, 1995).

In all the regions, women continue to be under-represented at union congresses, the unions' highest policy-making organs, unless women's meetings are convened just beforehand (ILO, 1993). Women are also unequally represented in non-elected union staff positions. There are a few exceptions in Europe. For example, the proportion of female departmental officials was 51 per cent in the FNV (Netherlands) and the LO (Norway), 67 per cent in the GSEE (Greece) and 42 per cent in the ICTU (Ireland). In the SGB (Switzerland), the TCO (Sweden) and the ICTU (Ireland), women formed 50 per cent of the heads of departments (Braithwaite and Byrne, 1994).

Union measures to expand women's representation

While the principle of equality is now accepted by most unions, in reality efforts made to pursue it, together with the degree of commitment, have not yet led to the existence of full equality in many unions. Many trade unions do not even keep statistics disaggregated by sex and, therefore, cannot adequately monitor the impact, if any, that these efforts are having on women.

In all regions, measures adopted by unions continue to include equality policies/programmes, changes in union constitution, creation of women's departments, appointment of equality or women's officers, targeted female recruitment and information campaigns, allocation of a number of leadership seats to women, organization of special seminars/congresses for women, and adoption of other affirmative action measures. Campaigns have been launched on issues of particular interest to women, child-care facilities at union meetings have been provided by some unions and publications and information materials produced. Some national trade union centres, for example, have an Equal Opportunities Committee with various tasks, such as advising and initiating relevant policy discussions with unions. Efforts have also been made by a few to incorporate women's concerns and gender equality issues in collective bargaining with employers (O'Regan and Thompson, 1993; Dickens, 1993). But the unions' commitment to the implementation and monitoring of the measures varies; it is not very high in many instances (Hastings and Coleman, 1992). Furthermore, unions differ in the range of measures adopted. For instance, a survey of 38 unions in the United Kingdom in late 1993–early 1994 (SERTUC, 1994), found that no national women's committees existed in 13 of them and that child-care arrangements at conferences were not provided by six. In the different regions, attempts are currently being made by a few unions to inform women about their rights and also to mobilize domestic, farm and other unorganized workers, the bulk of whom are women. Resolutions and plans of action have been adopted by several unions to guide their coverage of women's issues and promotion of women's representation into leadership positions. The problem of sexual harassment has also been recognized by several unions, which have adopted guidelines, codes of practice and other measures to tackle it (see Chapter 6).

Proposals for further action to empower women in the unions

Empowerment of women in unions and the strengthening of the unions' role in the promotion of gender equality at work will not occur without the unions' adoption of conscious and deliberate policies to extend women's membership, influence and power within their structures. The persistence of inequalities between women and men in membership and leadership of many unions could be attributed to the inadequacy of measures so far adopted, the extent of their implementation and monitoring and the unions' insufficient adjustment to changes in the socio-economic environment. Also of significance are the limited role models for women, especially in union leadership positions, and inadequate supportive measures by employers, governments, national women's machineries and women workers themselves. Employers, for example, by their policies and practices, can assist or hamper women's participation in unions. Governments can make a significant contribution through enacting appropriate labour and equality legislation that can enhance women's attachment to the market, promote women workers' rights and the unions' coverage of workers in all economic sectors – both formal and informal. Discrimination and job segregation at the workplace deserve to be tackled by employers and governments, together with unions, through adoption and implementation of pay equity and comparable-worth programmes, positive-action measures and training (Eaton, 1992).

Sustained research (for example on the impact of current trends in the amalgamation of trade unions), the development of appropriate materials on effective techniques for organizing women workers, and training more women as workers' education instructors are necessary. Intensified assistance by international organizations such as the ILO, international trade union federations like the International Confederation of Free Trade Unions (ICFTU) the World Confederation of Labour (WCL) and the World Federation of Trade Unions (WFTU), international trade union secretariats, regional trade union bodies (e.g. the European Trade Union Confederation and the Organization of African Trade Union Unity) and others is necessary. It can include provision of advisory services, conduct of research, preparation of appropriate training materials, dissemination of data and organization of workers' education.

Other relevant measures are organization of awareness-raising campaigns on equality issues and women's rights; modifications in the unions' traditional structures, male culture, methods and hours of work to suit women; provision of child-care facilities by more unions at their meetings; strengthening of women's committees and departments within unions to play a more active role in articulating women's concerns; launching recruitment campaigns; undertaking gender training of union members and leaders to ensure that due consideration is taken of women's views and needs in union decision- and policy-making and in collective bargaining. Building women's confidence in trade unionism requires focus through training. Women's unequal share of family and domestic responsibilities also requires attention to enhance their availability for leadership and other demanding positions within unions.

The collection of gender-specific data by unions deserve strong focus to permit adequate monitoring of women's unionization trends. Furthermore, the unions' commitment to equality policies they have adopted should be reflected in the resources − staff and funds − allocated to this work. The unions should acknowledge the value of, and adequately tap, the differences in women's and men's experiences to enrich and strengthen their work and structures. They can intensify their organizing of women through house-to-house calls, big publicity campaigns on such matters as child-care leave, setting up information centres to offer advice readily to women workers and increasing women's access to workers' education (Phillips, 1995). In addition, an action plan for European women trade unionists calls for 'mentorship' schemes to be encouraged, through which a senior official 'oversees the development of a woman's career'.

Other measures, proposed for example by the ICFTU at its Sixth World Women's Conference, include the unions' continued 'work for the adoption of strong equality legislation and the elimination of discrimination in the labour market', reaffirmation of 'their commitment to the (ICFTU) Programme of Action for the Integration of Women into Trade Unions' and elimination of sexist language from their constitutions, functions and titles. Women trade union leaders are urged to build networks among themselves for mutual support and to 'overcome their isolation'. The unions must adopt diverse positive-action measures to remove barriers hindering women's access to decision-making levels. In particular, they should create additional seats, set some of the existing seats aside, have a quota system or numerical targets for women, include women in negotiating teams, promote gender sensitivity among the unions' male leaders and monitor the implementation of such affirmative-action measures. The trade unions in the Central and Eastern European countries undergoing transition to a market economy are specifically called upon to ensure that women's problems are taken into account and tackled in union activities. Also urged are: international solidarity through networking, contacts and exchange of information between trade unions in the different regions (ICFTU, 1994, Appendix p. 9) for mutual support; working women mobilizing themselves and encouraging each other to contest union elections for a wide range of offices; and putting significant pressure on union leaders to focus on issues of concern to women.

Finally, it is essential for unions to broaden the scope of their operations to assist and mobilize workers in the informal and rural sectors, where most women workers are concentrated in Africa and some other developing regions. These unorganized workers also tend to be the most disadvantaged in terms of poverty, precarious working conditions and inadequate social security coverage and protection.

The trade unions and women workers in the urban informal and rural sectors: Africa, a case-study[2]

The urban informal and rural sectors are very important in the labour market of Africa in terms, *inter alia*, of the large number of people who are engaged in them. Furthermore, in the current climate of economic restructuring and retrenchment in the formal sector, it is the informal sector that has become the 'shock absorber' in terms of absorbing some of those who have been laid off and providing sustenance to many households. By covering the informal sector and other unorganized and vulnerable groups of workers, in addition to formal sector wage-earners, the trade unions would thus be speaking on behalf of a very significant group of workers and could attempt to assist them. In addition, with the large numbers of women in the informal, rural and the other unorganized sectors, trade union coverage of these groups of workers is an essential aspect of making such unions women-friendly.

A number of advantages could also be gained by workers in the unorganized sectors through their association with, or involvement in, the trade unions. For example, membership of the union as a registered legal body entitles one to certain rights. Furthermore, trade unionism can help to build up the confidence of such workers through training. The development of confidence could in turn contribute to a change in the image of their work and also in the government's perception of such work, which could enhance the ability of these workers to obtain governmental and other forms of assistance. Furthermore, the trade unions can assist such workers, for example domestic workers, to obtain the rights enjoyed by formal sector workers, such as paid leave, maternity leave, minimum wages and a pension. Trade unionization could thus constitute an essential means of empowering the informal, rural and other unorganized workers.

It is to be envisaged that owing to the different characteristics of workers in the formal sector, who have traditionally been the focus of the trade unions, and those in the informal, rural and other unorganized sectors, the unions might have to adopt new strategies and approaches for this new work. A number of these workers are scattered and work in isolation. Furthermore, they tend to lack literacy skills because of limited access to training and education. Moreover, they tend not to be covered by existing labour laws or other relevant industrial relations instruments. In some instances, legislation does not allow unions to organize such workers. These and other characteristics make it difficult for trade unions to organize them using their traditional strategies and methods of work. In some cases, therefore, the strategies adopted by the unions have included the planning of group activities around training and special services on income-generating projects. The unions have sometimes linked up with co-operatives or similar activities to assist such workers. Others have found it necessary to establish working relationships with national women's machineries and non-governmental organizations already working with such groups.

Another major constraint is the unions' lack of adequate resources in terms of finance and personnel to enlarge the scope of their operation to include workers in the unorganized sectors. There is also the limited capacity of workers in the unorganized sector to make substantial contributions in terms of payment of dues for such work. This financial constraint makes the unions hesitant to broaden the scope of their work because of limited capacity. Resources are crucial because, owing to the limited stronghold of the unions in the unorganized sectors, attempts at organizing there will tend to be long-term. They will also require considerable patience. Technical assistance and support by bodies such as the ILO and the international trade union confederations or secretariats could thus greatly facilitate the work of local or national unions in this area.

Union activities with such workers require education programmes and training materials that are adapted sometimes to illiterate people. Furthermore, such workers are not in an employee-employer relationship, so that traditional collective action through unions will not be directed to an employer, but more towards government decision-making organs or financial institutions granting credit, and so on. Thus, the workers will not require training in shop-floor bargaining procedures but in tackling the constraints and the discrimination encountered in their work through collective action. They will need access to credit, relevant skills in the management of small-scale businesses, appropriate technology, marketing opportunities, and also child-care, to enable them to combine their work with their family responsibilities. The attraction of workers to trade unions in the informal and rural sectors will depend upon whether membership leads to identifiable benefits and also enables some of their specific needs to be met.

In Africa, a few attempts have been made by the trade unions to organize these unorganized workers, such as domestic workers, urban informal sector women workers and rural workers.

Domestic workers and unions

In several countries around the world, trade unions have assisted domestic workers, despite the scattered nature of their work locations, to organize themselves to seek an improvement in their very poor working conditions, including very long working hours, very low wages and no job security. In Namibia, for example, in 1990 – before independence – domestic workers were assisted by the National Union of Namibian Workers (NUNW) to form the Allied Workers' Union, which is currently affiliated to the NUNW. Despite its short history, about a third of the total number of domestic workers in the country are already members of the union. Information on the union is provided regularly by the Namibian Broadcasting Corporation and, through this, a number of domestic workers have learned about it and applied for membership. The union has branches in each region and a section steward at the local levels, not a shop steward. The Namibian Domestic

Allied Workers' Union (NDAWU) assists its members to negotiate with their employers, organizes literacy and income-generating activities and also places considerable emphasis on the provision of education about trade unionism. By organizing, therefore, some improvements are beginning to occur in the working conditions of Namibian domestic workers.

Informal sector women workers and unions

In Burkina Faso, the Association of Women Market Traders in Ouagadougou and the Cissin-Natenga Women's Association (together with other informal sector groups) have been affiliated to the central trade union body, the Organisation Nationale des Syndicats Libres (ONSL), since the inception of the union. The ONSL is quite progressive: five women are represented on its executive board of 37 members and it also has a women's committee, which is responsible for training, organization and implementation of various projects for women. Furthermore, it has organized several seminars specifically for women. The ONSL Women's Committee has set up a Market Women's Committee and also organized seminars for women's leadership in various trading activities in the informal sector. When the rents for market stalls were raised following renovation of the market place, the union approached the relevant authorities on behalf of its members to have such rents reduced, in some cases by half the original amount.

A number of women of Cissin-Natenga have also become literate and acquired a trade through functional literacy programmes run by the women's associations. In addition, the ONSL has assisted with selling products from the association's activities, such as tablecloths, bracelets and woven cloth, to enable the members to earn an income. Furthermore, it has organized courses in trade unionism, together with the market women in Ouagadougou, and obtained a loan from the bank for these women workers' activities.

The ONSL, through its efforts with informal sector workers, has increased its membership and also tried to adapt to the socio-economic context within which it operates.

Women and rural workers' organizations

An ILO/IFPAAW[3] project in several African countries focused on including more women in rural workers' organizations in the region.[4] The project set out to promote a corps of women workers' specialists with adequate training to improve women's participation in rural workers' organizations.

In the project's pilot phase, seminars organized for women covered women's participation in trade union activities, gender training, social security and women, support services for working parents, sexual harassment at work, occupational health and safety, and selected special services such as child-care centres, literacy training and income-generating activities for rural women.

Potential women leaders among the participants were selected at the end of the pilot phase to undergo training on trainers' courses, with a focus on women's leadership roles, the development of organization-based services and self-help activities for women members, trade union administration, education, labour laws, international labour standards, appropriate technology, health and family education.

Drama was perceived to be an effective channel for adult learning and was therefore emphasized in the project and also recommended as an effective approach to rural workers' education. A participatory approach to learning was used and taught to the trainers. This covered group discussions, role-playing and chairing of meetings to enable the women to express their needs.

Women's committees were encouraged and formed in all the project's participating unions. Some special services were promoted, including adult literacy classes, child-care facilities and other social activities such as dancing, drama and music. Through such joint activities, the women were able to meet regularly to discuss their common problems and how they could be tackled. The women were also taught their civic responsibilities, which helped to raise their awareness.

While none of the project's five unions had women on their executive councils before the project, three of them now have women on these councils. Interaction was promoted among women in different countries, and even regions, to share and compare experiences in this area in order to enhance understanding of the similarity of their problems and stimulate ideas on how to tackle them.

The strategies adopted, and the benefits and scope for more action

Similar trade union efforts to organize the unorganized women workers have also been undertaken in other regions, both developing and developed (Martens and Mitter, 1994). There is clearly great potential for such action.

A number of strategies have been adopted. In some cases, the workers formed an association and approached the trade union for help. In other cases, the central trade union body perceived the need to organize informal sector workers. In all cases, informal sector workers involved in the unions have derived clear benefits such as training, access to funds, improved work sites and even marketing outlets. This demonstrates the relevance of trade unionism for these workers. Even greater gains have been documented in other parts of the world, including extension of the minimum wage, paid leave and maternity provisions to domestic workers in Recife, Brazil (Anderfuhren and Cisse, 1993).

While the initiative can come from either the workers or the unions, outside support is needed in terms of finance for the organization of training and other activities, design and production of appropriate workers' education materials, sponsoring and organization of relevant training courses, seminars and other meetings to examine critically the efforts being made and to plan for the future. The smooth development of such work further requires an appropriate social and political setting with labour laws and other instruments that also cover informal and rural workers, as well as the ratification and observance of relevant international instruments. Governments and other actors also have a contribution to make towards this endeavour.

Trade union coverage of informal, rural-sector and other vulnerable workers is an important means of strengthening the capacities of these groups and giving them the protection and avenues for development that they desperately need. It is also an essential means of empowering the trade unions themselves through expansion of their membership and diversification of their work, which could enhance their relevance to the society in which they operate. Further work in this area could contribute to making the trade unions more representative and, thus, more democratic.

Notes

1. See, for example, Council of Europe, 1994.
2. For detailed analysis of the situation worldwide, see Martens, M. and Mitter, S., 1994. For a review of the situation in Africa, See Date-Bah, 1993.
3. IFPAAW is the International Federation of Plantation, Agricultural and Allied Workers.
4. See Maloba-Caines, 1994.

References

Anderfuhren, M. and M. Cisse (1993) *Les syndicats et les travailleuses dans le secteur non structuré: Le cas des travailleuses domestiques à Recife, Brésil, et des vendeuses sur les marchés à Ouagadougou, Burkina Faso*, Geneva, ILO, IDP Women WP-6.

Balliache, D. and C.E. Febres (1993) *Participación de la mujer en los sindicos de Venezuela*, Geneva, ILO, IDP Women WP-11.

Braithwaite, M. and C. Byrne (1994) *Women in decision-making in the trade unions*, Brussels, European Trade Union Confederation.

Clark, R. (1993) *Women in trade unions in Trinidad and Tobago*, Geneva, ILO, IDP Women WP-17.

Council of Europe (1994) *Equality and democracy: Utopia or challenge*, Strasbourg.

Date-Bah, E. (1993) 'African trade unions and the challenge of organizing women workers in the unorganized sectors', in *Labour Education*, Geneva, ILO, 92-1993/3.

— (ed.) (1995) 'Towards gender equality in the unions: A worldwide overview', draft manuscript, Geneva, ILO.

Dickens, L. (1993) *Collective bargaining and the propmotion of equality: The case of the United Kingdom*, Geneva, IDP Women WP-12.

Donlevy, V. (1995) 'Women in trade union movement in the countries of the European Union', thesis presented for the degree of Master of European Studies, Bruges, College of Europe.

Eaton, S. (1992) *Women workers, unions and industrial sectors in North America*, Geneva, ILO, IDP Women WP-1.

Hastings, S. and M. Coleman (1992) *Women and trade unions in Europe*, Geneva, ILO, IDP Women WP-4.

ICFTU (1991) *Report on 5th World Women's Conference*, Ottawa.

— (1994) *Changing the world through equality: The trade union vision*, The Hague, Sixth World Women's Conference of the ICFTU, October.

ILO (1993) *World labour report*, Geneva.

— (1994) *Promoting gender equality in employment in Lesotho: An agenda for action*, Turin.

Institute of Study (ed.) (1995) *No democracy without women*, Salzburg.

Maloba-Caines, K. (1994) 'Workers' education programme for women members of rural workers' organizations in Africa', in Martens and Mitter, 1994.

Martens, M. and S. Mitter (1994) *Women in trade unions: Organizing the unorganized*, Geneva, ILO.

Olney, S.L. (1996) *Unions in a changing world: problems and prospects in selected industrialized countries*, Geneva, ILO.

O'Regan, C. and B. Thompson (1993) *The unionization of women workers in different industrial sectors in South Africa*, Geneva, ILO, IDP Women WP-10.

Phillips, K. (1995) 'Women workers and trade unions in Asia', draft report, Geneva.

SERTUC (1994) – Southern and Eastern Region of the (British) Trade Union Congress, *Struggling for equality: A survey of women and their trade unions*, London.

Trebilcock, A. (1991) 'Strategies for strengthening women's participation in the trade union', in *International Labour Review*, Vol. 130, No. 4, Geneva, ILO.

11

The role of employers' organizations and other bodies in the promotion of gender equality in employment: the case of Malaysia

YOKE WAN LEE

This chapter first provides a descriptive sketch of women's economic participation in Malaysia, including their role in managerial and entrepreneurial positions. Secondly, it reviews the policies, programmes and activities adopted by government and both the private and public sectors to promote gender equality in employment. It then offers guidelines to employers' organizations in the development of programmes and activities geared towards the promotion of equality in employment.

Brief overview of women workers in Malaysia

Malaysian women seem to be making use of the new economic opportunities emerging from the present economic growth of their country. Their labour force participation rate increased from 37.2 per cent in 1970 to 47.8 per cent in 1990. However, this participation rate continues to lag behind that of men, whose rates were 81.3 per cent and 85.6 per cent respectively. The contributory factors to this trend are varied. Among them are:

- the rapid growth of the Malaysian economy, which has undergone tremendous structural changes, as it evolved from a primary commodity producer into an increasingly diversified economy with an expanding export-oriented industrial base. This has important implications in terms of demand for skilled and unskilled labour;
- the improvement of education and training facilities under the National Development Policy, aimed at producing an educated, skilled and trained labour force. Wider and higher levels of education have opened up employment opportunities for women;
- social, cultural and religious factors, such as the acceptance of marriage at a later age and the gradual erosion of traditional reservations, that used to inhibit women from joining the labour force have undergone changes.

Over the last two decades, the proportion of women workers classified as employees rose from 38.9 per cent in 1970 to 62.9 per cent in 1990, indicating the growing significance of formal sector employment for women. Women, however, are still under-represented at the administrative and managerial levels and tend to be concentrated in the areas of clerical, sales, service, agriculture and production work.

Women continue to face a number of constraints before entry into the labour market, such as in education, choice of disciplines and skills, and within the labour market itself. In the face of a rapidly tightening supply of labour in certain sectors and locations, it is a matter of concern that the involvement of women in economic activities continues to be inhibited by a number of constraints, such as the following:

- the dual and often competing responsibilities of family and career restrict the mobility and increased participation of women in the labour market; to take the example of job transfers, it is more acceptable for a wife to request a transfer to follow her husband. Inflexible ideas of gender roles in the domestic sphere and in the labour market constrain and inhibit efficient deployment of human resources. Sharing of family responsibilities between men and women has not been promoted;
- the tendency of women to opt for non-technical areas has limited the adaptability and participation of women in the labour market;
- social mores and other socio-cultural prejudices regarding the role and status of women in society and in the labour market restrain their involvement and attainment of their full potential in economic activities. Women are perceived as secondary earners who supplement family incomes rather than as co-earners whose economic activities are crucial to the family. Consequently, income-generating programmes targeted at women generally reinforce their homemaker roles, providing few opportunities for the acquisition of new and more marketable skills. The mass media continue to portray traditional roles for women, which do not reflect present reality;
- lack of appropriate management training, inadequate access to credit and other productive resources, and a paucity of relevant market information also hinder the participation of women in the economy;
- working conditions and environment are generally not conducive to the sustained employment of working wives and mothers. Employers are reluctant to invest in skills' upgrading and to introduce flexible working hours;
- limited attention has been paid by the male-dominated trade unions to women's situation in the labour market;

- there are high costs and difficulties in obtaining stable and trust-worthy child-care for their children. The support of the extended family in this sphere is eroding and domestic help is becoming more expensive. The provision of child-care should not be viewed as solely a woman's problem, but as a joint concern of husband and wife and indeed of the whole society;
- lack of supportive legislation guaranteeing equal employment opportunities for men and women (ILO/EASMAT, 1996).

A recent assessment of women's situation in the Malaysian labour market summarized the measures required to tackle women's constraints as follows: 'promoting an integrated child-care policy, creating a more enabling work environment, providing gender-sensitive skill training, helping women return to work, stepping beyond gender blindness and empowering women in the workplace' (ILO/EASMAT, 1996, p. vii).

There are few women in management. They are dispersed across sectors and are uncommon in most organizations. Most women in Malaysia make the decision to commit themselves to their career relatively late in life — usually in their thirties. When first joining the employment market women tend to accept whatever position is offered. Women may fear success, especially in a traditionally male-dominated organization — a classic double-bind situation, the fear that success in competition may lead to a loss of femininity. In addition, the scarcity of successful female managers has made it difficult for women in general to have role models demonstrating appropriate and effective work styles that allow them to combine work and family responsibilities.

In addition to male employers' prejudices against women occupying managerial positions, many women are also unaware of their potential in management. There are relatively more women in entrepreneurial and small business operations than in corporate hierarchies. Nevertheless, women entrepreneurs in Malaysia are few. In 1984 only 0.65 per cent were classified as employers and about 16 per cent were own-account workers. There are no available data on the size of businesses owned by women. The age group with the highest figures for both categories (employer and own-account worker) is the 40–54-year-old group. In one study (Lang and Sieh, 1990), it was found that 18 per cent of the women entrepreneurs covered in the survey were involved in retail trade, and more than 40 per cent were involved in various diverse services such as insurance, recreational, community and household services. About 60 per cent were in sole control of their enterprises, while less than 15 per cent had a superior in the organization. About 70 per cent had 10 employees or less while only 3 per cent had

50–100 employees. In terms of their needs, more than 55 per cent felt that they needed improvement in the functional areas of marketing, finance, management, budgeting and planning.

Existing policies, programmes and activities for promoting gender equality in employment

Government role

There is a National Policy for Women, formulated in 1989, which reflects the government's commitment to optimizing the potential of women in the social and economic development of the nation and establishes guidelines for integrating women's contribution to the process of national development. The overall objectives are:

• to ensure equitable sharing in the acquisition of resources and information, and access to opportunities and benefits of development, for both men and women;
• to integrate women in all sectors of national development in line with their abilities and needs, in order to improve the quality of life, eradicate poverty, abolish ignorance and illiteracy and ensure a peaceful and prosperous nation.

Concrete measures are required to ensure that the government's commitment to integrating women in the development process is realized.

Under the Sixth Malaysia Plan (1991–95), the government took cognizance of the multiplicity of women's roles in the family, society and economy and recognized that specific strategies must be formulated to incorporate women effectively in the process of development. The National Advisory Council on the Integration of Women in Development (NACIWID) was set up in the Prime Minister's Department in 1976 to translate the Declaration adopted by the World Conference, convened in International Women's Year in Mexico in 1975, into the national context. In 1983 a Secretariat for Women's Affairs (HAWA) was established to monitor and evaluate services for women provided by the public and private sectors. The government has allocated RM 20 million (RM 2.42 = US$1,1995) under the Sixth Malaysia Plan to support programmes and projects to be implemented by HAWA. To enhance the role and awareness of women in development and to assist in the planning, monitoring and evaluation of development programmes for women, the Information and Resource Centre for Women in Development was officially launched as a national network in August 1993.

Even though there is no explicit gender equality legislation, there is the Employment Act of 1955, which covers issues also of relevance to women. Workers employed in manual labour (irrespective of pay) and those whose pay exceeds RM 1,250 per month are within the scope of this Act. Employers in agricultural and industrial undertakings who wish their female employees to work between the hours of 10 p.m. and 5 a.m. have to obtain the approval of the Director-General of Labour. This approval is subject to conditions such as the provision of free transport to and from the workplace, 11 consecutive hours free from such work before commencement of work for the next day, and payment of a shift allowance.

Apart from the Ministry of Human Resources, other government organizations such as Kemajuan Masyarakat (KEMAS), Federal Land Development Authority (FELDA), Rubber Industry Smallholders Development Authority (RISDA) and some regional development authorities also provide various support services – including educational, social and religious programmes.

Role of non-governmental organizations including women's associations

Several NGOs have been playing relevant roles. The National Population and Family Development Board (NPFDB) conducts courses on family life, parenting and counselling techniques and also implements programmes related to the promotion of happy families through family togetherness. The Islamic Economic Development Foundation of Malaysia assists women with small business loans without collateral under the Ikhtias Project Fund. This Fund, managed by Amanah Ikhtiar Malaysia (AIM), which is a non-governmental trust agency, has further facilitated the increasing involvement of women in economic activities. Preliminary studies indicate that not only do women account for the majority of the clientele of AIM's credit scheme but they are also better debt repayers. Their repayment rate is as high as 99.9 per cent. Other non-governmental organizations, such as the National Council of Women's Organizations (NCWO), Women's Institute (WI), Islamic Women's Action Organization (PERTIWI), Women's Aid Organization and the Islamic Women's Welfare Board, have instituted various self-help development programmes and provided support facilities to promote women's participation in economic and social activities.

Although there are many women's organizations, they are mainly welfare-oriented. Hence there is a need to establish women's trade or business associations to provide assistance and support to business-women. Of the few that already exist, the most active is the Persatuan Perniagaan Wanita Bumiputra. It has been very active in helping Malay businesswomen solve their problems through the provision of training courses in different aspects of management, motivation and instilling of self-confidence in their business dealings.

The Women and Media Network for Asia and the Pacific Regions, located in Kuala Lumpur, has initiated a series of dialogues with women's groups and media organizations to pursue a more positive and realistic image of women and women's issues.

Employers' organizations

Employers' organizations in Malaysia have, at tripartite discussions, been supportive of government efforts to encourage women's participation in the workforce. This is especially so in view of the tight labour market and the shortage of human resources to meet increasing demand. Recently the National Labour Advisory Council, the highest tripartite consultative body comprising the social partners – government, employers and workers – considered the issues relating to the introduction of child-care centres and the concept of flexible time into human resources management. A survey was carried out by the Ministry of Human Resources which covered 400 factories in peninsular Malaysia employing more than 200 workers. The objective of the survey was to gauge the feasibility of child-care centres at the workplace.

The potential role of employers' organizations in promoting gender equality

Much more can be done by employers' organizations to provide guidelines to member companies on women-related issues. In general, sex discrimination legislation in developed and developing countries has not always effectively compelled employers to take positive measures to combat inequality in employment. Among the reasons why employers voluntarily embark on positive action are the following:

- the question of public image – managers and owners like their organization to look progressive and socially responsible;
- within a tight labour market, employers realize that they will be obliged to compete with each other for unemployed or under-employed groups;
- women are fighting discrimination and employers do not relish the idea of being dragged through the courts;
- there is pressure from government and non-governmental organizations for changes in the workplace.

Employers' organizations can assist in promoting equal opportunity policies in enterprises, providing training and technical assistance and establishing guidelines for employers in the promotion of gender equality in employment. Equal opportunity policy in an organization means ending the sexual division of labour, and breaking down the barriers that prevent vertical and horizontal movement by women into non-traditional jobs and into different levels and locations in the organizational hierarchy. The implications of such policies entail widening access to the organization by fair recruitment practices; supplementary training courses for women; a review of procedures for appraisal and promotion and ultimately an acknowledgement of the abilities of women, thus enabling them to develop as managers, technologists and professionals.

Such a policy is not easy to implement, since it requires confronting established practices and intervening in gender, class and race rivalries. Although some employers are genuinely concerned with justice, it is often clear that they have organizational ends primarily in mind. They aim to improve recruitment and retention of women whose qualities they perceive themselves as needing. The majority of women feel that prejudice against women exists, although it is less institutional than personal, and difficult to pin down.

Employers' organizations can persuade their members to adopt an equal opportunities policy as a means of maximizing the effective use of human resources that would be in the best interests of both the company and the employees. Guidelines for employers could include the following:

- develop a general policy statement underlying the commitment to be an equal opportunity employer;
- promote and publicize the advantages of such a policy as a means of attracting and retaining personnel;
- evolve action plans and strategies to achieve the objectives of the policy, taking into account the nature of the industry and local conditions. Periodically review the progress of the plans to ensure that the relevant issues are given higher priority;
- assist in identifying staff to implement the strategies and monitor progress towards specific objectives;
- publicize the existence and promotion of equal opportunities for women employees at all levels; and
- assist in the development of policies and procedures that provide for prompt and fair consideration and resolution of grievances relating to sexual discrimination and harassment.

Training programmes for management development and small enterprise development are called for. Women perceive themselves as having a greater need for management training. This may be due to the lack of confidence that they feel in assuming managerial responsibilities. The employer can assist women by being sensitive to their development and training needs. However, it should be noted that it is difficult to devise finely tuned training strategies that respond to women's needs and the subtle systemic discrimination they encounter. Training should also instil confidence and self-esteem and enlarge opportunities and functional areas for the placement of women in the workplace.

There is a need for organizations to develop a more differentiated approach to meeting training needs and to tailor different training opportunities (corporate-based, educational institution-based, contracted-out, intensive, experimental, etc.) to different individuals and groups. Employers' groups can assist in drawing up training strategies related to the achievement of equality of opportunity. The following points should be considered in the development of training courses:

- cover not only management development but also confidence building and assertiveness;
- aim to achieve defined objectives such as promotion prospects and the opening up of career opportunities.

The government and employers' organizations could help women entrepreneurs by taking the lead in establishing a national women's business association which could further encourage the participation of women in business. A possible model to emulate is the American Women's Economic Development Corporation in New York, which is a non-profit organization dedicated to teaching potential entrepreneurs how to start a business and providing them with management training. Seminars on topics such as cash-flow management, marketing, preparation of business plans, loan applications and business organization would provide women entrepreneurs with the capability necessary to establish themselves in business. Seminars can be organized by employers' organizations and held in collaboration with governmental and non-governmental organizations to ensure greater participation and a multifaceted approach to issues relating to women in employment.

Women proceed into the lower and middle management levels in a fairly orderly fashion, but they must work twice as hard to gain the confidence and trust of their managers in order to be promoted to a higher position. There is a need to familiarize women adequately with human resources, awareness of acceptable behaviour, and other relevant information to help them build important linkages at an early stage of their careers. Strategies that give women information, social contacts and power can help them demonstrate their competence, talents and abilities to overcome organizational barriers and be more productive.

This also applies to women entrepreneurs to enable them to establish networks for the exchange of information and experience.

Employers' organizations can enhance women's career development through promoting the idea of mentoring to their members. While career mentors who supply coaching, exposure, visibility and sponsorship are more important for men, psychological mentors providing moral support, friendship and an example or role model are just as important for women. The use of mentoring systems would be more suited to public sector organizations since the more competitive culture of private organizations is less conducive to mentoring.

Flexible work patterns and hours need to developed. Career advancement in Malaysia tends to correspond to women's child-bearing years. Hence a large number of women would forgo promotional opportunities rather than face family conflict or feelings of guilt regarding their children. Women's multiple roles and responsibilities affect their job prospects, opportunities and behaviour, and also affect the way that organizations view their women employees. Therefore, the workplace has to become more sensitive and supportive in enabling them to play multiple roles.

Alternative work arrangements and a supportive work culture that allows women to combine a successful career with a rich and meaningful family life must be promoted. 'Flexi-time' in its true form remains only an idea yet to be translated into action in most organizations. In this regard, employers' organizations can advise employers of the benefits of such schemes, and assist in training and implementation.

At the organizational level, it is opportune to take into consideration the type of measurement that can be used to assess an individual's performance objectively. Because of their nurturing tendencies women are often perceived as being soft, loving, attentive, emotional and intuitive and unable to make tough decisions. Although these perceptions may in fact be inaccurate, they have a subtle influence on the way women are perceived and on what is considered as appropriate work for women and the proper role for women in a work group. Increased use of job evaluation by employers' organizations as a method of analysing and assessing jobs in order to determine their relative worth can be considered by employers. It is one way of dealing with the issue of equal pay for work of equal value, called for by International Labour Convention No. 100 on equal remuneration.

Studies can be undertaken by employers' organizations regarding women's issues, such as the level of participation, wage differentials, fringe benefits, work organization and problems faced so as to identify priority areas for the development of strategies. These studies can be conducted in collaboration with other organizations in order to solicit greater response and a diversity of opinions and ideas.

Men need to be made aware of the problems women face, since their support and consideration are often crucial to the development and advancement of women. Senior management could provide sponsorship within the organization to help the female manager meet colleagues and understand better the informal customs and procedures in the organization. Women managers in particular must be made to realize that focusing on self-improvement as the critical determinant of career advancement is not enough, as decisions concerning promotion and other rewards are not always based solely on individual competence. Women aspiring to enter the higher levels of management must be made to realize the importance of informal networks in their career advancement. Just as women need training, so men should be reoriented to look at family and household duties as shared responsibilities. Perhaps a concerted effort at national level is needed to develop programmes and conduct seminars attended by men and women where they discuss the issue of shared family responsibilities.

A directory of successful businesswomen would be useful to provide data on visible role models and mentors for young entrepreneurs so that they can see how these women have been successful in business and prove a challenge to them. It would also serve as a reference to establish contacts and cultivate formal and informal networks where advice and exchange of information can be facilitated. The use of the media in highlighting these success stories and the organization of business clinics could help to bring together the women who have 'made it' and those aspiring to do so, thereby creating a continuous pool of entrepreneurs for the nation.

To facilitate implementation of the programmes suggested above, employers' organizations may consider setting up a women's committee or wing at council level to co-ordinate the various proposals, prioritize the programmes for action, and to lobby, monitor and advise on the implementation of equal opportunity policies by employers.

Women's struggle for equality in society has created a social environment in which it can no longer be accepted as legitimate to exclude women. To a degree, social and psychological contracts that are the basis of modern society are being autonomously rewritten by women in their own hand.

While men in powerful positions in organizations may see good reason to introduce fairer practices in recruitment and promotion, special training for women or more generous maternity leave, it is seldom that men raise these issues. In the case of recruitment, training and promotion of women, management today will be more willing both for pragmatic and moral reasons to try to remove bias in their human resources management practices and to open up to women careers in management, professional and technical fields. However, implementation is not monitored; non-compliance is not penalized nor is co-operation rewarded. In order not to make positive action for sex equality in organizations a passing fad, in addition to policy-making there should be emphasis on implementation and monitoring systems to ensure that organizational practices, management procedures and workplace cultures are really changing.

Despite cogent arguments, the degree of success has been limited because the sources of discrimination are embedded in social and organizational cultures and structures which have been constructed on gendered understandings of management, organizational power and leadership. These cultural values permeate organizations. It is argued that organizations will be able to maximize the opportunities for, and potential of, their female managerial workforce if they understand their lifestyles and responsibilities, their attitudes and aspirations, and customize their management policies to these differentiated groups or segments.

The management of a workforce consisting of diverse groups and demanding more flexible working patterns is undoubtedly one of the human resources management challenges of the new millennium. It requires policies to become more flexible and responsive. The role of employers' organizations as part of this emerging trend would boost their contribution to the promotion of equality of women in employment. The effects of affirmative-action legislation, greater equality in education and the gradual breakdown of structural and systemic barriers to women in management will produce aspiring women managers who have higher expectations of employers and of themselves. This group envisages upward progression and is prepared to face and accept changes in return for an attractive package of career development and flexible work benefits.

References

ILO/EASMAT (1996) – East Asia Multidisciplinary Advisory Team, *Malaysia's labour market: A woman's place*, Bangkok.

Lang Chin Ying and Sieh Mei Leng (1990) 'Women in business: Corporate managers and entrepreneurs', proceedings of the Colloquium on Women and Development in Malaysia – Implications for Planning and Population Dynamics, Kuala Lumpur.

PART V

12
Concluding observations

EUGENIA DATE-BAH

Together, the contributions in this volume demonstrate that gender inequalities at work and women's disadvantaged position in this sphere remain largely unresolved at the close of the twentieth century, despite significant strides in some areas, countries and regions. The persistence of this problem calls for urgent attention and action at the dawn of the twenty-first century. It calls for further consideration of strategies likely to speed up the process and address emerging challenges, new risks and persistent problems.

The essays in this book show that improving the status quo is complex. It requires consideration of a range of critical factors within a comprehensive integrated strategy. It calls for creating an enabling and supportive macro- and microeconomic environment and legal framework, poverty alleviation, action in social security coverage, and support for child-care and other family responsibilities. Furthermore, it involves action to improve working conditions and to strengthen women workers' group mobilization. There is a need for active and concerted roles to be played by the different bodies in society at different levels, including government, workers' and employers' organizations, national women's machineries, and other non-governmental bodies. Furthermore, regional and international organizations, such as the International Labour Organization, have important functions to perform. Other important elements of the strategy, mentioned in a number of the chapters, include attention to training, access to productive resources, unpaid work, occupational health and safety, job segmentation, and the situation of the more disadvantaged women's groups, including unemployed, rural and informal sector, casual, part-time and other precarious workers.

The diversity of factors and the challenges they pose make the attainment of the goal of gender equality and the advancement of women workers a very daunting task. The close links between the different elements make it imperative that action in each of them is not formulated or implemented in isolation. Piecemeal and segmented approaches should be discarded. The views and involvement of women should be sought. Furthermore, the growing interdependence of economies and the trend towards a 'global village' make it imperative for this comprehensive framework to involve action not only at national level, but also at regional and international levels.

Regular collection and analysis of gender-sensitive data is therefore identified as critical. Throughout the volume attention has been drawn to areas requiring more research, in order to bring to the fore the gender-differential impact of current socio-economic and other developments. Such data need to be widely disseminated to inform and guide meaningful action and policy-making. The analysis of the impact of recession and structural adjustment, for example, points to the limited availability of data on this issue and the need for more data collection for conclusions and regional variations to be drawn. The examination of the impact of the transition from centrally planned to market economies identifies further research as a major prerequisite for policy-making in the rapidly changing context of Central and Eastern Europe. This will bring understanding of the nature of the relationship between economic transformation and women's employment prospects. In relation to African women workers, globalization and AIDS, a call is made for a 'systematic attempt to tackle the dearth of data and analytical conceptual work ... and for the valuation and analysis of women's non-market (unpaid) activities ...' Furthermore, sex-disaggregated statistical data on poverty should be collected. The review on innovations in work organization at the enterprise level and changes in technology and women's employment call for strengthened co-operation between the various United Nations agencies and research institutions 'to monitor the impact of technological change in relation to women's employment in developed and developing countries'.

Empirical data on the extent of sexual harassment are limited in many countries. What is available is only the tip of the iceberg. The analysis of social security and protection points to the expanding diversity in the situations of women and their families. It is therefore necessary to embark on studies 'to accurately evaluate the needs of women and the impact that social security arrangements have on them'. A call is made in the review of legal frameworks to conduct analyses of the different components of the national legal framework to be able to identify the constraints they face in promoting women's advancement and gender equality. As regards enforcement, there is a need to assess 'the overall impact of administrative and judicial action' ... and to develop 'guidance material ... on the effective enforcement of non-discrimination and equal opportunity and treatment provisions'.

Monitoring changing trends regarding trade unions and women workers requires regular research and the compilation of sex-disaggregated figures and other records in the various countries and economic sectors. It is clear from the case-study on employers and the promotion of gender equality that employers have already begun work in this area. It is therefore proposed that this trend should be documented in the different countries to assess impact. Furthermore, conducting studies on wage differentials, fringe benefits and other work organization problems of women is identified as one of the roles that can be undertaken by employers in collaboration with research and other institutions. To all the above proposed areas of research can be added the need to document and analyse the innovative survival strategies of women, especially the more vulnerable groups, so as to guide the formulation of measures to strengthen them.

Research can be greatly facilitated by the development of relevant analytical concepts and statistical measurement instruments. This will, for example, allow for the adequate recording of women's work, both paid and unpaid, the assessment of their contribution and the extent of gender disparities in such areas as pay. It will help make women fully visible in official statistics to make possible their adequate consideration in the formulation and implementation of development and other plans. There is, for example, no universally accepted best method of analysing wage differentials between men and women. A variety of methodologies exist, which do not all measure the same thing, and this creates difficulties, for example in comparisons between countries. There is, therefore, a need for appropriate methodologies to disentangle the variety of factors contributing to women's wage disadvantage, including discrimination in the labour market, lower educational attainment and other human capital traits, seniority, productivity, non-pecuniary benefits and differences in employment patterns and in length of service.[1] Conceptual and statistical measurement work, in addition to data collection, constitutes an essential part of the required comprehensive strategy. This is among the recommendations contained in the Platform for Action adopted by the Fourth World Conference on Women, as well as by a number of other meetings held in recent years.

It is hoped that the broad, comprehensive and integrated approach portrayed in this volume will contribute to enlightened debate and to the elaboration and implementation of an effective policy and action agenda to turn our vision into reality in the near future.

Notes

1. See P. Gonzalez, 'Measuring wage differentials', in P. Gonzalez and M.J. Watts, *Measuring gender wage differentials and job segregation*, IDP Women WP-24; Geneva, ILO, 1996.

Annex
Output of the ILO Interdepartmental Project on Equality for Women in Employment

I. Published books, articles and manuscripts

R. Anker, *'Occupational sex segmentation in the world'*, draft manuscript (Geneva, 1995).

E. Date-Bah (ed.) 'African trade unions and the challenge of organizing women workers in the unorganized sectors', in *Labour Education*, 92-1993/3 (Geneva, 1993).

— 'Women's empowerment in trade unions: Recent data from the ILO IDP Project on Equality for Women in Employment', in *Labour Education*, 90-1993/1 (Geneva, 1993).

— *'Towards gender equality in the trade unions: A worldwide overview'*, draft manuscript (Geneva, 1995).

— *Promoting gender equality at work. Turning vision into reality for the twenty-first century* (London, Zed Books Ltd., 1997).

M. Gunderson, *Comparable worth and gender discrimination: An international perspective* (Geneva, ILO, 1994).

B. Husbands, 'Sexual harassment law in employment: An international perspective', in *International Labour Review*, Vol. 131, No. 6, 1992.

ILO, *Combating sexual harassment at work: A conditions of work digest* (Geneva, 1992).

— *International labour standards and women workers' rights* (Turin, 1993).

— *Promoting gender equality in employment in Lesotho: An Agenda for Action* (Turin, 1994).

— *Training package on women workers' rights* (Turin, 1994).

— *Conditions of work: Maternity and work* (Geneva, 1995).

M. Martens and S. Mitter, *Women in trade unions: Organizing the unorganized* (Geneva, ILO, 1994).

S. Olney, *'Collective bargaining and equality'*, draft manuscript (Geneva, 1994).

J. Siltanen *et al.*, *Gender inequality in the labour market* (Geneva, ILO, 1995).

C. Thomas, *'Positive Action'*, draft manuscript (Geneva, 1994).

II. Working papers

IDP Women/WP-1: 'Women Workers, Unions and Industrial Sectors in North America', Susan C. Eaton

IDP Women/WP-2: 'Gender Inequality in the Labour Market: Occupational Concentration and Segregation, A Manual on Methodology', Janet Siltanen, Jennifer Jarman, Robert Blackburn

IDP Women/WP-3: 'Statistical Measurement of Gender Wage Differentials', ILO Bureau of Statistics

IDP Women/WP-4: 'Women Workers and Unions in Europe: An Analysis by Industrial Sector', Sue Hastings, Martha Coleman

IDP Women/WP-5: 'Women and Social Security in Latin America, the Caribbean and Sub-Saharan Africa', Nancy Folbre

IDP Women/WP-6: 'Les Syndicats et les travailleuses dans le secteur non structuré: le cas des travailleuses domestiques à Recife, Brésel et des vendeuses sur les marchés à Ouagadougou, Burkino Faso', Marie Anderfuhren, Mamounata Cisse

IDP Women/WP-7: 'Organizing Homeworkers in the Informal Sector in Australia, the Netherlands and Canada', Jane Tate

IDP Women/WP-8: 'Collective Bargaining and the Promotion of Equality: The Case of South Africa', Catherine O'Regan, Clive Thompson

IDP Women/WP-9: 'El Hostigamiento Sexual en el Empleo: Qué se ha hecho hasta ahora en Badilla Costa Rica?', Marta E.Solano, Anan Elena

IDP Women/WP-10: 'The Unionization of Women Workers in Different Industrial Sectors in South Africa', Catherine O'Regan, Bee Thompson

IDP Women/WP-11: 'Participacion de la Mujer en los Sindicatos de Venezuela', Dilcia Balliache, Carlos E. Febres

IDP Women/WP-12: 'Collective Bargaining and the Promotion of Equality: The Case of the United Kingdom', Linda Dickens

IDP Women/WP-13: 'Occupational Segmentation by Sex in the World', Debra Barbezat

IDP Women/WP-14: 'Négociation Collective et Promotion de l'Egalité en France', Annette Jobert

IDP Women/WP-15: 'Affirmative Action in the United States and its Application to Women in Employment', Fania E. Davis

IDP Women/WP-16: 'Positive Action in the Public Service and the Education and Training Sectors in Zimbabwe', Unity Chari

IDP Women/WP-17: 'Women in Trade Unions in Trinidad and Tobago', Roberta Clarke

IDP Women/WP-18: 'Investigación sobre las actividades emprendidas por las organizaciones de trabajadores/as rurales de algunos países de América Central y República Dominicana para fortalecer la participación de la mujer', Lic Martiza, Delgado González

IDP Women/WP-19: 'The Impact of recession and structural adjustment on women's work in developing countries', Sally Baden

IDP Women/WP-20: 'Enforcement of equality provisions for women workers', Constance Thomas, Rachel Taylor

IDP Women/WP-21: 'Reorientación de la formación profesional para la mujer', Daniela Bertino, Sara Silvera

IDP Women/WP-24: 'Measuring wage differentials and job segregation', Pablo Gonzalez, Martin Watts

III. Organized Seminars/Workshops

Séminaire sous-régional d'éducation ouvrière sur la participation des femmes dans les syndicats, Abidjan, Côte d'Ivoire, 8–18 February 1993

Interregional seminar on 'Effective Strategies to Disseminate Information on Women Workers' Rights', Turin Centre, Italy, 22–26 June 1993

Course on 'The Measurement of Gender Wage Differentials and Occupational Segregation', Turin Centre, Italy, 15 Nov–5 Dec 1993

Tripartite Regional Seminar on Combating Sexual Harassment at Work, Manila, Philippines, 22–26 November 1993

Index

'added worker' effect, 11, 26, 36, 53
affirmative action, 4, 80-1, 101, 145, 190, 216, 218; legislation, 235
Afghanistan, Constitution, 203
Africa Development Bank, 102
Africa: cheap labour, 29, 95; desertification, 97; economic crisis, 90; foreign investment, 92-3; globalization impact, 85, 91; governments, 102; law systems, 88-9, 101, 175-7; poverty, 99; rural sector organization, 221-2; sub-Saharan, 25, 33-5, 40, 50; trade unions, 218-19; women workers, 86-8, 100-3
African Regional Federation of Commercial, Clerical, Professional and Technical Employees, 133
agriculture, 25, 49; African, 98; collective, 68; employment, 27, 52; exports, 31; incomes, 50; labour, 33, 64; unpaid labour, 39; wage rates, 51
AIDS, 13, 85, 96-7, 140, 236
Albania, 67-8
Algeria, 97
American Airlines, 111
American Women's Economic Development Corporation, 232
Angola, 97
Antrobus, P., 53
Appleton, S., 41
Argentina, 41-2, 118, 121, 123, 146; Civil Service Union, 149
Australia, 5, 143, 145, 190; Equal Opportunities Commission, 138, 142; industrial tribunals, 199, 201
Austria, 166
automation, 120-3
automobile industry, 108

Baden, Sally, 11
banana industry, 53
Bangladesh: trade unions, 213
Barbados, 111, 113; National Union of Public Workers, 148
Basotho women, 17, 175, 179
Belguim, 144-5, 158, 201; sexual harassment, 142
Benin, 43
berufstätigkeit, 74
biotechnology, 14, 95, 119-20, 125
Bolivia, 34; ESF, 53
Botswana, 43, 90
Brazil, 41, 108, 113-14, 116, 121, 125, 146; Recife, 223; São Paulo, 38, 45
'breadwinner' family, ideology, 65, 72-5
Bretton Woods, institutions, 90
Brocas, Anne-Marie, 15
Bulgaria, 67
Burkina Faso: maternity leave, 165; Organisation Nationale de Syndicats, 221
Burundi, 97

Calcutta, subcontracting, 108
Cameroon, public sector, 43

Canada, 143-5, 158, 194; Human Rights Act, 146; Labour Code, 147; Labour Congress, 132; Trade Union Congress, 134; trade unions, 211-214

careers: hierarchies, 63; mentors, 233

Caribbean, the, 33, 37, 111-12, 143; trade unions, 214

cash crops, 50-2

casualization, 25

Central African Republic, 42

centrally planned economies, ex-, 9, 11-12, 59-67, 71, 75, 80, 236

Chad, National Union of Workers, 148

Chambers G., 207

child-care provisions, 5, 12, 61-3, 65, 68-71, 73, 81, 89, 93-4, 101-2, 107, 160-1, 163, 166-7, 212, 215, 217, 222, 227, 230

child rearing, 87, 156

Chile, 32-5

China, 3, 112

civil strife, 13, 85, 96-7

class legal actions, 202-3

Côte d'Ivoire, 41, 50, 137; sexual harassment, 141

Coleman, M., 212

Common Market for Eastern and Southern Africa (COMESA), 102

Commonwealth of Independent States (CIS), 164

Commonwealth Secretariat, 38, 53, 143

comparative advantage, 121

computer technologies, 14, 119-125; training, 71

Congo, the, 47

constitutions, 174-5, 187

Costa Rica, 43, 143

credentialism, 41

credit, access, 5, 90, 98, 175, 220-1, 226; allocation schemes, 103; restrictions, 29; rotating societies, 49

customization, 124

Cyprus, 5; Equal Remuneration Law, 201

Czech Republic, 3, 66, 74, 77, 159

Czechoslovakia ex-, 64, 74; female labour, 61

data gathering, need, 8, 20, 25

data-processing, 109-10, 124; off-shore, 14, 111-13, 115, offshore, 112

Date-Bah, Eugenia, 18, 20

Declaration of the World Summit for Social Development, 6

demand restraint, policies, 27

democracy, notions of, 210

Denmark, 136, 139, 143, 201

deregulation, 29-30, 33, 47

'derived rights', 156, 168

deskilling, 71, 106, 113

devaluation, 28, 30, 44, 50

disabled, the, 6; benefits, 162

'discouraged worker' effect, 11, 27, 36, 53

displaced people, 85, 97

division of labour: domestic, 61, 213; international, 93; sexual, 97, 205, 231; traditional, 116-17

foreign investment, 91-2, 112, 121
Fourth World Conference on Women, 1-2, 7, 9, 20, 86, 155, 237
France, 136, 139, 142, 144-5, 158, 166, 170, 204; sexual harassment, 134
Francke, M., 37, 47
free trade zones (FTZs), 112-13
fructose, 119

Gabon, 90
Gambia, 42
gender-sensitive data, need, 236
Germany, 72, 74, 139, 158; DAG, 214; Democratic Republic (GDR),ex-, 60-4, 73, 79; east, 66, 68, 76-7; Federal Republic, 62; Institute for Economic Research, 74; Labour Code, 199; unification, 65, 73
Ghana, 49, 90, 94, 161; agriculture, 51-2; PAMSCAD, 53; public sector, 43; Trade Union Congress, 148
'glass ceiling', 4, 179
globalization, 9, 12-13, 85, 91-5, 236
governments, role, 223, 228-9
grass-roots associations, 103
Greece, trade unions, 215
Grindling, T.H., 42
group justice, perspective, 203; theories, 190

Hastings S., 212
headloading, 52
health and safety, occupational, 8, 13-14, 89, 94, 114-15, 118, 125-6, 131, 183, 185-6, 236; regulation, 193
health care, 98; access, 159, 162-3, 181; charges, 38; cover inequalities, 164; insurance, 69
heavy industry, fetishization, 64
Hein, C., 94
Hirata, H., 38, 45
homeworking, 30, 45
Horton C., 207
Horton, S., 35, 54
Human development report 1995, 99
Humphrey, J., 37-8, 45
Hungary, 63-70, 72-3, 77-9, 159

import substitution, 44
India, 112, 125, 136, 190, 203
indirect discrimination, 202
Indonesia, 34, 195; sexual harassment, 138
industrial tribunals, 199-200
informal sector, 2, 4, 6, 11, 16, 18, 25, 27, 29, 32-3, 37-9, 44-6, 49-50, 85, 90, 93, 95, 98, 103, 160, 213, 216, 218, 220, 222-3, 236; gender range, 48; growth, 47; heterogenity, 30; income spread, 50; trade unions, 219
information technology, 76-7, 125
injury benefit, occupational, 157
Institute for Gender Studies, Russian Academy of Sciences, 73
intellectual property rights, 120, 123